INVENTIONS
THAT DIDN'T CHANGE
THE WORLD

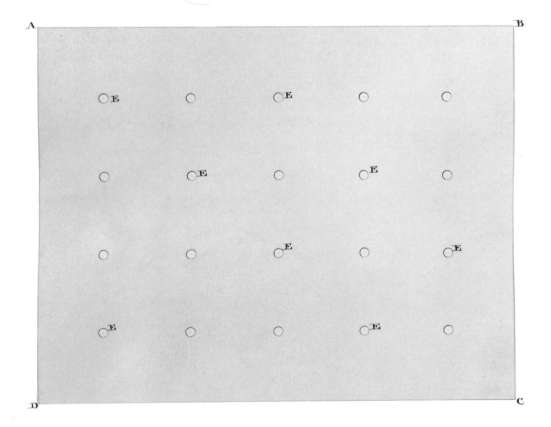

Design for a Spring Bible and Prayer Case

provisionally Registered for Mr Thomas Brindley.
of 2 Leonards Square, Finsbury.

DESIGNS OFFICE
SEP. 20
1853
REGISTERED
PROVISIONALLY.

DESIGNS OFFICE
SEP 24
1853
REGISTERED

3514

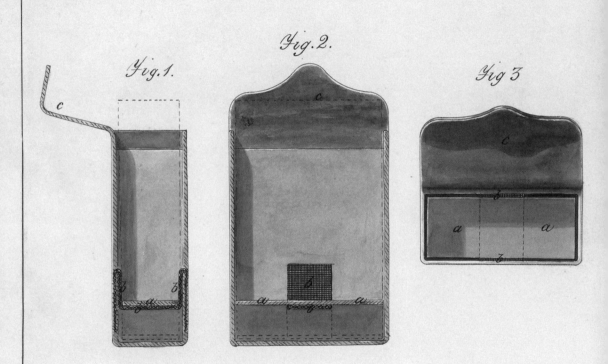

Fig. 1.   Fig. 2.   Fig 3

The above drawing which is drawn to a geometrical scale, represents a design for a spring Bible and Prayer case: fig. 1. shows a transverse vertical section of the spring case; fig. 2. a lateral vertical section, and fig. 3. a plan of the same. The object of the spring case is to facilitate the withdrawal of the book from the case, and to obviate the necessity of a ribbon for that purpose, a is a piece of stiff card-board, or other suitable material which slides loosely up and down in the case, this rests upon a piece of elastic webbing b, stretched across the case and made fast in the sides as shown. The elastic web b, stretches sufficiently to allow the loose piece a to be depressed to the bottom of the case which takes place when the Bible or Prayer book is introduced. The web b, exerts a constant tendency to thrust the book up and partially out of the case. The lid c, of the case when down and clasped, retains the book within the case, but immediately it is released the book is lifted out to the position of the dotted lines in which it is easily taken hold of & removed. Protection is sought for the shape & configuration of those parts of the design represented by the letters a & b which are new and never before in use, the rest being old.

INVENTIONS
THAT DIDN'T CHANGE
THE WORLD

◆ ◆ ◆

Julie Halls

WITH 240 ILLUSTRATIONS IN COLOUR

 **Thames & Hudson**

 The National Archives

FOR MY SON, OLIVER

THANK YOU TO MY FATHER, LAURIE; MY BROTHER, ROBIN;
ANN & MY FRIENDS BARBARA & LINDSEY FOR THEIR SUPPORT
AND ENCOURAGEMENT

JULIE HALLS *works in the Advice and Records Knowledge Department*
at The National Archives, London, and is a specialist in registered designs.

FRONT COVER: *Design for a portable cooking apparatus, 1845*

BACK COVER: *A miscellany of designs, registered 1843–55*

PAGE 1: *Design for a ventilating window pane, 1847*

PAGE 2: *Design for a Spring Bible and Prayer Case, 1853*

PAGES 4–5: *Design for a placard holder, 1848*

PAGES 6–7: *Design for a Fire Escape, 1846*

PAGE 8: *Cover binding of a volume of designs* BT 45/28, *1874–78*

PAGE 224: *A Tombstone Socket or Shoe, 1861*

First published in the United Kingdom in 2014 by
Thames & Hudson Ltd, 181A High Holborn, London WC1V 7QX

Published in association with The National Archives

The National Archives is the UK government's official archive
containing over 1,000 years of history. They give detailed guidance
to government departments and the public sector on information
management, and advise others about the care of historical archives.

www.nationalarchives.gov.uk

Inventions That Didn't Change The World
© 2014 Crown Copyright

Images reproduced by permission of The National Archives,
London, England 2014

The right of Julie Halls to be identified as the author of this work has
been asserted by her in accordance with the Copyright, Designs and
Patents Act 1988

British Library Cataloguing-in-Publication Data
A catalogue record for this book is available from the British Library

ISBN 978-0-500-51762-8

Printed and bound in China by Everbest Printing Co. Ltd

To find out about all our publications, please visit **www.thamesandhudson.com**.
There you can subscribe to our e-newsletter, browse or download our current
catalogue, and buy any titles that are in print.

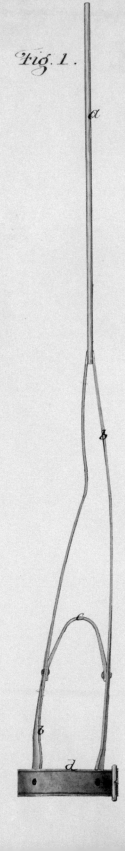

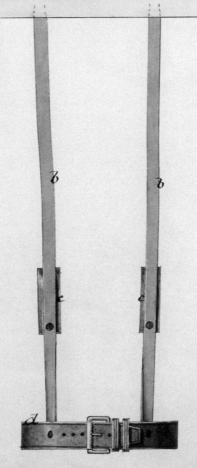

Fig. 2.

a

a

NEUBER'S

IMPROVED

LIQUID GLUE

WITHOUT SMELL.

For mending
WOOD GLASS CHINA METAL

Sold retail at
76 LONG ACRE
6d, 1s, and 1s.6d, *a bottle.*
Wholesale at the manufactory
4 Endell St, Broad St, Holborn.

b

b

c

c

d

Fig. I.

Reference.

A   a bracket bolt.
B   hook of dº.
C   eye of dº.
D   Collar or shank.
E   screw nutt.
F   short wire rope.

G   eyes or loops
H   Basket or cr
I   ropes or chain
K   eye or ring
L   an instrumen
M   screw socket
N   screw on
O   a rope.

Alexᵈ Prince. Registration Agent, 14 Lincolns Inn Fields.

- DESIGN-FOR-A-FIRE-ESCAPE -

Registered for James Walby of 59 Greek Street Soho London.

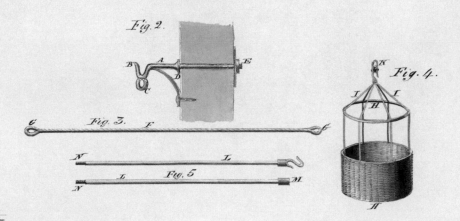

Fig. 2.

Fig. 4.

Fig. 3.

Fig. 5.

Description. — The drawing exhibits several views of the design drawn to a geometrical scale. — Fig. 1 represents a Front elevation of four houses shewing the application of the Fire escape thereto. The Fig.ˢ 2.3.4.5. represent portions of the design detached from each other and drawn upon an enlarged and geometrical scale, similar letters of reference are placed upon and denote corresponding parts in so far as such parts appear or can be seen at each of the Figures respectively. AA marks a wrought iron bracket bolt one end of which is formed with a hook B and eye C and there is a collar or shank D upon the said bolt which bolt when passed through the wall of a house may be securely fixed thereto by the end of the said bolt having a screw cut around it upon which fits a screw nutt E as shewn at Fig. 2. F marks a wire rope, at each end of which there is formed an eye or loop G as shewn at Fig. 3. for the purpose hereafter described, H marks a basket or cradle — of wicker or wire work to the upper part of the said basket there are attached ropes or chains I which terminate in a hook and pulley K. as shewn at Fig. 4. L marks an instrument formed of two or more parts and of certain convenient lengths which may be connected together by screw sockets M and screws N formed upon the ends of the said rods. The use of the parts above referred to is as follows. At the Fig 1. the hooks B.B are represented as disposed or arranged at the joints of houses and the rope F is attached thereto as shewn, the basket or cradle H ~~and railway~~ being afterwards attached to each end of the rope F ~~by which persons~~ ^to the said rope and there is a rope O.O. attached^ may remove themselves or be removed from the window of one house to that of the next or from one floor to another, or if necessary or found more convenient the basket or cradle may be lowered to the ground as represented by the dotted lines a b by means of the rope P and block Q which may be placed upon either of the hooks for that purpose or by the rope only as shewn at A Fig. 1. The Protection sought is for the general configuration resulting from the disposition of the several parts which taken collectively constitute an *entirely new design for a Fire Escape.* ——

DESIGNS

OFFICE.

CONTENTS

Preliminary Remarks   *10*

. . . .

I   **HOUSE & GARDEN**   *18*

II   **FIELD & FACTORY**   *54*

III   **HIS & HERS**   *86*

IV   **OUT & ABOUT**   *116*

V   **PREVENTATIVES & PANACEAS**   *142*

VI   **SPORT & LEISURE**   *166*

VII   **SAFETY & SECURITY**   *190*

. . . .

Picture Credits   *218*

Index   *221*

Acknowledgments   *224*

PRELIMINARY REMARKS

The inventions in this book tell a story of nineteenth-century enterprise, enthusiasm and, above all, optimism. Each gadget, machine or 'apparatus', however bizarre it might seem now, was copyrighted by an inventor filled with hope that it would prove popular, useful and – if others shared his vision – profitable. The Victorian era was one of amazing inventiveness, and many inventions of the period were so successful that they changed the way we live – such as the telephone, steam engine, railway and light bulb. However, there were also thousands of inventions that we have long since forgotten or that never saw the light of day.

Everyone who applied to copyright an invention had to provide two identical drawings of the design to the government's Designs Registry at Somerset House, London. If successful, one copy of the drawing would be stamped and returned to the copyright holder. The other would be pasted into a huge, leather-bound volume of designs and retained by the Registry, part of the Board of Trade. These volumes are now in the care of The National Archives, which look after more than 1,000 years of UK government records. Most of the inventions, dating back to 1843, have never been seen by any but a few determined researchers. This is partly because of the complex system of numbering adopted by the Registry, which can make it difficult to track down specific designs, and perhaps also because the volumes are large, dusty and extremely heavy. Although the documents are now carefully stored in temperature-controlled conditions, this was not always the case during their long history, as can be seen by the damage to some of the drawings.

Spine of a single volume of designs, BT 45/14, 1850–51

Although some inventions have now been catalogued and the details of the proprietor (the copyright holder), date of registration and a brief description of the design can be found on The National Archives's online catalogue, few of the images have been digitized.

The activities of the inventors, many of them amateurs, were part of a wider culture that celebrated as a national triumph the technological achievements and industrial advances made in Britain. By the middle of the nineteenth century it was both the greatest manufacturing nation and the greatest trading nation in the world. The process of industrialization that began in the eighteenth century paved the way for a period of immense industrial productivity based on steam technology. Huge advances were made in the mining of coal, minerals and other raw materials, and in the production of iron, textiles and manufactured goods. These advances allowed Britain to mass-produce goods more efficiently and sell them more cheaply than any other nation.

This powerful position was further strengthened by improvements in transport and communication technologies. The railways moved freight and passengers around the country at great speed, providing new opportunities for commerce and leisure activities. The *Illustrated London News* described the railways as 'the grandest exponent of the enterprise, the wealth and the intelligence of our race',[1] and their rising importance is reflected by a number of railway-related designs. Britain's steam ships dominated the seas, making international trade faster and the administration of the growing Empire more efficient. The electric telegraph aided the smooth running of the railways, and undersea telegraph cables helped Britain to control a vast empire that provided raw materials for British factories and markets for the goods they produced.[2] Men like Richard Arkwright, credited with creating the modern factory system, George Stephenson and Richard Trevithick, pioneers of steam transport, and the visionary engineer Isambard Kingdom Brunel, were all national heroes.

As the prosperity of the nation increased, a greater proportion of the population than ever before had disposable income to spend on the huge range of goods being produced. The affluent and expanding middle classes, in particular, helped ensure a strong domestic demand for goods, fuelled by an increase in advertising along with lifestyle books and journals.

The press in general expanded hugely at this time, and the sense of excitement and widespread interest in technological innovations were reflected in the growth of popular magazines and journals aimed at ordinary mechanics and artisans as well as highly qualified engineers. There was an intense

A registration stamp. Blue ink was used until mid-1852

An example of a provisional registration stamp

Provisional Spiral Grooved Candle*, 1870

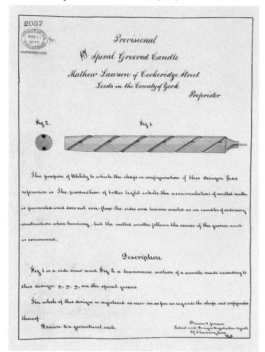

interest in how things worked, which crossed the barriers of class. Publications such as *The Mechanics' Magazine*, *Popular Science Monthly* and *The Engineer* contained highly technical articles about the latest inventions and technological developments and lively letters demonstrating that readers had a sound understanding of the subject.

The Victorians tended to imbue every aspect of life with a sense of morality, which included a powerful belief in individualism, self-respect and self-reliance – there was a feeling that people should make their own way in the world. Each issue of the *Mechanics Magazine*, for example, had on its title page a morally improving quotation designed to inspire its readers.

This belief in self-reliance was encapsulated in Samuel Smiles's best-selling book *Self-help; with illustrations of character and conduct*, published in 1859. There is a strong emphasis on industry – meaning the human quality of industriousness, as well as machine production – and inventors and engineers

are described in heroic terms. There are numerous homilies describing the determination of successful inventors to succeed in the face of setbacks. Smiles emphasized that the fruits of labour could be enjoyed by people at any level in society who were prepared to work hard and persevere. Individual effort could enable inventors to rise from the lowest social ranks. In this environment – where technology was a source of fascination and admiration – inventors were seen as heroic and morally superior individuals, and ordinary men were encouraged to work hard in order to achieve success.

Having come up with an idea, the inventor would want to make sure that it was not immediately copied. Until the Designs Registry was established by the Designs Registration Act of 1839, the only way to protect an invention was by taking out a patent. Registration of designs was established in part to address shortcomings in the patent system, as well as to give copyright protection to (at first) 'ornamental' designs. To this day patents and registered designs remain two separate methods of protecting intellectual property; designs are today registered at the Intellectual Property Office.

By the first half of the nineteenth century the patent system had become hopelessly expensive and inefficient, giving rise to a vociferous reform movement. Its administrative machinery was labyrinthine and was described in a discussion in the House of Lords in 1851 as 'calculated…to baffle and paralyse the efforts of a class so essential in maintaining the commercial pre-eminence' of the country.[3]

Before an inventor was granted a patent, his application had to go through as many as ten offices, with a fee payable at each. Petitions, warrants and bills were prepared several times over, signed and countersigned, before a patent was finally approved. At any stage in the process an application could be opposed by a competitor, causing delays of up to six months and increasing the possibility of details of the patent leaking out. The cost of a patent was prohibitively expensive and out of the grasp of many small manufacturers. Between 1750 and 1852 patents could cost up to £400, with separate costs for taking out the patent in England, Scotland and Ireland.[4]

Charles Dickens's short story *A Poor Man's Tale of a Patent*, published in *Household Words* in 1850, tells of one man's efforts to patent his invention. The story exaggerates the process, describing thirty-four steps, but the desperation and confusion felt by the would-be patentee as he negotiates the system is echoed by contemporary accounts. Dickens writes: 'Is it reasonable to make a man feel as if, in inventing an ingenious improvement meant to do good, he had done something wrong? How else can a man feel, when he is met by such difficulties at every turn? All inventors taking out a Patent *must* feel so.'

Calls for reform of the patent system coincided with calls for the protection of what were termed 'ornamental' designs. This came about because of the huge increase in mass-produced goods, especially textiles. Piracy of designs was common, and could mean major financial losses for manufacturers.

As the production of goods sped up, so did the rate at which designs could be copied. In 1787 the Calico Printers' Act was passed, giving protection to textile designs, and in the years that followed manufacturers of other types of goods started to demand protection for their designs.[5]

The Act of 1839 extended copyright to all ornamental designs – so that as well as textiles, decorative items made from any other material could also be registered. However, inventors were also registering their work – inappropriately in the eyes of the Registrar – and in part to address this problem, and also to extend the period of copyright for printed fabrics, the 1839 Act was replaced in 1842 by the Ornamental Designs Act. This created thirteen 'material classes' – metal, wood, glass and so on – each with its own period of copyright protection. Either because of genuine confusion, or because registering a design was cheaper and easier than taking out a patent, the 1842 Act failed to stop 'the incessant attempts on the part of inventors of utilities to squeeze in along with their more fortunate brethren the inventors of ornament. Patents were, from their expense, in a multitude of cases quite out of the question'.[6]

The 1843 Utility Designs Act, which provided copyright protection for designs 'not being of an ornamental character', but instead for 'any new or original design for any article of manufacture having reference to some purpose of utility', gave proprietors copyright protection for three years. The Act also addressed a growing feeling that the patent system should be reserved for 'important' inventions, and not 'snuffers, stirrups, lamps, cork-screws, and other articles of domestic use'[7] – although in reality many 'significant' inventions were also registered.

"THE WANTS OF SOCIETY CALL FOR EVERY MAN'S LABOUR. NO ONE IS PERMITTED TO BE A BLANK IN THE WORLD. NO RANK NOR STATION EXEMPTS ANY MAN FROM CONTRIBUTING HIS SHARE TO THE PUBLIC UTILITY AND GOOD. THIS IS THE PRECEPT OF GOD; THIS IS THE VOICE OF NATURE; THIS IS THE JUST DEMAND OF THE HUMAN RACE ONE UPON ANOTHER."

MECHANICS MAGAZINE, OCTOBER 1839–MAY 1840

Although there was still some confusion between what should be covered by a patent and what should be registered as a design – this hinged on the fact that protection for non-ornamental designs was based on a new 'shape or configuration' of a useful object, while a patent covered its utility, or function – the law struggled to find a logical basis for distinguishing between the two categories.[8] The Act was widely perceived as a cheaper and quicker form of protection for small tradesmen than the convoluted patent system. As the barrister Thomas Turner explained: 'As regards all the minor inventions, and therefore the majority of them, the patent, from its enormous and inflexible cost, afforded no protection at all. It is insisted on that the [1843] act was expressly provided to remedy this, and to such inventions it has been widely applied.'[9]

In practice the decision as to whether to register an invention as a design or to apply for a patent was left to the applicant. It was felt unlikely that the inventor of a design which ought to be patented would forego fourteen years' patent

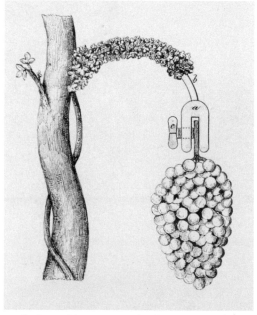

A Clip for attaching grapes or other fruit to Epergnes, 1870

> ## "WE OFTEN DISCOVER WHAT *WILL* DO BY FINDING OUT WHAT WILL NOT DO; AND PROBABLY HE WHO NEVER MADE A MISTAKE NEVER MADE A DISCOVERY."
>
> SAMUEL SMILES, *SELF HELP*, 1859

protection in favour of the three years offered by registration. Thousands of inventors chose to register their designs, resulting in the unique documents seen in this book.

Having decided to register his design, the inventor had to take or send to the Designs Registry 'two exactly similar drawings or prints [of the design] made on a proper geometric scale'. He also needed to provide the title of the design; his name and address; explanatory text; and to state which parts were (or were not) new and original.

Although some inventors produced their own drawings and applications, others used the services of a registration agent. Patent agents had begun to appear at the end of the eighteenth century, as the numbers of patent applications and court cases began to increase along with industrialization, and as applicants found it increasingly difficult to negotiate the system. By 1851 patent agents had become an established service industry, and dealt with around 90 per cent of all patents. Many were engineers and patentees themselves, while others had a legal background.[10]

While some patent agents saw the introduction of the Designs Registry as a threat, others saw it as an opportunity to expand their businesses and were quick to rebrand themselves as both patent and registration agents.

Unsurprisingly, it tends to be the case that where particularly detailed and professional drawings have been submitted, a registration agent was used. They would either have made the drawing themselves on behalf of their clients,

Design for a Pedo-manu-motive, c. 1848

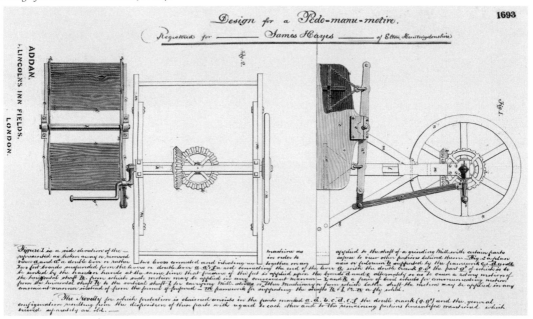

or employed a professional draughtsman to do so. The accompanying explanation of the designs tends to be carefully worded to avoid any suggestion that the object should have been patented instead of registered as a design. Words such as 'principle', 'action' or 'invention' were avoided, and instead the object was described using terms such as 'shape', 'form' and 'configuration'. The 'object of utility', or purpose of the design, would always be described.

The fee for registering designs of utility (useful designs) was set at £10. It was hoped that the relatively high cost compared with ornamental designs would avoid making registration of designs too attractive to inventors whose designs should be the subject of patents, and would also act as 'a safeguard against the Registrar being inundated with merely trifling or insignificant designs'.

Trifling or otherwise, these designs provide a fascinating insight into the social history and technology of the period. Some seemingly inexplicable inventions make sense within their historical context. One example is the 'Design

for a Flying or Aerial Machine for the Artic [*sic*] Regions', which was registered at a time when exploration of the Arctic, and in particular attempts to find a trade route through the Northwest Passage, was the subject of sensational news stories. There are several designs registered around the time of the gold rushes, and the 'Anti-Garotting Cravat' coincided with a national scare about incidents of robbery. The Victorians seem to have been preoccupied by personal safety, judging by the number of items designed to protect life and limb. Some of these seem as perilous as the dangers they hoped to mitigate: the 'Design for a Fire-Escape', for example, is intended to catch a person jumping from the window of a burning building.

Contemporary crazes can also be found – such as hydropathy, or hydrotherapy – which involved mineral or vapour baths, cold plunges and sitz baths, and were thought to cure a wide range of ills. The designs for therapeutic baths often refer to users as 'patients'. The 'Hydro Vapour Bath' promises 'an instantaneous ablution of cold or tepid water whilst immersed in the steam'.

Design for "Cantab" Braces, 1850

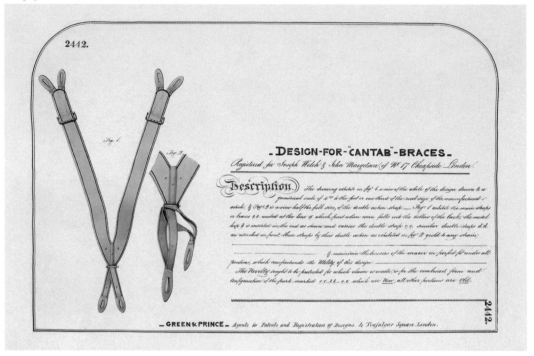

A number of the designs were displayed at the Great Exhibition of the Works of Industry of all Nations, one of the wonders of the Victorian age, held in 1851 in London's Hyde Park. Pressure for reform of the patent system increased in the run-up to the Great Exhibition, as manufacturers feared that their exhibits would be copied by competitors. Although patent reform did not take place until the Patent Law Amendment Act of 1852, the Designs Act of 1850 provided copyright protection of one year (termed 'provisional' protection) for designs to be exhibited.

The Great Exhibition was the first world fair and marked the high point of British economic power, consolidating Britain's position as 'the workshop of the world'. Over six million visitors flocked to see the huge machines that powered industry, as well as the vast range of commodities on offer. Although the more spectacular exhibits received the most publicity, thousands of items made by small-scale tradesmen and manufacturers were also on display.

This meant that as well as being awestruck by power-looms, the Jacquard lace machine and steam-powered threshing machines, visitors could also admire the 'Somapantic Bath' registered by Samuel Gilbert of Stamford, Lincolnshire, a gravy dish registered by John Gray from Edinburgh, and the 'Cantab' braces (which 'yield to any strain and maintain the trousers of the wearer in perfect fit under all positions'), registered by Welch, Margetson & Co, of Cheapside, London.

Pseudo-scientific names were often attached to the names of objects, presumably to impart a sense of gravitas. Examples include the 'Epanalepsian Advertizing Vehicle', the 'Pedo-manu-motive'

"THRIFT IS THE BASIS OF SELF-HELP, AND THE FOUNDATION OF MUCH THAT IS EXCELLENT IN CHARACTER."

SAMUEL SMILES, *THRIFT*, 1875

(for grinding mills), and the 'Amphitrepolax Boot'. Objects are often described as 'improved' (the 'Improved Pickle Fork', the 'Improved Sausage Machine'), 'economic' (an 'Improved Economic Button for Ladies Wear') or 'portable' – all considered selling points. A look at the designs described as 'portable' tells us the word then had a different connotation, as clearly items such as the 'Portable Economic Fire proof Building', the 'Portable Sheep House' and the 'Portable Smelting Apparatus' could not be picked up and carried. The term can refer to objects that could be taken apart and reassembled elsewhere, or to equipment that could be towed to different sites of work. Portable forges, kilns and similar equipment could be used in the building of railways, in quarrying and mining, and on the battlefield, where military blacksmiths and farriers were employed to shoe horses and repair equipment.

Many inventors attempted to find solutions to small everyday problems, many of which have long ceased to be an issue. Top hats, worn by most men throughout the nineteenth century, posed various problems, notably related to over-heated heads and storage. The 'Design for a boot or shoe warmer', and the lethal-looking 'Portable Bed Warmer' remind us of the problems of keeping cosy in unheated Victorian homes. The 'Spring Bible and Prayer Case', which 'obviates the

necessity of a ribbon' for removing the book from the case, suggests the need for urgent moral guidance of a kind few of us turn to today.

Other items that at first sound pointless make more sense when the proprietor's occupation is known. The 'Combined Knife and Fork', which sounds like an attempt to improve on an already perfectly good system, was registered by surgical instrument makers, and was presumably intended to help amputees. Whereas now inventions are the province of specially trained engineers, in the nineteenth century they were often thought up by people who would have used them within their own professions. The 'Mechanical Poultry Feeder', for example, was designed by a cook, and the 'Pneumatic Inhaler' by a surgeon. Items with a combination of functions seem to have been particularly popular, reflecting a fondness for small, ingenious objects – the 'Cigar-Holding Pencil Case Knife' is just one example.

In the nineteenth century anyone who had an idea that might solve a problem or speed up a task could come up with a technical solution. Inventors were ingenious, imaginative, sometimes misguided, but, in the unexpected world of Victorian inventions, ever hopeful.

Note to reader: *All titles for illustrations marked with an asterisk (*) denote* provisional *registration only.*

[1] Michael Snodin and John Styles, *Design & the Decorative Arts: Victorian Britain 1837–1902*, London: V&A Publications, 2004, p. 122.

[2] Herbert Sussman, *Victorian Technology: Invention, Innovation and the Rise of the Machine*, Oxford: Praeger, 2009, p. 74.

[3] *Sessional Papers of the House of Lords*, XVI, 1851, pp. 456–58, quoted in H. I. Dutton, *The Patent System and Inventive Activity During the Industrial Revolution 1750–1852*, Manchester: Manchester University Press, 1984, p. 34.

[4] H. I. Dutton, *The Patent System and Inventive Activity During the Industrial Revolution 1750–1852*, Manchester: Manchester University Press, 1984, p. 35.

[5] J. Halls, 'Questions of attribution: registered designs at The National Archives', *Journal of Design History* 26(4), p. 417.

[6] T. Turner, *On Copyright in Design in Art and Manufactures*, London: F. Elsworth, 1851, p. 24.

[7] J. Farey, *1829 Select Committee on Patents*, 141, quoted in Brad Sherman and Lionel Bently, *The Making of Modern Intellectual Property Law*, Cambridge: Cambridge University Press, 1999, p. 88.

[8] Brad Sherman and Lionel Bently, *The Making of Modern Intellectual Property Law*, Cambridge: Cambridge University Press, 1999, p. 92.

[9] Turner, *op. cit.*, p. 45.

[10] Dutton, *op. cit.*, pp. 86–88.

DESIGN FOR A SOMAPANTIC BATH

1848

Fig. 1

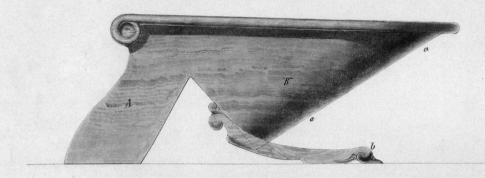

Fig. 2

Fig. 3

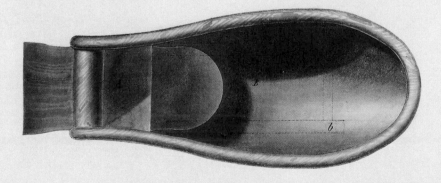

*The shape of the bath means that much less water is required to cover
the body when in a recumbent position than when an ordinary bath is used.*

HOUSE
& GARDEN

"THE MACHINE
SAVES LABOUR,
SOAP AND FIRE..."

• • •

Advertisement for Bradford's
'Vowel' Washing Machine
As appears in Dickens's Dictionary of London

1879

The word 'gadget' originated in the nineteenth century, and nowhere was the Victorian love of gadgets more apparent than in the home. As large-scale industrial inventions changed work and society beyond recognition, a host of less eminent inventors were inspired to produce ingenious domestic objects. Some of these have stood the test of time better than others – who now, for example, soaks in a 'Somapantic Bath' (see p. 18) or uses a '"Jack" for putting on and pulling off Boots' (see p. 26)?

The spread of industry meant that factories were now mass-producing objects for the home more quickly and cheaply than ever before. Commodities previously available only to the rich were now much more widely affordable. At the same time social changes, especially the rise of the middle classes, led to a huge increase in consumerism. Britain had become the wealthiest nation in the world, thanks to its industrial dominance and the income generated by the colonies. The middle classes in particular benefited from this wealth. Not surprisingly, the poorer classes spent a lot of their income on housing and food, but even in the poorest households status was marked by the ability to possess goods.

People were anxious that their homes should reflect their social status, and this meant conspicuous consumption and ostentatious display – the acquisition of 'things'. Wealth began to be measured by the possession of material goods, as the machine had made commodities inexpensive and more widely available.[1] Ever-changing fashions and a demand for novelty added to the huge numbers of items being manufactured for the home.

The range of objects with which the house could be decorated and equipped meant that the question of taste became a matter of intense

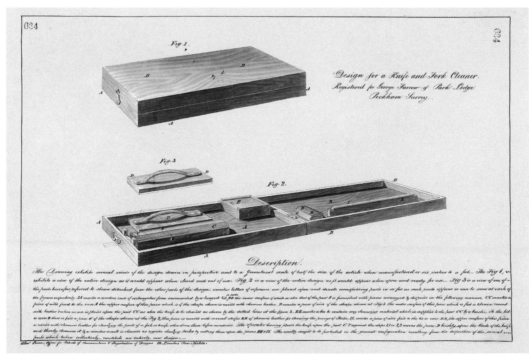

Design for a Knife and Fork Cleaner, 1846

Design for an Extending Table, 1853

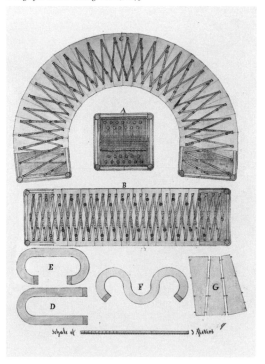

discussion and debate. Correct etiquette, immensely important, was also a source of great anxiety, especially among the upwardly mobile. To assuage – or perhaps feed – these anxieties, advice books and journals proliferated, aimed at readers at different social levels and with a range of incomes. What to choose became a fraught area – living up to your station was as important as not being thought pretentious. The influential lifestyle writer Mary Stickney Ellis thought it: 'Scarcely necessary...to point out...the loss of character and influence occasioned by living below our station'.[2] Small things mattered: for example, another writer of advice books, Jane Ellen Panton, felt that if well decorated, the hallway would 'disclose immediately to the eyes of the caller that here is the abode of people who care for their home, and who wish it to be pretty, and who thus denote that they are worth cultivating, for no doubt they will turn out to be desirable friends'.[3] People were socially categorized, and the items that they owned helped to signal their place in the hierarchy.[4]

The gallery of manufactures at the Great Exhibition of 1851 showcased the rise of consumerism in the machine age. In the 'metallic, vitreous and ceramic' section, for example, the subdivision of 'cutlery and edge tools' displayed the metal knives and tableware of Sheffield; other cities specialized in different products, as specialist suppliers and skilled labour congregated together. The cutlery section contained a multitude of utensils used by middle-class Victorian diners – fish knives and fish forks, fish carvers, game carvers, dessert knives and dessert forks.[5]

This plethora of dining accoutrements helped to make dinner parties, always an opportunity to display taste and propriety, even more of a minefield. They were the most popular middle-class social event, with consequences for the host's reputation.[6] According to advice writer Mrs Loftie, there was heated debate over 'the knife and fork

question'. On forks, she writes, 'the "three-prongians" hold their own against the "four-prongians", except in the matter of young peas'.[7] The designs for extendable dinner tables also reflected the desire to entertain on a certain scale even within a smaller home (see above and p. 52).

This increase in the number of objects meant that there were many more things to keep clean. Other factors also made housekeeping difficult. Coal stoves and fireplaces meant that soot and black dust within the house were a constant problem. To avoid airborne infections and dirt brought in from outside, doctors recommended

"THERE IS A SERIOUS QUESTION ANXIOUSLY DEBATED AT MANY DINNER PARTIES AS TO THE SUPERIORITY OF THREE PRONGS TO FOUR."

MRS LOFTIE, *ART AT HOME*, 1876

Design for Bar of Soap, 1865

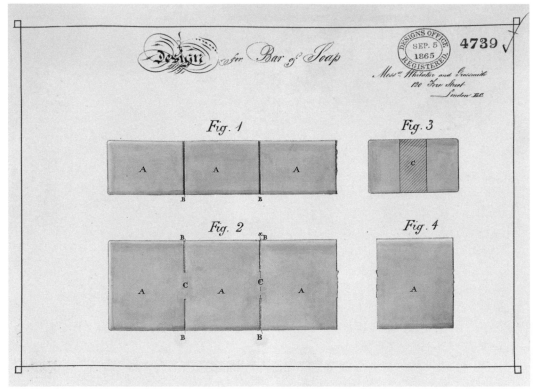

that curtains be replaced with blinds that could be wiped down. Many houses had both curtains and blinds: the blinds had the added advantage of preventing carpets and curtains from fading.[8]

Although a challenge, keeping a clean, ordered house was considered a sign of moral rectitude. Since a respectable wife could not be seen to do too much around the house, servants were needed. Not everyone could afford servants who were properly trained, or even full-time, but many employed a workhouse child, or a charwoman, to come in from time to time. The wife of an assistant surgeon in 1859 said: 'I must not do our household work, or carry my baby out: or I should lose caste. We must keep a servant'. It is estimated that in London between 1851 and 1871 around 60 per cent of the population had at least one servant.[9] The plethora of new objects created not only a need for servants but also a market for labour-saving devices:

the registered designs include early attempts to save on washing up in the form of knife and fork cleaners – which appear more labour intensive than the conventional method (see p. 20).

The nineteenth century saw other major developments within the home, some of which had effects far beyond questions of social status. The most important of these was improved sanitation. By the 1840s people were becoming aware of the link between poor sanitation and contagious disease, although the mechanism for this was not understood (see chapter V).

The increasing popularity of flush lavatories (the word was used by the Victorians to mean the place where they washed – the object itself was known as a water closet) exacerbated the problem of polluted drinking water and the consequent spread of waterborne diseases such as cholera. By the 1840s water closets were commonly built in wealthy districts; the contents went into the drainage system, which discharged into the rivers – a major source of the population's drinking water. Many rivers in urban districts became, in effect, open sewers. This famously culminated in what became known as the Great Stink of 1858, when the smell from the Thames was so atrocious that members of the House of Commons considered relocating upstream to Hampton Court. Curtains coated in chloride of lime were hung to try to counteract the problem.

Many people experienced a flush water closet for the first time at the Great Exhibition. They were a source of great interest, so much so that Parliamentary Papers concluded that they 'strongly impressed all concerned in the management with the necessity of making similar provisions for the public wherever large numbers are congregated, and with the sufferings which must be endured by all, but more especially by females, on account of the want of them'.[10]

In the early days water closets were malodorous and unhygienic, and for that reason they were often positioned in extensions at the back of the house.[11] As the designs shown here suggest, these problems taxed many engineers (see this page and p. 43). One of the best known of these was Thomas Crapper, who introduced a very successful improved flushing system in 1861 ('a certain flush with every pull').

For much of the first half of the nineteenth century most houses either had a well with a pump in the scullery, or more often a water tank or barrel kept full from a neighbourhood pump or standpipe. Middle-class homes in urban and suburban areas had a cistern that was regularly filled by a waterman with a horse-drawn water cart. By the middle of the century most middle-class homes would have had access to running water, although the system was intermittent, with water often only provided for two hours a day and, until 1872, never on Sundays.[12]

Until the 1870s, the middle and upper classes would wash in their bedroom or dressing room, at a washstand on which stood a basin and ewer. Water would be brought up from the kitchen, bucket by bucket. From the 1840s more expensive properties began to pipe hot water upstairs, and by the 1870s hot-water pipes began to appear in middle-class homes. However, soaking in hot water was viewed as morally suspect: baths of a similar shape to our own were used for vague therapeutic purposes, with bathers being referred to as 'patients' (see pp. 42, 44).

Many commentators recommended daily cold baths.[13] Separate bathrooms and water closets increased in popularity as the century progressed, and by the 1880s they were installed in many homes. There was some distaste for sharing the bathroom, and it was often used by everyone but the lady of the house, who continued to use the washstand in her bedroom.[14] By the end of the century, gas geysers were often used to heat water in bathrooms. Like early kitchen ranges, they were dangerous and prone to explode.

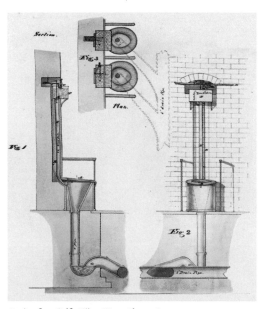

Design for a Self-Acting Water Closet, 1849

Although the shower, or shower-bath, did not arrive in middle-class homes until the 1890s, there are some very early examples of the shower concept among the registered designs. They used cold water contained in a tank – a cord was pulled to release a rush of water onto the user's head (see p. 45). Even at the end of the century it seems there was still some way to go before showering became an enjoyable experience. In her memoir of childhood, the engraver Gwen Raverat described the family bathroom, which 'had a sort of grotto containing a shower-bath at one end; this was lined with as many different stops as the organ in King's Chapel. And it was as difficult to control as it would be for an amateur to play that organ.'[15]

Changes in lighting, too, had an impact on home life. At the beginning of the century candles were the main source of illumination, until oil for lamps became more affordable. Oil lamps remained popular throughout the century, although their smoke created yet more soot inside the house. Gas lighting was used as early as 1798 in factories, and it was commonly used in cities for street lighting and in public places by the

"PIERCING JETS OF BOILING, OR ICE-COLD, WATER CAME ROARING AT ONE FROM THE MOST UNEXPECTED ANGLES, AND HIT ONE IN THE TENDEREST SPOTS."

GWEN RAVERAT, *PERIOD PIECE*, 1952

middle of the century. It began to be used in middle-class homes around the 1840s, and had many advantages – for example, evening parlour games became very popular. However, it was also dirty, emitting fumes which could damage household items, as well as depleting oxygen, causing problems such as headaches and fainting. Gas explosions were a common cause of household accidents. The aspidistra famously became popular at this period because it was one of the few plants that could survive gas in the atmosphere. Paraffin was discovered in the United States in 1859. It was safe, clean and gave a good light, and paraffin lamps became very popular. Electric lighting was introduced in the 1880s, but was rarely used until the invention of the modern tungsten filament bulb in 1907.[16]

As well as having a greater disposable income, the Victorians began to separate their world into the public sphere of work and trade, and a private sphere of home life and domesticity. More and more, work was moving outside the home; for example, piecework, which was produced at home, changed to factory work, and professionals such as doctors and lawyers worked in offices rather than from home.[17] Those who could afford it moved to the suburbs to escape the disease, pollution and overcrowding of the city.

Although city homes had gardens – the lifestyle guru Mrs Haweis wrote a book called *Rus in Urbe: or Flowers that thrive in London Gardens and Smoky Towns*[18] – it was with the advent of suburban life that gardening became

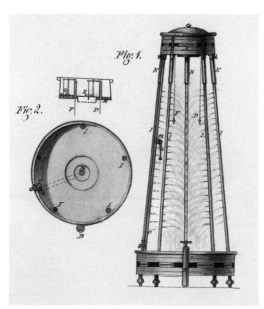

Omnidirective Shower Bath, 1843

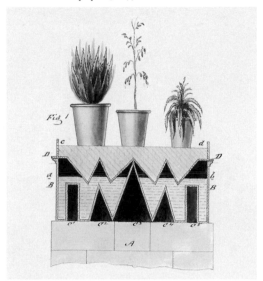

Design for a Hot Water Circulator suitable for Horticultural Domestic and other purposes, 1844

a popular middle-class recreation. There was general agreement that gardening was a virtuous, and even Christian, activity, the seasonal growth of plants being the work of God. The middle classes encouraged gardening among the working classes, believing it would keep them out of the pubs, reduce political unrest and improve their morals. Allotment societies were promoted and horticultural societies set up: by the end of the century a garden was considered an essential part of life.[19] This gave scope for ingenious outdoor inventions, including gadgets for picking hard-to-reach fruit and flowers, tools for pruning, new ways to water the plants, and a device for killing insects on trees that looks as if only a gymnast could successfully put it in place (see pp. 46–51).

Improvements in lighting, sanitation and the move towards suburban living transformed the character of many homes over the course of the nineteenth century. From candlelight, cesspools and a relatively restricted number of household objects at the beginning of the century, to electricity, indoor bathrooms and a host of labour-saving devices, the home became the focal point of family life – and the showcase for new inventions, large and small.

[1] Herbert Sussman, *Victorian Technology: Invention, Innovation, and the Rise of the Machine*, Oxford: Praeger, 2009, p. 67.

[2] Mary Stickney Ellis, *The Wives of England: Their Relative Duties, Domestic Influence, & Social Obligations*, London: Fisher, Son & Co, 1843, p. 219. Quoted in Judith Flanders, *Inside the Victorian Home*, London and New York: W. W. Norton & Company, 2003, p. 168.

[3] Mrs [Jane Ellen] Panton, *Homes of Taste: Economical Hints*, London: Sampson Low, Marston, Searle, & Rivington, 1890. Quoted in Judith Flanders, *Inside the Victorian Home*, London and New York: W. W. Norton & Company, 2003, p. 168.

[4] Rachel Rich, 'Designing the dinner party: Advice on dining and décor in London and Paris, 1860–1914', *Journal of Design History*, 16(1), 2003, p. 49.

[5] Sussman, *op. cit.*, p. 70

[6] Rich, *op. cit.*, p. 49.

[7] Mrs Loftie, 'The Dining Room, "Art at Home"' series, London, 1876, quoted in Rich, *op. cit.*, p. 57.

[8] Flanders, *op. cit.*, pp. 191 and 192.

[9] Flanders, *op. cit.*, p. 131.

[10] 'First report of the Commissioners of the Exhibition of 1851', *Parliamentary Papers*, 1852, vol 26, Appendix 30.

[11] Flanders, *op. cit.*, p. 335.

[12] Anne Hardy, 'Parish pump to private pipes: London's water supply in the nineteenth century', *Medical History*, Supplement No 11, 1991: 76–93.

[13] Helena Barrett and John Phillips, *Suburban Style: The British Home, 1840–1960*, London: Little, Brown and Company, 1993, p. 120.

[14] *Ibid.*

[15] Gwen Raverat, *Period Piece: A Cambridge Childhood*, [1952], London: Faber & Faber, 1987, p. 183. Quoted in Flanders, *op. cit.*, p. 328.

[16] Barrett and Phillips, *op. cit.*, p. 64.

[17] Flanders, *op. cit.*, pp. 6–7.

[18] Mary Eliza Joy Haweis, *Rus in Urbe: Or, Flowers That Thrive in London Gardens and Smoky Towns*, London: Field and Tuer, 1886.

[19] Barrett and Phillips, *op. cit.*, p. 169.

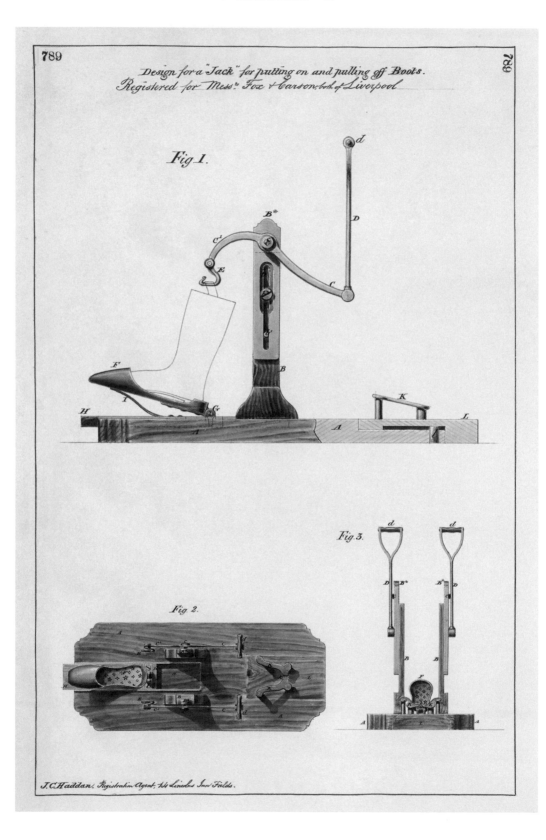

Design for a "Jack" for putting on and pulling off Boots.
Registered for Messᵣ Fox & Carson, both of Liverpool

Fig 1.

Fig. 3.

Fig. 2.

J. C. Haddan. Registration Agent; 44 Lincolns Inn Fields.

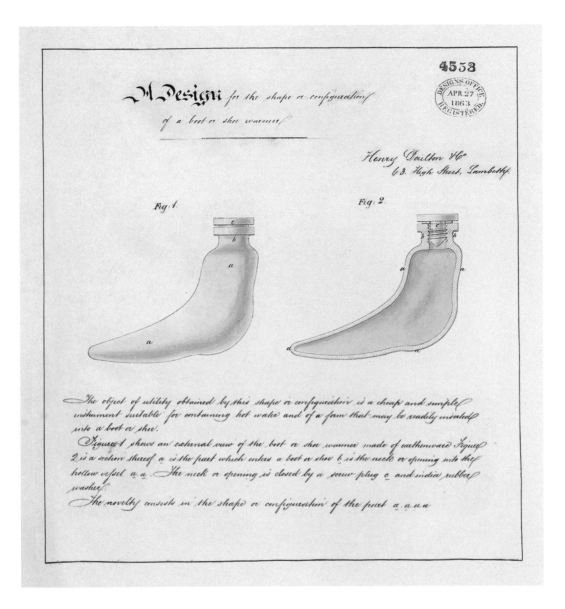

OPPOSITE

DESIGN FOR A "JACK" FOR PUTTING ON AND PULLING OFF BOOTS

1846

Fig. 1. side elevation • *Fig. 2.* plan view. • *Fig. 3.* end view

Boots can be pulled on and off by attaching them to the hook (E) and using the levers (D). The slot in the central section (B*, Fig. 1.) contains a screw (B²) whereby the height of the standards (B) may be adjusted to suit the height of the person. Spaces are allowed (K) in case the person's boots should have spurs attached thereto.

ABOVE

A DESIGN FOR THE SHAPE OR CONFIGURATION OF A BOOT OR SHOE WARMER

1863

Fig. 1. external view of the boot or shoe warmer made of earthenware • *Fig. 2.* section thereof

This is a cheap and simple instrument suitable for containing hot water and of a form that may be readily inserted into a boot or shoe. The instrument can be opened and closed by means of the screw plug (C) and an india rubber washer.

BELOW

DESIGN FOR THE SHAPE OR CONFIGURATION OF A SPATULA

1847

The novelty of this design is that configuration of the blade (a) of a Spatula which consists of the blade being hollow so as to receive a heater in place of being solid as heretofore.

OPPOSITE

KNIFE AND FORK CLEANER

1850

Fig. 1. front elevation • *Fig. 2.* end elevation

The drums (C, D & E) are turned by (B), a cranked shaft attached by a rod (G) to a treadle (F). The first drum (C) is covered with buff leather for cleaning the sides of the blades of knives, the second (D) is for cleaning the backs of blades, and the third (E) has its periphery covered with bristles or wires and forms a cylindrical brush suitable for the cleaning of forks.

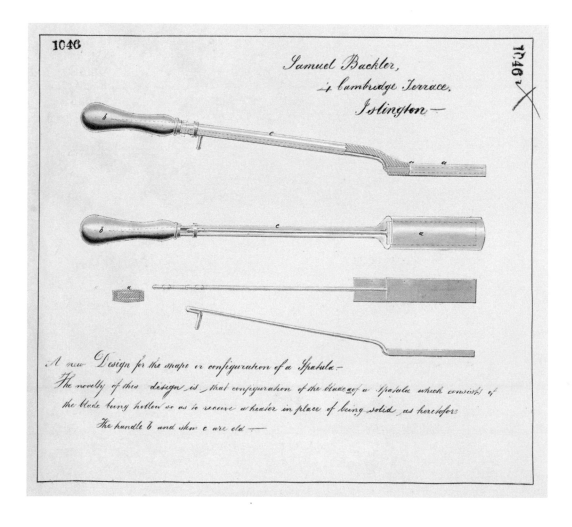

Knife and Fork Cleaner.

2504.

Thomas Parker, of Kensington, Middlesex, Gentn

Fig. 1.   Fig. 2.

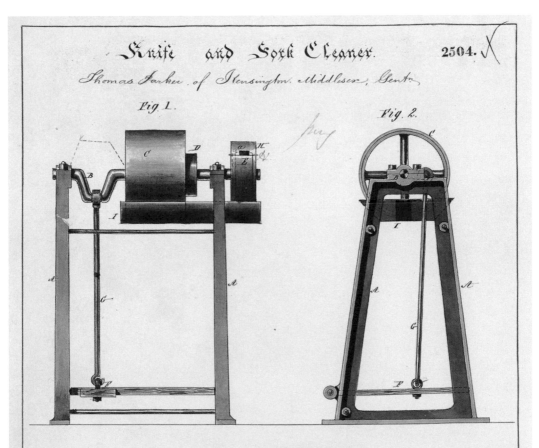

Description

Figure 1 is a front elevation and Figure 2 an end elevation of this knife cleaner, A A is the frame work, B B a cranked shaft which has its bearings in the top of the frame and has fitted upon it three drums or pullies C, D, & E. F is a treadle connected with the crank upon the shaft B by a rod G. — The first Drum C is covered with one or more plies of buff leather and is employed for cleaning the sides of the blades of the knives; the second drum D is used for cleaning the backs of the blades, and the third drum E has its periphery covered with bristles or wires and forms a cylindrical brush suitable for the cleaning of forks, which in cleaning are introduced through a hole a in the covering H of the circular brush, I is a trough for holding emery or brick dust. — The purpose of utility to which this Design has reference is the cleaning of knives & forks by one machine.

The parts of this Design which are not new or original are all the parts separately considered, but the configuration resulting from their combination in the manner described is registered as forming a new Design for a knife & fork cleaner.

Messrs. J. C. Robertson & Co
Registration Agents

1305 **1305**

Design for a Counterbalance Candle Holder.

by
James Mellin
Levengrave near Rochdale.

Half Size.

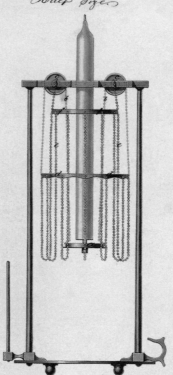

In this design the candle is fixed into the socket *a* suspended by the chains *b b* passing over the pulleys *c c* and is counterbalanced by the ring *d d* and chains *e e* the upper ends of which are attached to the stationary ring *f f* by which means the flame of the candle is always kept at one uniform height.

All new.

NEWTON & SON del^t Patent Office MANCHESTER.

OPPOSITE

DESIGN FOR A COUNTERBALANCE CANDLE HOLDER

1847

In this design the candle is fixed onto the socket (a) suspended by the chains (bb) passing over the pulleys (cc) and is counterbalanced by the ring (dd) and chains (ee), the upper ends of which are attached to the stationary ring (ff) by which means the flame of the candle is always kept at one uniform height.

BELOW

ILLUMINATED NIGHT CLOCK

1847

A helical spring (b) is placed at the bottom of the candlestick, (a); (c) is the support on which the candle rests, which is forced up by the spring; (d) is a cap which prevents the candle rising excepting as it burns away; (e) is a slot in the candlestick through which the pointer (f), which is attached to the candle support (c) passes; as the candle burns away the support (c) and pointer rise, and the latter traversing the dial (g) indicates the time.

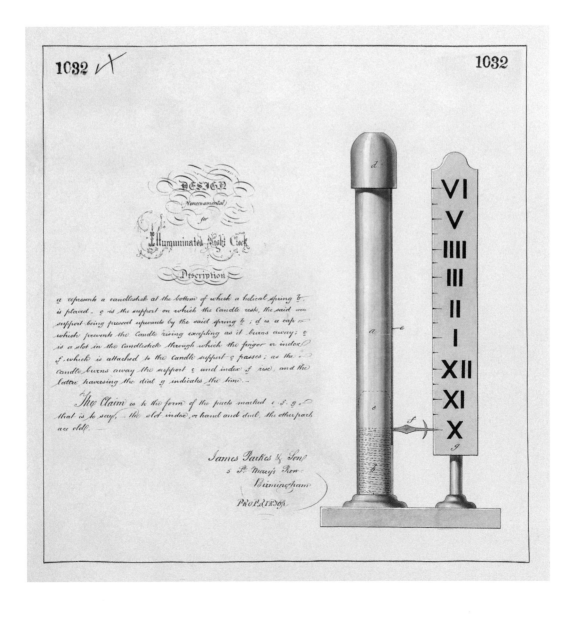

ABOVE

IMPROVED BREAD KNIFE

1846

(A.A.A) *is an iron stand with two upright pillars
between which are suspended from the point* (B) *two
straight bars or levers supporting a knife moving freely
upon the point* (C). (D) *is a board on which the loaf
or other substance to be cut is placed. The claim is for
all the parts except the knife* (E) *and the board* (D).

OPPOSITE

THE DESIDERATUM COMBINED KNIFE AND FORK*

1881

Figs. 1. & 2. the combined knife and fork in an open
position, from each side • *Fig. 3.* in the closed position

The fork has a blade (b), *and a barb* (e), *which prevents
food from slipping when being cut. When in use the food
is cut with one hand, and when so cut, the instrument
is closed, assuming the position shown at* Fig. 3. *when
it can be used as a fork.*

THE

DESIDERATUM

Combined Knife And Fork

Messᵣₛ Arnold & Son
Surgical Instrument Makers
West Smithfield
London
Proprietors

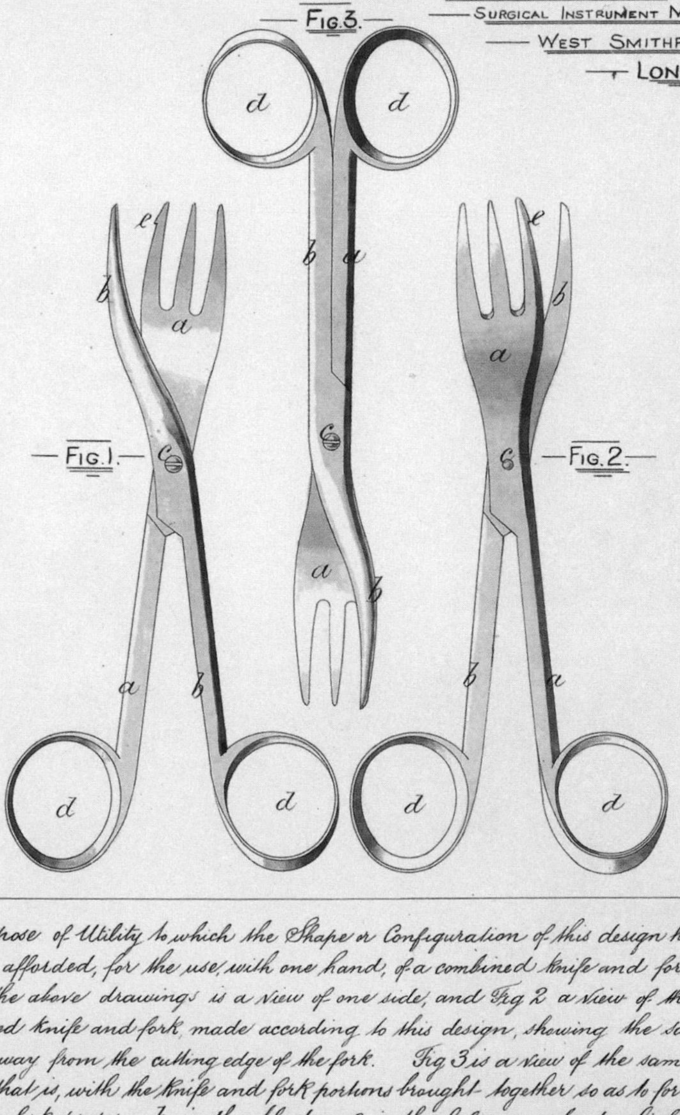

Fig. 3.

Fig. 1.   Fig. 2.

The purpose of Utility to which the Shape or Configuration of this design has reference is, the facility afforded, for the use, with one hand, of a combined Knife and Fork.

Fig 1 of the above drawings is a view of one side, and Fig 2 a view of the other side of a combined Knife and Fork, made according to this design, shewing the same open, or the blade away from the cutting edge of the fork. Fig 3 is a view of the same Instrument but closed, that is, with the Knife and Fork portions brought together so as to form a Fork.

a is the fork proper, b is the blade, c is the fulcrum about which the shanks or parts a and b work. d d are the rings in which the fingers are inserted, for simultaneously operating the blade or Knife b, and fork a. e is a "barb" on the cutting edge of fork a, to prevent the food being cut, from slipping.

When in use the food is cut with one hand, and when so cut, the instrument is closed, assuming the position shown at Fig 3, when it can be used as a fork.

The whole of this Design is New, in so far as regards the shape or Configuration thereof.

BELOW

DESIGN FOR A GRAVY DISH

1849

Fig. 1. top plan view ◇ *Fig. 2.* section taken through the line (AB) at *Fig. 1.*

The Gravy gradually runs down to reservoir (C) the carver having cut the meat and being ready to serve the gravy, he withdraws the Cork (F) with the point of his fork by passing it through the ring thereon. The pure gravy runs through the passage into reservoir (D) leaving the grease &c in the reservoir (C).

OPPOSITE

DESIGN FOR AN OYSTER OPENER

1852

Fig. 1. side view ◇ *Fig. 2.* plan view of the improved instrument

A knife (c) is attached to a bell-crank lever (b), which is pushed whilst the operator holds the oyster, positioned in a cup (f), in position. A spring (h) allows the position of the oyster to be adjusted. The design consists in a novel configuration constituting an improved Oyster Opener the object being to open Oysters with greater facility than heretofore.

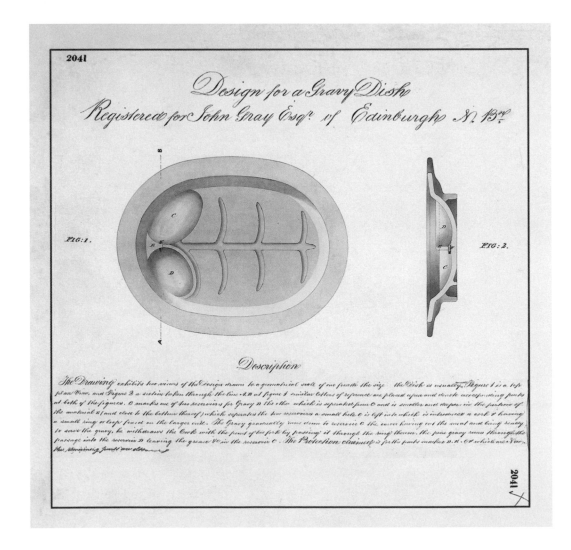

Design for An Oyster Opener

Registered by

Adolph Aubert   Nantes France

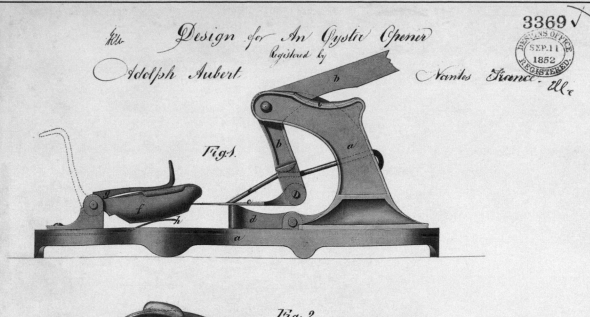

Fig. 1.

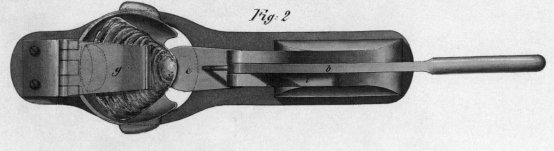

Fig: 2

This Design consists in a novel configuration of parts constituting an improved Oyster Opener the object being to open Oysters with greater facility than heretofore. In the Drawing Fig 1 is a side view and Fig 2 a plan view of the improved Instrument. *a a* is the bed and frame for carrying the several parts. *b b* is a bell-crank lever to the lower limb of which a knife *c* is jointed; the longer limb forms a handle for working the knife. *d* is an adjustable bed for keeping the knife to a proper level and *e* is a spring affixed to the frame *a* and passing through the lever *b* to press upon the knife for the purpose of keeping it in its position. *f* is a cup jointed to a bracket on the bed and formed so as to receive the oyster and *g* is a hinged piece lying over the cup and intended to receive the pressure of the hand of the operator, and thereby hold the oyster firmly so that it may be pierced by the knife *c*. Below the cup is a spring *h* which gives it a tendency to rise and thus admits of the position of the oyster being adjusted to meet the thrust of the knife. For the purpose of removing any rock or other excrescence from the oyster that might impede the operation of opening the same a substitute for a pair of shears is formed by chamfering off the upper part of the frame to a cutting edge as shewn at *i*, and similarly shaping the under side of the handle.—

Under this Registration I desire to secure the peculiar configuration of parts as shewn and described: All new

Newton & Son del. 66 Chancery Lane.

Design for a Curved Roller Blind

BY

Rudolph Lindenzweig and William Jolly
Islington.

4813

DESIGNS OFFICE
SEP. 20
1856
REGISTERED.

The purpose of utility to which the shape or configuration of this Design has reference is to provide a roller blind that will fit a curved window as for example the curve of a Brougham front and will yet roll up with the same facility as an ordinary spring roller blind. The chief novelty consists in providing a flexible case (to which the curtain or blind is attached) in place of the ordinary rigid case in which the axle and coiled spring are contained. This flexible case is constructed of a wire helix and covered with cloth or other flexible material as shewn in the Drawing which represents the blind rolled up but a portion of the roller laid bare to expose the interior. <u>a</u> is the spindle or central rod curved to correspond to the curvature of the window frame. This rod is squared at its ends and inserted into square holes in metal brackets <u>b b</u>. Two short barrels <u>cc*</u> run freely on the spindle <u>a</u> and to these barrels are connected the ends of the wire helix <u>d</u>. The coiled spring is shewn at <u>e</u>. It is connected at one end with the barrel <u>c*</u> and at the other with the fixed spindle as usual. As therefore the curtain or blind is drawn down it will rotate the barrel and wind up the spring <u>e</u> which will be retained in that position by the ordinary catch <u>f</u>. On releasing the catch the spring <u>e</u> will roll up the blind as usual. In order however that the case may revolve around the fixed curved spindle it is necessary that its form shall continually change while it revolves. To effect this therefore the case is formed of a flexible tube as described and to prevent the covering of the coiled wire or helix from slipping on the wire it is not only stitched on the helix but coblers wax or other adhesive substance is in addition applied thereto. The cylindrical case thus formed takes its curve from the spindle and as it revolves it adapts itself to the constrained figure it receives from the spindle.

The parts of this Design which are not new or original as regards the shape or configuration thereof are marked <u>b cc* e</u> and <u>f</u>.

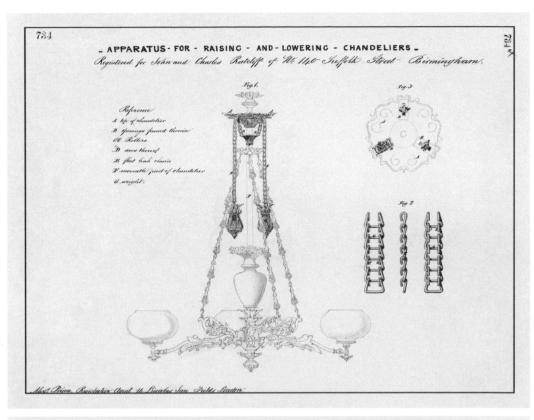

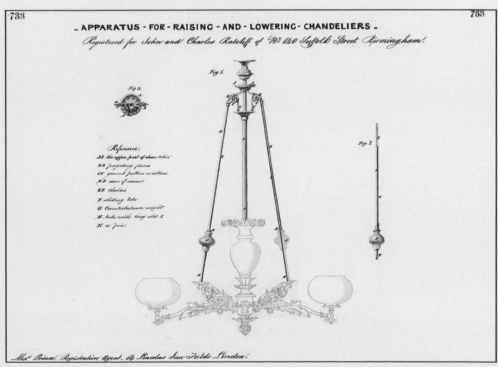

PREVIOUS LEFT

DESIGN FOR A CURVED ROLLER BLIND
1866

A wire helix covered with cloth is connected with the barrel (c*) and with the fixed spindle. When the blind is drawn up it will rotate the barrel and wind up the spring which will be retained in that position by the catch (f).

PREVIOUS RIGHT, ABOVE & BELOW

APPARATUS FOR RAISING AND LOWERING CHANDELIERS
1846

PREVIOUS RIGHT, ABOVE

Fig. 1. the design • *Fig. 2.* detached from chandelier
Fig. 3. top plan view

Rollers (CC) are attached to the chandelier (BB); the rollers revolve on axes (DD), over which the chain (E) passes. One end is attached to the moveable part (F) of the chandelier and the other to a counterbalance (G).

PREVIOUS RIGHT, BELOW

Fig. 1. the design • *Fig. 2.* edge view • *Fig. 3.* top plan view

A chain (EE) passes over grooved pullies or rollers (CC). A counterbalance (G), slides up and down a tube (H).

OPPOSITE

[...]SUPPORTER OR BED REST
1850

Fig. 1. view of the supporter shewing the manner in which it is applied • *Fig. 2.* perspective view of it as detached

The device is attached (CC) to the foot posts of the bed. Buckles (ee) allow the position to be adjusted; the design aims to provide a firm and efficient but at the same time pliant and easily adjustable support to invalids and others when reclining or sitting up in bed.

BELOW

DESIGN FOR A PORTABLE BED WARMER
1844

Fig. 1. the whole configuration of the stand in one general view • *Fig. 2.* view of the configuration of the Lamp
Fig. 3. the wire gauze chimney section shewn separately

(E) is the chimney and (F) its socket by which it is set on the Lamp at (G), the Lamp being then placed in the cavity (H) of Fig. 1. The Lamp is lighted with Spirits of Wine.

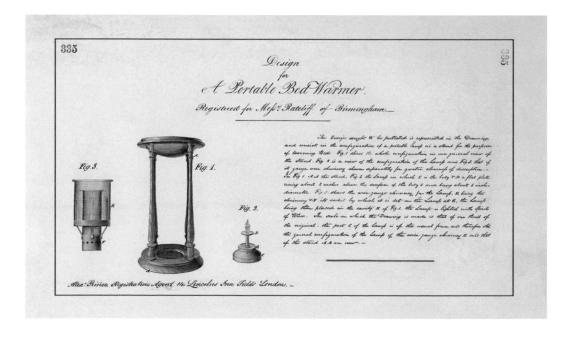

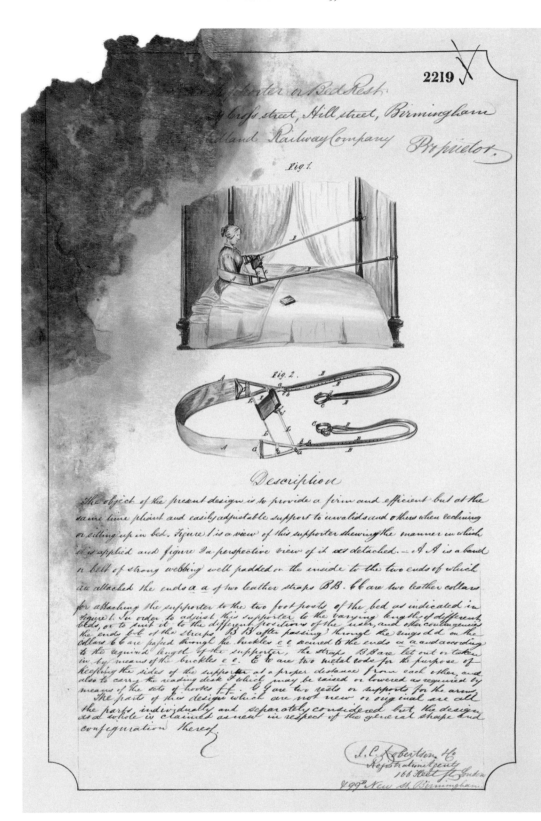

2219

...porter or Bed Rest.

...cross street, Hill street, Birmingham

...Midland Railway Company Proprietor.

Fig 1.

Fig. 2.

Description

The object of the present design is to provide a firm and efficient but at the same time pliant and easily adjustable support to invalids and others when reclining or sitting up in bed. Figure 1 is a view of this supporter shewing the manner in which it is applied and figure 2 a perspective view of it as detached. — A A is a band or belt of strong webbing well padded on the inside to the two ends of which are attached the ends a a of two leather straps B B. C C are two leather collars for attaching the supporter to the two foot posts of the bed as indicated in figure 1. In order to adjust this supporter to the varying length of different beds, or to suit it to the different positions of the user, and other contingencies the ends b b of the straps B B after passing through the rings d d on the collars C C are passed through the buckles e e secured to the ends a a and according to the required length of the supporter, the straps B B are let out or taken in by means of the buckles e e. E E are two metal rods for the purpose of keeping the sides of the supporter at a proper distance from each other, and also to carry the reading desk F which may be raised or lowered as required by means of the sets of hooks f f. G G are two rests or supports for the arms.

The parts of this design which are not new or original are all the parts, individually and separately considered but the design as a whole is claimed as new in respect of the general shape and configuration thereof.

J. C. Robertson &c
Registration agent
166 Fleet St. London
& 99 New St. Birmingham.

BELOW

DESIGN FOR A NURSE'S ASSISTANT OR "BABY JUMPER"

1847

Fig. 1. exhibits the Design complete and as it would appear when in use; the remaining figures are drawn to a larger scale for the sake of clearness ❧ *Fig. 2.* the jacket

Having placed the Child in the jacket shown in Fig. 2. *the elasticity of the spring* (E) *will cause the Child to rebound continually from the floor the distance being so adjusted that its feet just touch the floor thus affording a safe healthy and pleasing exercise for Children.*

OPPOSITE

NON-ORNAMENTAL DESIGN FOR A ROCKING HORSE

1850

Fig. 1. side view of the Rocking Horse complete
Fig. 2. side view with parts in section ❧ *Fig. 3.* plan with the Horse and rockers removed

(A) *is the horse,* (BB) *are the rockers working on the platform* (C). *It will be evident that this arrangement allows of the rocking of the horse, but at the same time prevents it from shifting backwards or forwards or sideways from its proper position.*

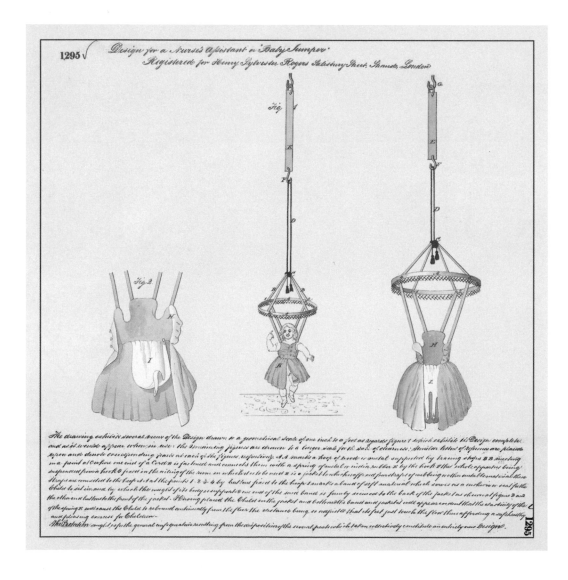

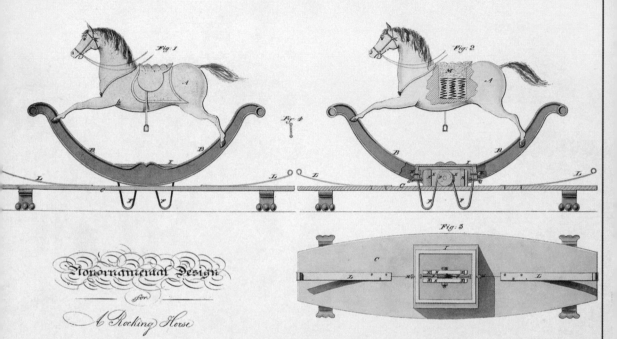

Fig: 1

Fig: 2

Fig: 4

Fig: 3

Nonornamental Design

for

A Rocking Horse

Figure 1 is a side view of the Rocking Horse complete. Figure 2 is a side view with parts in section, and Figure 3 is a plan with the Horse and rockers removed. Similar Letters refer to similar parts in all the figures. A is the horse. B. B. are the rockers working on the platform C. These rockers are made of cast iron of the section shewn in Figure 4. D is a roller or pulley whose axis is carried by the two supports or guides E. E fixed to the platform. F is a bent piece of iron passing over the roller D and attached by four screws G. G. H. H. to the box I which is fixed to the rockers B.B. The cover of this box is removed in the plan Figure 3. On the supports E. E. are fixed pieces of leather K. K. K. K. which serve as guides to the iron bar F. It will be evident that this arrangement allows of the rocking of the horse but at the same time prevents it from shifting backwards or forwards or sideways from its proper position. L. L are two springs which prevent the ends of the rockers from striking the platform. If the two screws H. H. are taken out, the bar F may then be turned on one side on the other screws G. G. and the horse may then be used without the platform if desired, and it then acts like an ordinary rocking horse. The back of the horse M is formed with a recess containing three spiral springs N. N. N. over which is placed the stuffing of the saddle which is thus rendered elastic.

The form and configuration of the arrangement for preventing the shifting of the horse, consisting of the roller D, supports or guides E. E, and bent piece of iron F, are new and original. The form of the combination of the platform C with the springs L. L, and the form of the combination of the springs N with the recess in the back of the horse M and the form of the section of the rocker Figure 4 are new and original. The remainder of the design is not new.

appᵈ

Registered for John Allen
Clarence Place
Hackney Road

Charles Cowper
Patent Agent
20 Southampton Buildings
Chancery Lane

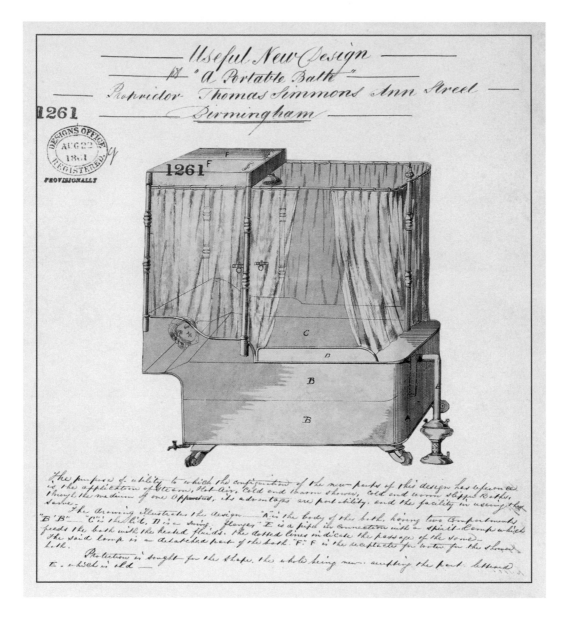

ABOVE

USEFUL NEW DESIGN FOR "A PORTABLE BATH"*

1861

(A) *is the body of the bath, having two compartments*
(BB) – (C) *is the lid,* (D) *is a swing flange,* (E) *is a*
pipe in connection with a spirit lamp which feeds the bath
with heated fluids. The dotted lines indicate the passage
of the same. (FF) *is the receptacle for water for the*
shower. The purpose of utility is the application of steam,
Hot Air, cold and warm shower, cold and warm Slipper
Baths, through the medium of one Apparatus.

OPPOSITE

IMPROVED SELF-ACTING SERVICE CISTERN
FOR WATER CLOSETS

1852

Fig. 1. front elevation • *Fig. 2.* end elevation

(A) *is the pan and* (A') *the trap for sealing the pan.* (C)
is the cistern, divided into (D) *and* (E) *each of which*
is supplied with a valve (b) *and* (c): *valve* (b) *is for*
opening a communication between the two compartments;
(c) *is for allowing the water to flow into the pan* (A).

Improved Self acting Service Cistern & Water Closets.

Thomas Crump of Derby Plumber

Proprietor.

3392

DESIGNS OFFICE
NOV. 24
1852
REGISTERED.

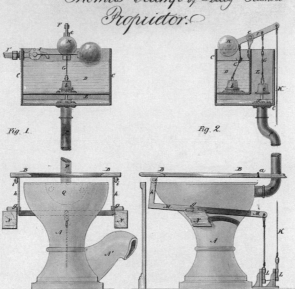

Fig. 1.   Fig. 2.

Description

Figure 1 of the above drawings represents a front elevation of this Closet apparatus and *Figure* 2 an end elevation of the same A is the pan and A' the trap for sealing the pan B is the seat which is hinged at a. C is the cistern which is divided into two compartments D and E each of which is supplied with a valve b and c: the valve b is for opening a communication between the two compartments while c is for allowing the water to flow into the pan A . F is a lever centred at e the two arms of which carry the links G G connected to the valves b. c . H is a counterbalance weight upon the end of the lever F. I is the ball cock upon the end of the service pipe I'. K is a wire connecting the lever F with the cranks L. L. which are likewise connected by a wire to the forked lever M centred at g upon the wood bearer N . The ends h. h. of the lever M are turned up as shewn and carry two friction rollers i. i. upon which the front of the seat B rests . The action of this water closet is as follows: Upon pressure being applied to the front of the seat B the lever M is depressed and through the intervention of the wires and cranks the lever F is brought down which closes the valve c and opens the valve b when the water in the compartment D flows into E at the same time the falling of the water opens the ball cock I and allows the water from the service pipe to flow into D and keep both compartments full . When the pressure is taken off the seat B the counterbalance H restores the position of the lever F when the valve B is closed and the valve c opened when the water in the compartment E flows down the pipe P through the scatterer Q and cleanses the pan A . The soil water &c passes through the trap A' to the sewer or other receptacle.

The purpose of utility to which the ~~parts~~ shape of the new design have reference is the more effectual cleansing of water closets by self acting apparatus.

The parts of this design not new or original in so far as regards the shape and configuration thereof are the parts marked A A'. I. I'. and Q.

J. C. Robertson &C°
Registration Agents
166 Fleet Street
City

Drawn to a geometric scale

1863

Design for "The Hydro Vapour Bath".

by

John Goodman, M. R. C. S.

Manchester.

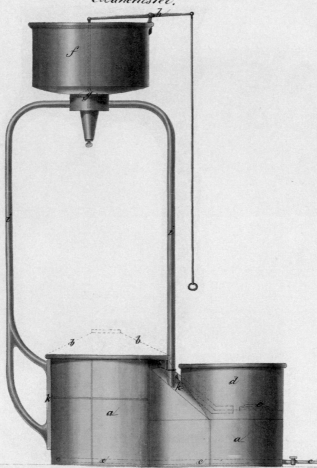

The novelty of this Design consists in the peculiar configuration or arrangement of parts whereby a shower Bath and Vapour Bath are combined, and a Patient may be submitted to an instantaneous ablation of cold or tepid water whilst immersed in the steam or vapour bath without any exposure of the body to the atmosphere. a. a. represents externally a tub bath "of nearly the ordinary construction but with a perforated pipe or g to admit steam to the interior. In this Bath the Patient is seated with the legs extended forward in the usual manner. To the upper part of the "dry bath" a flexible covering shewn by dots at b. b. is adapted and furnished with an elastic ring in the ends which by closing airtight round the neck prevents the vapour from escaping. d. is a reservoir for cold or tepid water which may when required be admitted into the interior of the Bath, by opening the valve e. f. is another reservoir for cold or tepid water which upon raising the valve g by means of the cord and lever h, will flow down the pipe or tubular pillars i. i. through perforated slots k k into the bath where it strikes or impinges upon the body of the Patient in a shower.

The parts e, b, i. i. and k. k. are new, all the rest are old.

OPPOSITE

DESIGN FOR "THE HYDRO-VAPOUR BATH"

1849

*To the upper part of the "sitz bath" a flexible covering
shown by dots at (bb) is adapted and furnished with an
elastic ring in the centre which by closing airtight around
the neck prevents the vapor from escaping. (f) is another
reservoir for cold or tepid water which will flow down
the pipes in (ii) through perforated plates in (kk) into
the bath where it strikes or impinges upon the body
of the Patient in a shower.*

BELOW

DESIGN FOR A PORTABLE SHOWER-BATH

1845

Fig. 1. vertical section of the reservoir through the
line (AB) in *Fig. 2.* ◦ *Fig. 2.* plan view of the upper
side of the machine ◦ *Fig. 3.* profile view ◦ *Fig. 4.*
plan view of the underside

*(A) is a reservoir of any elastic and waterproof material,
attached to the concave plate (B) by the holes (CC).
The valve (F) is opened by either pulling it downwards
or pushing it upwards. Fig. 4. shews perforations for
the escape of water.*

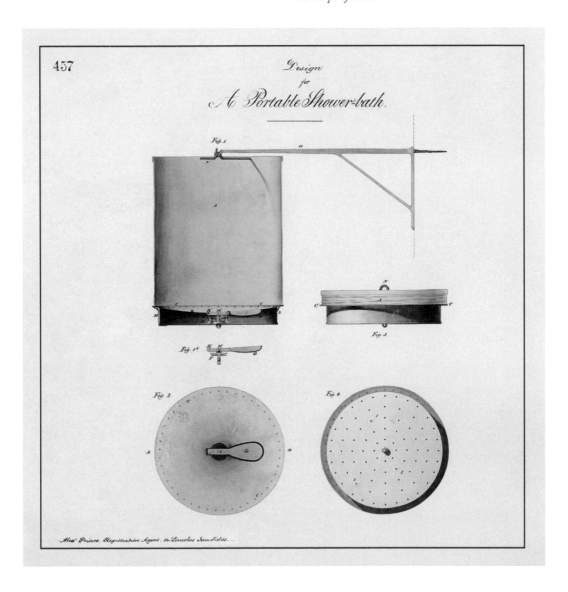

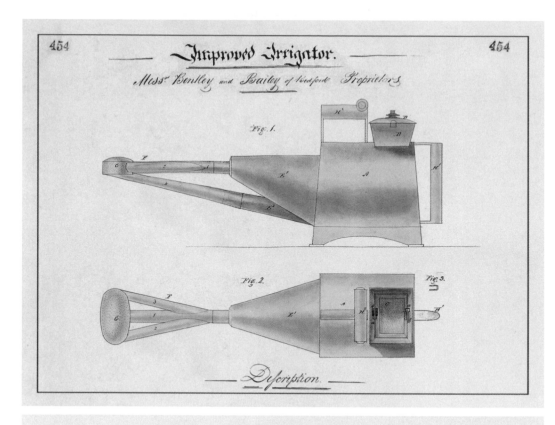

454   454

Improved Irrigator.

Messrs. Bentley and Bailey of Bedford, Proprietors

Fig. 1.

Fig. 2.   Fig. 3.

Description.

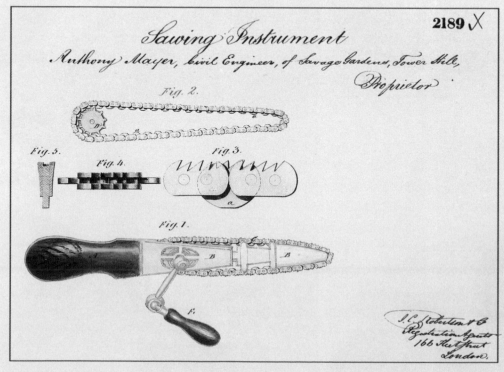

2189 ✓ X

Sawing Instrument

Anthony Mayer, Civil Engineer, of Savage Gardens, Tower Hill,

Proprietor

Fig. 2.

Fig. 5.   Fig. 4.   Fig. 3.

Fig. 1.

J. C. Robertson & Co.
Registration Agents
166 Fleet Street
London.

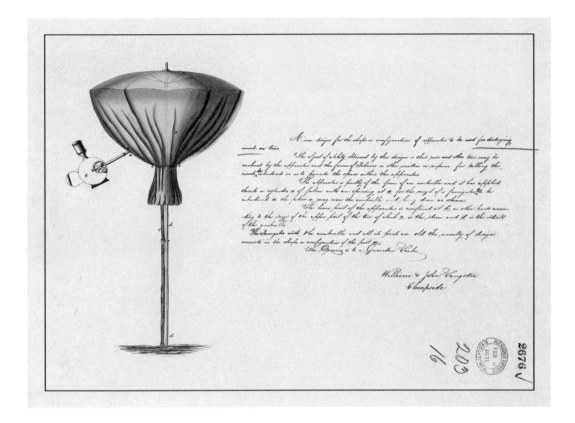

OPPOSITE ABOVE

IMPROVED IRRIGATOR

1845

Fig. 1. side elevation ❖ *Fig. 2.* top view, cover removed

(A) *is the water case and* (B) *is the funnel-shaped head through which the case is filled. The water as it passes through the pan* (C) *is freed from any sand or stone which may happen to be intermingled with it.* (F) *is a nozzle piece of four branches three of which* (1, 2, 3) *unite in one common tube which fits onto the spout* (E').

OPPOSITE BELOW

SAWING INSTRUMENT

1850

Fig. 1. elevation in its complete state ❖ *Fig. 2.* side elevation ❖ *Fig. 3.* side elevation of three links *Fig. 4.* plan of the teeth ❖ *Fig. 5.* cross section

(A) *is the handle,* (BB) *a frame for carrying an endless saw. For surgical and other purposes.*

ABOVE

APPARATUS TO BE USED FOR DISTROYING INSECTS ON TREES

1851

Rose and other trees may be enclosed by the apparatus and the fumes of Tobacco or other matters or vapour for killing the insects be introduced so as to pervade the space within the apparatus. The apparatus is partly in the form of an umbrella and has applied thereto a cylinder (x) *of fabric with an opening at* (a) *for the nozel of a fumigator* (e) *to be introduced.*

OVERLEAF

PEACH PROTECTOR, GREENHOUSE

1850

Fig. 1. showing the interior ❖ Fig. 2. side elevation

For a Peach growing against a wall: (aa) *is a glass dome formed with a lip* (bb) *for keeping a wire* (c) *in position and which wire is twisted so as to form two loops* (dd), *by which the dome may be fastened over the fruit.*

2239

Fig 1.

Fig 2.

for Christopher Hatterman of
Gardener.

The drawing is made to a geometric
the full size and represents two vie
of the design as applied to a Peach
against a Wall.— Fig.1 is a fac[e] [vi]
side elevation with part removed to [shew]
a,a, is a glass dome formed with a lip
keeping a wire C in the position she[wn]
wire is twisted so as to form two lo[ops]
d, by which the dome may be faster[ed]
to the surface against which the tree [is]

The Novelty for which protecti[on]
consists in the shape & configuration of [dome]
& wire C.— The remaining parts d,d, [are]
shewn for the purpose of explaining [ ]
of the Design.—

387   387

Fruit Gatherer.

Thomas Dray of Chiswell Street Finsbury Ironmonger Proprietor.

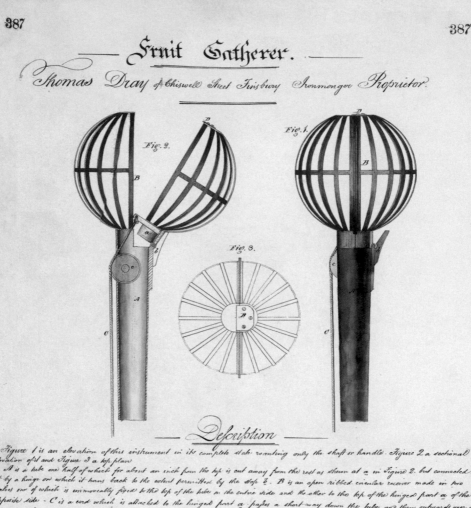

Fig. 2.   Fig. 1.   Fig. 3.

Description

Figure 1 is an elevation of this instrument in its complete state, wanting only the shaft or handle. Figure 2 a sectional elevation of it and Figure 3 a top plan.

A is a tube one half of which for about an inch from the top is cut away from the rest as shewn at a in Figure 2, but connected to it by a hinge on which it turns back to the extent permitted by the stop b. B is an open ribbed circular receiver made in two halves one of which is immoveably fixed to the top of the tube on the entire side and the other to the top of the hinged part a of the opposite side. C is a cord which is attached to the hinged part a, passes a short way down the tube and then outwards over a pulley c fixed in the tube, by pulling downwards of which cord the moveable half of the receiver when it has been thrown back for the reception of the fruit can be again closed upon it. D is a knife edge attached to the front of the moveable half at top, which serves on bringing the two halves together to sever the fruit from any stalk by which it is attached to the tree. A shaft of any convenient length is inserted into the under end of the tube.

The whole of this instrument is registered as new in respect of the shape and configuration thereof.

J.C. Robertson & Co
Registration Agents
166 Fleet Street
London

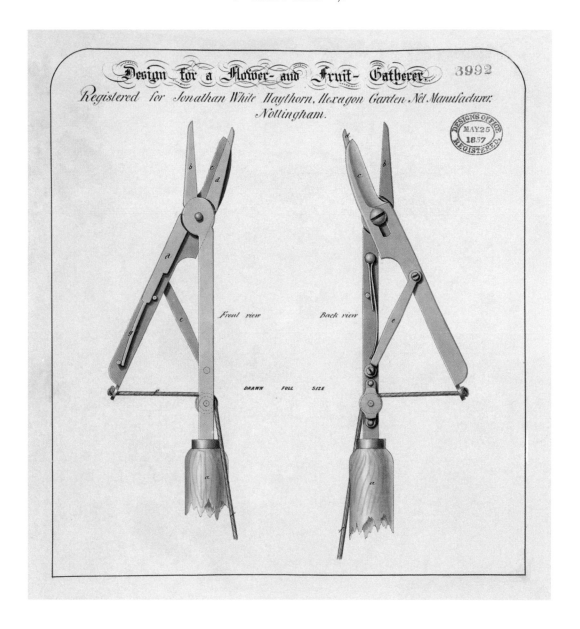

Design for a Flower- and Fruit- Gatherer. 3992

Registered for Jonathan White Haythorn, Hexagon Garden Net Manufacturer. Nottingham.

DESIGNS OFFICE MAY 25 1857 REGISTERED

Front view *Back view*

DRAWN FULL SIZE

OPPOSITE

FRUIT GATHERER

1845

Fig. 1. elevation of the instrument in its complete state
Fig. 2. sectional elevation • *Fig. 3.* top plan

(A) *is a tube one half of which is cut away from the rest,
forming a hinged section* (a). *By pulling the cord* (C)
the device opens to receive the fruit. (D) *is a knife edge
which serves on bringing the two halves together to sever
the fruit from any stalk by which it is attached to the tree.*

ABOVE

DESIGN FOR A FLOWER- AND FRUIT-GATHERER

1857

The "Gatherer" is fixed in a stem or handle (a) – (b)
is a stationary nipper against which the moveable blade
(c) *cuts* – (d) *is a moveable upper connected to the
blade* (c) – (e) *is a link to cause the blade* (c) *to have
a sliding or sawing motion whilst closing* – (f) *is a string
by pulling and closing which the flower or fruit may be
cut. The purpose is to enable a person to gather and hold
flowers or fruit from a distance.*

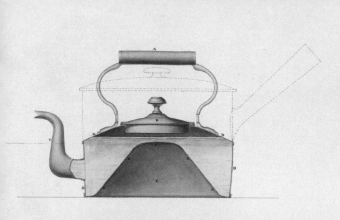

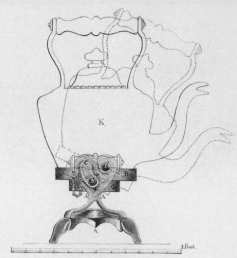

**DESIGN FOR THE BOTTOM OF A KETTLE
OR SAUCEPAN**

1846

**DESIGN FOR A SWING
KETTLE-STAND**

1858

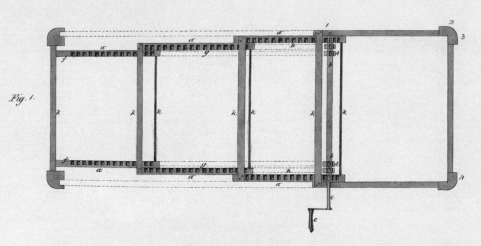

Fig. 1.

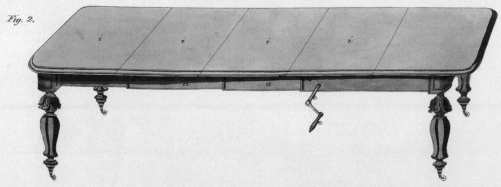

Fig. 2.

DESIGN FOR AN EXPANDING DINING-TABLE*

1851

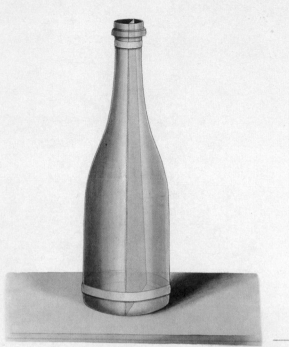

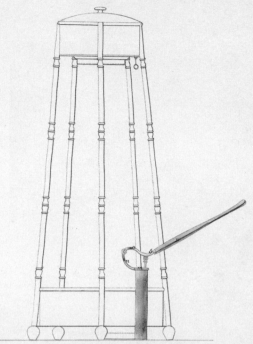

DESIGN FOR SPLIT BOTTLE*

1861

DESIGN FOR SHOWER-BATH

1849

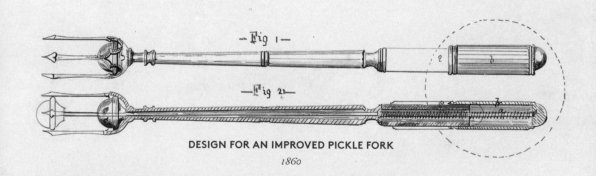

DESIGN FOR AN IMPROVED PICKLE FORK

1860

DESIGN FOR NOISELESS CORNICE-POLE AND RING*

1852

DESIGN FOR THE HAND HARD LABOR MACHINE

1852

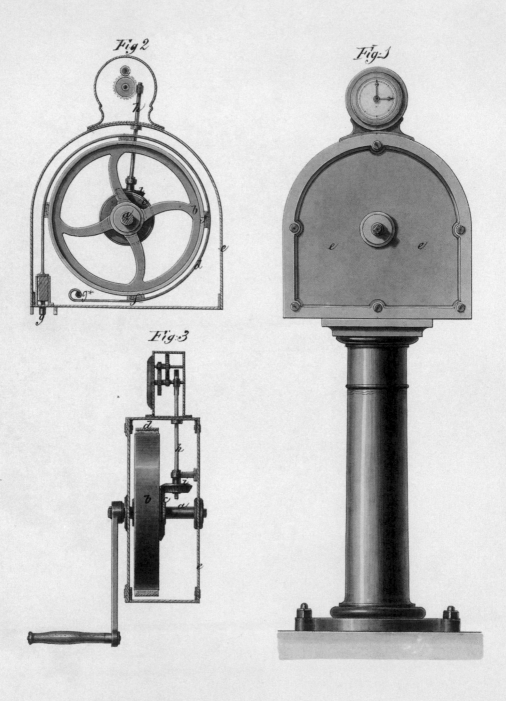

This design consists in a novel configuration of an Instrument
intended to be worked by Prisoners who are condemned to hard labour.

FIELD & FACTORY

"THE LIFE OF A MAN
IN THIS WORLD IS FOR
THE MOST PART A LIFE
OF WORK"

• • •

Samuel Smiles
Life and Labour
1887

The world of work was transformed for most social groups over the course of the nineteenth century. New places of work and methods of working – in factories, offices and shops – changed society and traditional ways of life. Most dramatic was the shift from agricultural labour towards work in the cities. In the first half of the century agriculture was the largest single area of employment, but by 1901 it accounted for only 6.4 per cent of national income. By that time 80 per cent of the population lived in urban areas – a greater number than in any other European country.[1]

Agricultural work was poorly paid and insecure, a situation that grew worse as steam-powered agricultural machinery became more widely used. The huge growth in the manufacturing industries – including textile mills, mining and iron works – and increasing opportunities for work in a huge range of industries in London meant that urban populations grew dramatically as labourers left the land to look for more secure and better-paid work.

A series of Factory Acts sought to improve the appalling conditions that existed in factories in the first half of the century. Legislation was introduced to protect children from abuse and mistreatment, reduce working hours (to ten a day), improve health and safety, and introduce routine inspections. Despite this legislation, the work could still be brutal. The health of workers could be permanently damaged by repetitive movements performed over many hours, by inhaling cotton dust or other fragments, and by heat or damp. Exposure to chemicals such as the lead in pottery works or the white phosphorus in matchmaking, which caused the condition known as 'phossy jaw', could lead to horrific diseases and disabilities.[2]

The workforce in the textile mills was made up primarily of women aged between fourteen and twenty-five. By contrast, in the iron and steel

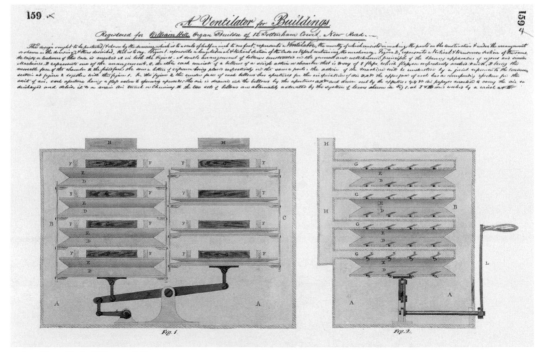

A Ventilator for Buildings, 1844

industries the heavy and dangerous work was done almost entirely by men. Segregation between masters and factory hands was often absolute: one worker told the *Morning Chronicle*: 'I have worked in that mill, sir, these nineteen years, and the master never spoke to me once.'[3] Factory workers always lived close to their places of work and would be called to their shifts at set times by whistles. Although highly regimented, with hard work and long hours, factory work offered reliable wages and freedom at the end of the working day.

As manufacturing machinery became more sophisticated, more and more processes became industrialized, so that as well as the major industries there were increasing numbers of smaller factories making consumer goods. This trend is reflected in the inventions registered for copyright, which attempt labour-saving solutions for a range of tasks, from folding paper bags (see p. 67) to feeding poultry (see p. 68).

The rise in machine-made goods also changed the way of life of existing urban populations. Many working-class families used to produce 'piecework' – items or parts of items were produced within the home – but with work increasingly factory-based, working life became more regimented. Among the middle classes, too, work and home became increasingly separated as people chose to move out to the suburbs and commute into work in the cities.

The class-consciousness that pervaded all aspects of Victorian life was nowhere more evident than in attitudes towards people's occupations. All groups were anxious to live in the style appropriate to their social station, and in all social groups a desire to maintain 'respectability' was paramount. A junior clerk might earn less and have less regulated working conditions than a skilled manual worker, but he would consider himself to be a member of the middle classes because he did not work with his hands. The expansion of the middle classes

Design for an Improved Sausage Machine, 1853

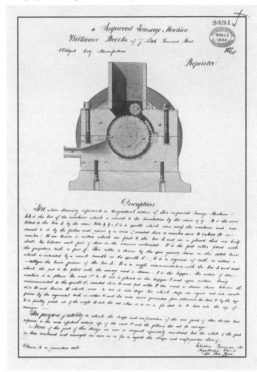

led to a rise in the number of people able to afford servants, who became a sign of social status. By 1901 domestic service was not only the largest employer of women in the country, but with over one and a half million people, it formed the largest occupational grouping of any kind.[4]

In the middle of the nineteenth century the middle classes consisted of members of the professions – such as doctors and lawyers – plus businessmen, bankers, and proprietors of large

"THE GREATEST KINDNESS WE CAN EXERCISE TOWARDS [SERVANTS] IS TO ENDEAVOUR, BY A MILD REIN, TO KEEP THEM IN THE PATH OF DUTY."

A PRACTICAL MISTRESS OF A HOUSEHOLD, *DOMESTIC SERVANTS AS THEY ARE AND AS THEY OUGHT TO BE*, 1859

Design for a Portable or Stationary Kiln, 1846

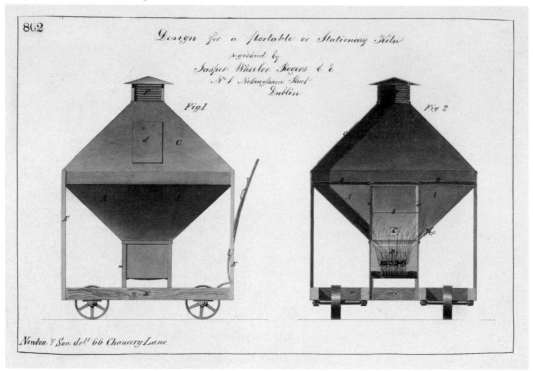

stores. A gulf existed between this group and the working classes. After 1850, however, a further group, the lower middle class, came into existence as the service sector of the economy grew and became more complex. As commerce started to become as important as industry, a huge growth in middle-class and lower-middle-class occupations took place, most notably in office work and retailing.[5]

At the beginning of Victoria's reign most retail shops were small family-run businesses. Urbanization, the railways and factory production contributed to the development of larger shops and department stores. Shop assistants were a new kind of employee and were considered to be lower middle class. Their lives were extremely hard, but this fact was not always obvious to the public because they were required to dress smartly and maintain a respectable appearance at all times.

In the larger clothing and department stores most employees were aged between sixteen and twenty-two and were required to 'live in', either in the upper floors of the shops or in nearby lodging houses. This meant that they could work long shifts – an eighty-five-hour week was normal – and that they were available to be exploited if the shop was busy. This institutionalized living was organized along rigid lines, with strict discipline and numerous rules. Writing about the store in Liverpool where he worked, a shop assistant named Edward Flower wrote that the assistants were not allowed to go out at all except on Sundays. There were as many as sixteen people sleeping in one room. He suggests that the mortality rate was high, but because the assistants were sent home if they became ill, where they often died, the public was not aware of their poor conditions.[6] There was no job security: seasonal trade meant that shop assistants were frequently dismissed when they were no longer required. Men were also often dismissed if they married, 'for it is considered an axiom that a married man is not so effective a salesman as one who is single'.[7] It went without saying that women assistants would not continue to work after marriage.

The situation did not improve over the course of the century. A host of petty rules was enforced: in one shop anyone with a light on after eleven p.m. on weekdays or midnight on Saturdays could be dismissed; no pictures could be put on walls and no assistant should enter any bedroom but her own. One shop in Holloway, north London, had seventy-five rules for assistants in the shop. They could be fined for 'gossiping, standing in groups, or lounging about in an unbusinesslike manner', or for bringing a newspaper into the shop; and if they allowed a customer to go out without making a purchase they would be reported. In some shops an assistant could be instantly dismissed for not making a sale. The famous London department store Whiteley's had 159 separate rules for staff.[8]

Attempts to form trade unions were unsuccessful, in part because the rigid hierarchy among shop assistants prevented them coming together to form a united front. Will Anderson, a former grocer's assistant who wrote a book called *The Counter Exposed* (1896), wrote: 'The draper's assistant affects a certain superiority over the grocer's assistant, the grocer's assistant has his own idea about the draper's assistant, the ironmonger's assistant is criticized by both.'[9]

The dreary lives of the workers could not have been in greater contrast to the magnificent appearance of the shops in which they worked. Plate glass began to be used, which reflected the gas lamps arranged outside, and window dressing grew ever more skilled and artistic. The growth in advertising in the second half of the century – one of the new service industries – helped lure customers into the shops. They were often attracted by the efforts of imaginitive advertising agents. Although agents had existed in the eighteenth century, the huge growth in periodical publishing and the rise in consumerism in the nineteenth century greatly increased their numbers.

Merchandising tie-ins became popular – for example, fans of Wilkie Collins's novel *The Woman in White* could buy *Woman in White* perfume, cloaks and bonnets.[10] Proprietary brand names were first introduced by Victorian firms, and newspapers and magazines were filled with advertisements for every kind of product imaginable. Celebrity endorsements became popular – Robert Baden-Powell, founder of the Scout movement, and the writer Rudyard Kipling were recruited to sing the praises of Bovril beef extract, and Oscar Wilde lent his support to Madame Fontaine's Bosom Beautifier ('Just as sure as the sun will rise tomorrow, just so sure it will enlarge and beautify the bosom').[11]

Magic lanterns projected huge images advertising anything from Pears' soap to London's tourist attractions onto giant curtains, and posters were plastered across every available space. The sandwich man was a familiar sight, and the advertising van (see p. 76–77) appeared in the middle of the century.[12]

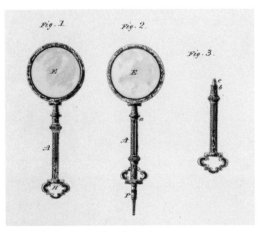

Design for the Optical Pencil, 1846

The boom in trade and the new sophistication of banking methods meant that every business and factory needed a small army of clerks. Every invoice and ledger entry had to be accurately, quickly and legibly written by hand. It was estimated that the 44,000 clerks, accountants and bankers in 1851 had grown to 449,000 in 1891.[13]

Junior clerks were members of the lower middle class, while the most senior staff would be members of the professional, or upper middle, class. In many businesses the clerk could expect his pay and status to rise throughout his working life – he had 'prospects'.

The clerks became a familiar sight in the commercial centres of cities. The journalist George Sala described them arriving at their various destinations in the City of London: 'So the omnibuses meet at the Bank and disgorge clerks by the hundred; repeating this operation scores of times between nine and ten o'clock…. Then, for an instant, Thames Street, Upper and Lower, is invaded by an ant-hill swarm of spruce clerks, who mingle strangely with the fish-women and the dock-porters. But the insatiable counting-houses soon swallow them up.'[14]

As elsewhere, conditions of work could vary enormously depending on the employers. Clerks often worked in damp, draughty and overcrowded offices, with inadequate sanitation, and were particularly prone to 'phthisis', more commonly known as consumption. The cramped posture that they maintained for hours at a stretch also created a range of health problems.[15]

However, not all working conditions were so difficult. Bank clerks formed the elite of the clerical class. A fear of scandal within the banking community ensured that these employees showed an ardent devotion to Victorian standards of respectability. They were employed based on social standing and recommendations from family and influential contacts. This moral dimension to bank employment was felt by some commentators to extend to the moral fabric of society as a whole: 'Banking exercises a powerful influence on the morals of society….

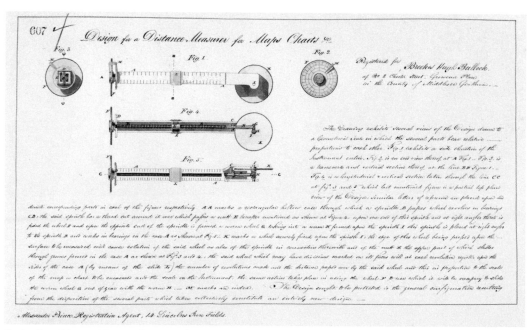

Design for a Distance Measurer for Maps Charts &c, c. 1845

The establishment of the bank in any place immediately raises the pecuniary value of a good moral character'.[16]

The private bank Hoare and Company, based in Fleet Street in London, adopted a highly paternal attitude towards its clerical staff, some of whom lived within the bank's building. Clerks were forbidden from getting into debt, and had to wear a white neck handkerchief and black coat and waistcoat. They were to conduct 'no business outside the bank except in top hats' and smoking in the building was forbidden. Private conduct was also under scrutiny: in 1825 a clerk was dismissed for having a relationship with an actress.

Despite these rules and regulations, conditions at the bank were exemplary compared to many other places of employment. Financial rewards could be generous and career prospects good. Papers from 1841 show that employees got four weeks' holiday, and all clerks were given lunch and dinner daily at the bank's expense.[17]

Towards the end of the century more women entered the clerical workforce. The Post Office started employing large numbers of women in 1876, and in 1881 the government established a new Civil Service category of woman clerk, albeit with a separate entrance examination and a lower pay scale. By the time of the 1901 census, around 60,000 women were in clerical jobs. The women's social background, however, seems to have been as important as their qualifications. The Prudential Insurance Company, in *The Office*, a magazine for clerks, stated: 'They must all be the daughters of professional men'.[18]

For many people, standards of living improved between the boom years of 1880 and 1896: during this time wages went up by almost 45 per cent. From 1880 onwards, a significant proportion of the population had time and money to spend on leisure activities.[19] Industrialization, urbanization and the expansion of the middle classes had transformed the experience of work and the structure of society. Millions of people adapted to work in factories, as servants, in shops or offices, and in the hundreds of other occupations needed by the thriving economy.

[1] Christopher Harvie and H. C. G. Matthew, *Nineteenth Century Britain*, Oxford: Oxford University Press, 2000, p. 77.

[2] Sally Mitchell, *Daily Life in Victorian England* (2nd ed.), Westport, Conn. & London: Greenwood Press, 2009, p. 57.

[3] Richard Dennis, *English Industrial Cities of the Nineteenth Century: A Social Geography*, Cambridge: Cambridge University Press, 1984, p. 17.

[4] Pamela Horn, *The Rise and Fall of the Victorian Servant*, London: Macmillan, 1990, p. 14.

[5] Harvie and Matthew, *op. cit.*, p. 94.

[6] Wilfred B. Whitaker, *Victorian and Edwardian Shop Workers*, Newton Abbot: David and Charles, 1973, p. 9.

[7] *The Early Closing Advocate*, 1854, quoted in Whitaker, *op. cit.*, p. 11.

[8] Whitaker, *op. cit.*, pp. 19–20.

[9] Whitaker, *op. cit.*, p. 25.

[10] Matthew Sweet, *Inventing the Victorians*, London: Faber & Faber, 2001, p. 39.

[11] Sweet, *ibid.*, p. 43.

[12] Sweet, *ibid.*, pp. 43–44.

[13] Mitchell, *op. cit.*, p. 68.

[14] George Augustus Sala, *Twice Round the Clock, or The Hours of the Day and Night in London*, London: Houlston and Wright, 1859.

[15] Gregory Anderson, *Victorian Clerks*, Manchester: Manchester University Press, 1976, pp. 18–19.

[16] *The Banker's Clerk*, 1843, p. 158, quoted in Ingrid Jeacle, 'The bank clerk in Victorian society: The case of Hoare and Company', *Journal of Management History*, 16 (3), 2010, p. 314.

[17] Jeacle, *ibid.*, p. 321.

[18] Gregory Anderson (ed), *The White-blouse Revolution: Female Office Workers Since 1870*, Manchester: Manchester University Press, p. 80.

[19] Harvie and Matthew, *op. cit.*, pp. 86–87.

Cordwainer's Standing or Sitting

Registered for William Warne of Lark-hall Lane

The Novelty of the Design sought to be protected consists in constructing a Mach...
inches to a foot. This Machine is designed for the purpose of enabling persons to work e...
the position of his work to himself in a ready & efficient manner and by thus afford...
favorable manner than has hitherto been the case. The nature of the machine will be b...

FIG.3   FIG.1

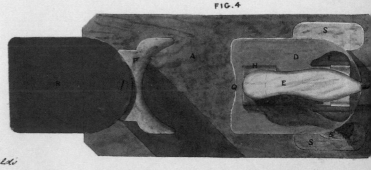

FIG.4

Alex. Prince
Registration Agent
14 Lincoln's Inn Fields

hine

harne

...he shape or configuration represented by the drawing which is to a scale of two
...sitting or standing posture: it likewise affords to the workman every facility of accommodating
...the free use of his limbs he is enabled to exert his strength in a more convenient and
...stood by referring to the drawing and to the figures and letters marked thereon. Fig. 1

FIG. 2.

represents a side elevation of the machine. Fig. 2. a front
elevation thereof. Fig. 3 a back elevation. Fig. 4 a plan view.
Similar letters are placed upon corresponding parts in all the
Figures. A A a block of wood to which is attached an upright B B
at whose upper end a circular top or piece of wood C is firmly
fixed and supports the revolving piece or table D which is connected
to the aforesaid top by passing a pin through them and which serves
as a fulcrum for the piece D to turn upon. The Drawing represents
the machine as ready for use. the last E which is of the ordinary
shape is kept steady by the front prop F which has pins G G at
its under side (see dotted lines in Fig. 2) fitted into holes formed
in the revolving piece D. — H the back prop formed of elastic
material such as cork. I a hook fixed to the last upon this hook
a hooked piece K is suspended and carries at its other end
a strap L which passes through holes formed in a stirrup iron
or foot plate M and terminates through a buckle attached to
the strap as shewn N the fulcrum of the foot plate, O an iron
upright at the upper end of which a curved piece P is made
fast serving as a prop or abutment for the legs of the workman
when in a standing position: the front of the revolving piece is
likewise hollowed out as shewn at Q in Fig. 4 to lean the
breast against when necessary. R a revolving seat attached to
the piece P by a screw see fig. 4. at which Fig the seat is shewn
thrown back or out of use, S S S' foot rests. T a trap or rack
for holding the foot iron fast. The workman having
adjusted his work to the last. places it upon the revolving
table and connecting it by the hooked piece inserts the
foot iron in the trap. the last is thus firmly held and the
table upon which it rests may be turned entirely round
or in any required position. the torsion or twisting of the

...ap keeping it in close contact with the fixed circular top. thus it will be seen that the feet
...the workman are at full liberty and may be brought to the required height for sitting
...placing them on the rests: the rest S' is designed to be used in cases when the workman requires
...s knee to be brought above the surface of the revolving table. The parts sought to be protected and
...ich are themselves new are represented by the entire drawing with the exception of that
...rt marked E.

PREVIOUS PAGES
CORDWAINER'S STANDING OR SITTING MACHINE
1844

Fig. 1. side elevation • *Fig. 2.* front elevation
Fig. 3. back elevation • *Fig. 4.* plan view

This machine enables persons to work either in a sitting or standing position: it likewise affords to the workman every facility of accommodating the positions of his work to himself and to exert his strength in a more convenient and favorable manner.

BELOW
DESIGN FOR A PORTABLE SCAFFOLD*
1860

Fig. 1. view of the apparatus closed • *Figs. 2. & 3.* the apparatus elevated and supporting a scaffold (S)

(AA) *are a series of jointed levers, folding up within the box* (B), *and capable of being raised by depressing the weighted levers* (CC), *which are held in position by pins* (dd), *passing though holes in the quadrants* (EE).

OPPOSITE ABOVE
DESIGN FOR A PORTABLE SMELTING APPARATUS
1850

Fig. 1. plan view • *Fig. 2.* side view • *Fig. 3.* longitudinal section on line (ZZ), (*Fig. 1.*) • *Fig. 4.* view of the leading end from which the apparatus is drawn
Fig. 5. back or end view

(AA) *marks the carriage on which furnace* (BB) *and magazine* (CC) *rest & are carried;* (aa) *are wheels on which the carriage runs;* (vv) *is a cranked rod and handle for drawing the apparatus to any required destination for use.*

OPPOSITE BELOW
DESIGN FOR A PORTABLE FORGE
1844

The portable forge may be removed from place to place with great facility; (aa) *is the bed of the forge, and* (b) *the blast pipe through which air is forced to the fire by means of a rotary fan or blower contained in the box* (cc). *The apparatus is mounted on a running wheel* (i) *and legs or supports* (jj) *similar to the ordinary wheelbarrow.*

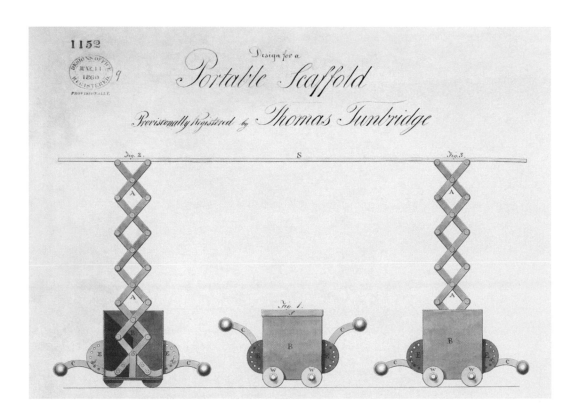

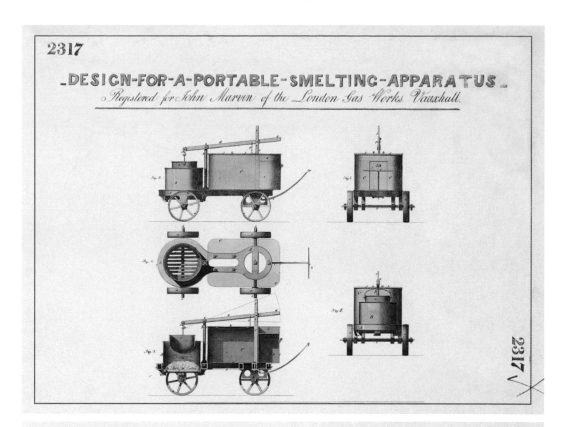

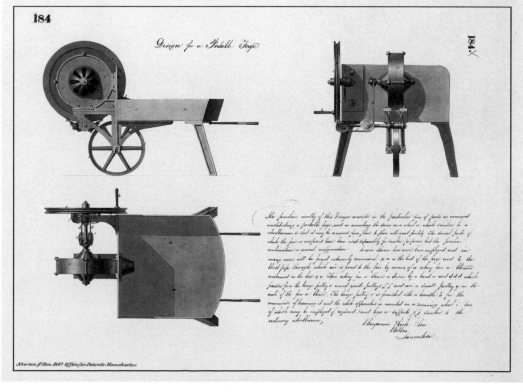

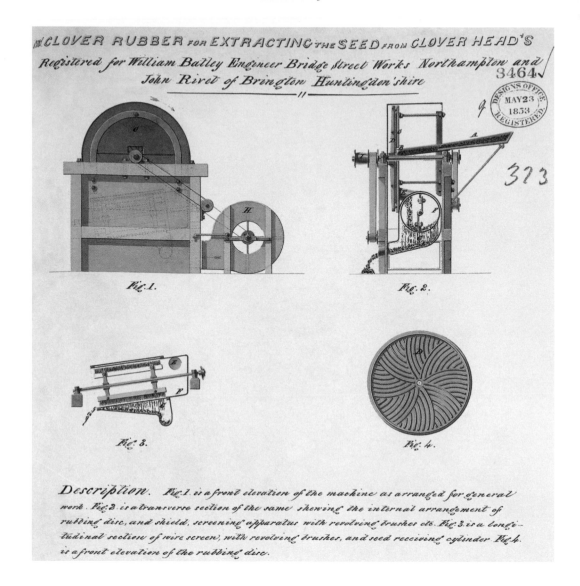

Fig. 1. Fig. 2. Fig. 3. Fig. 4.

Description. Fig. 1. is a front elevation of the machine as arranged for general work. Fig. 2. is a transverse section of the same shewing the internal arrangement of rubbing disc, and shield, screening apparatus with revolving brushes etc. Fig. 3. is a longitudinal section of wire screen, with revolving brushes, and seed receiving cylinder. Fig. 4. is a front elevation of the rubbing disc.

ABOVE

CLOVER RUBBER FOR EXTRACTING THE SEED FROM CLOVER HEAD'S

1853

Fig. 1. front elevation · *Fig. 2.* transverse section of the same · *Fig. 3.* longitudinal section · *Fig. 4.* front elevation of the rubbing disc

The clover heads are placed on the feeding board (A) and are rubbed between the cast iron revolving disc (D) and the wire surface on the wood shield (C) covered with coarse wire gauze, by which means the seed is completely liberated from the husk, clean and ready for use.

OPPOSITE

DESIGN FOR A MACHINE FOR FOLDING PAPER BAGS

1852

Fig. 1. front elevation · *Fig. 2.* side elevation partly in section · *Fig. 3.* plan view

The blue lines in Fig. 3. represent the shape of the paper which has to be folded into a bag. When the attendant begins, the handle (n) is turned partly round in the direction of the arrow in Fig. 1. The treadle is depressed so as to elevate the plate into position shewn by red lines. The purpose is to economise time in making paper bags.

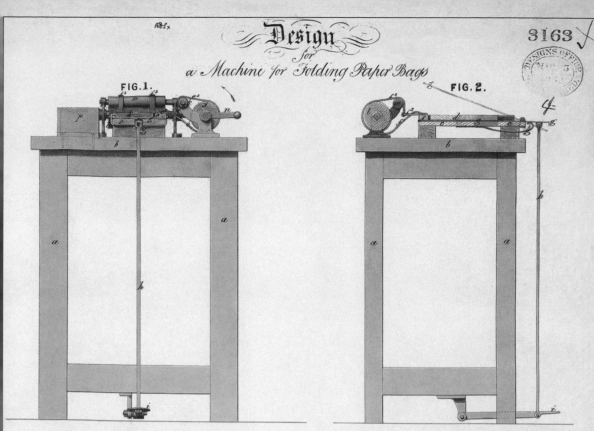

Design

for

a Machine for Folding Paper Bags

3163

FIG. 1.

FIG. 2.

FIG. 3.

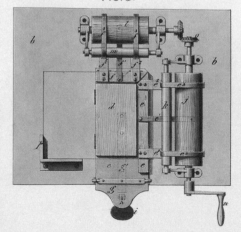

Peter Pearson *of Manchester in the County of Lancaster Proprietor*

The purpose of Utility to which the shape or configuration of this Design has reference is to economise time in making paper Bags.

Fig.1 is a front elevation of the Machine, Fig 2 is a side elevation partly in section and Fig 3 is a plan view of the same. The drawings are made to a scale of two and a half inches to one foot. a, is the framing supporting the table b. c is the bed plate seen best in Fig 2, to this bed plate are hinged the flap d, the side rail e and the end rail f, these two rails are united at one corner as seen in Fig 3, g is a thin plate also hinged to the bed plate, to the under side of the front of the plate g is connected a rod h, the lower end of which is jointed to the treadle i, the spring g' acts against the under side of the plate g. To the side rail e is attached one end of a shaft e² the other end of which is made fast to the roller j and the two levers e³ are also fixed to the side rail e, the shaps e⁴ are fixed to the levers e³ and are guided over the roller k and then made fast to the roller j. The end rail f is also furnished with a shaft f' attached to the roller l and with two levers f² the shaps f³ from which are carried over the roller m and then made fast to the roller l. The handle n is placed on the end of the shaft of the roller j and to the other end of the same shaft is fixed a mitre pinion o gearing into a similar pinion on the shaft of the roller l. To the table b is fixed an angle shaped guide p. The blue lines in Fig 3 represent the shape of the paper which has to be formed into a bag. When the attendant begins to make a bag the handle n is turned partly round in the direction of the arrow in Fig 1, by so doing the shaps e⁴ and f³ when the side rails e and f, the flap d is then opened by hand and the treadle i depressed so as to elevate the plate g into the position shewn by red lines in Fig 2. the attendant then slips the sheet of paper between the bed plate c and the plate g taking care that the left hand corner of the paper fits into the guide p. On letting go of the treadle i the spring g' causes the plate g to drop on the paper and hold it while the attendant with one hand throws over the flap d and with it that portion of the paper which was lying above it and with the other hand he moves the handle n so as to bring the rails e and f into the position shewn in the drawings, by this means the edges of the paper which had previously been pasted are doubled over the other part of the paper and the bag is completed. The end of the plate g is cut out to enable the attendant to take the bag off when it is completed.

The parts of this Design which are not new or original as regards the shape or configuration thereof are all the parts taken separately but as here combined form a new Design.

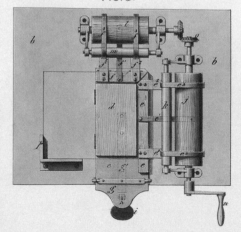

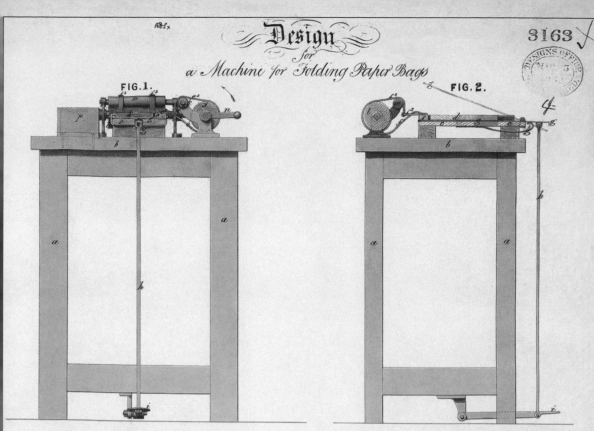

H.B. Barlow. Dacie Place Manchester.

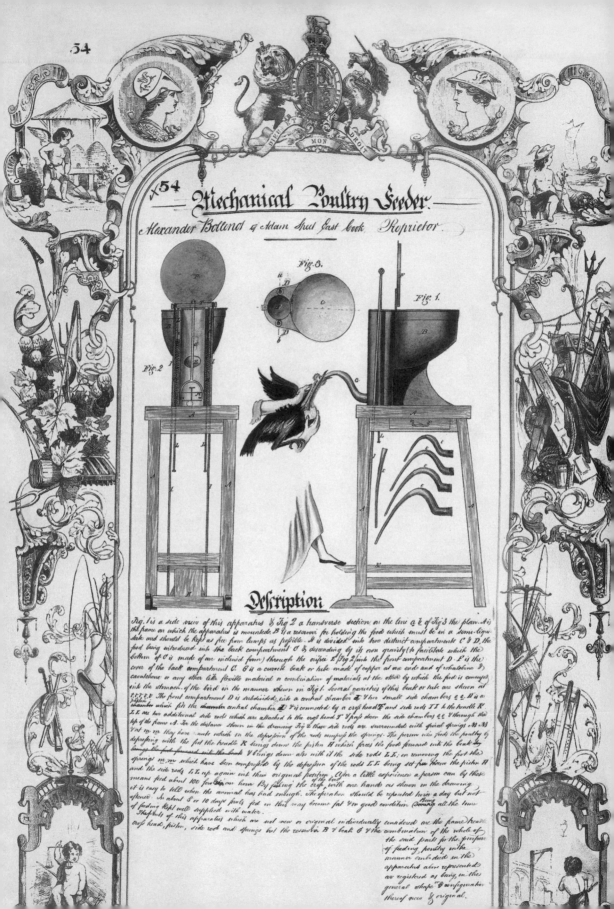

No 54

Mechanical Poultry Feeder.

Alexander Bottona of Adam Street East, book, Proprietor.

Fig. 3.

Fig. 2

Fig. 1.

Description

OPPOSITE

MECHANICAL POULTRY FEEDER

1843

Fig. 1. side view ◆ *Fig. 2.* transverse section on line (ab) of *Fig. 3.* ◆ *Fig. 3.* top view

(A) *is the frame; (B) is a reservoir for holding the food which must be in a semi-liquid state; (G) is a curved beak or tube made of copper at one end and whalebone and caoutchouc at the other. Food is pumped into the beak using the treadle (K). After a little experience a person can by these means feed about 100 fowls in an hour. The operation should be repeated twice a day. In about 8 or 10 days fowls fed in this way become fat and in good condition.*

BELOW

DESIGN FOR IMPROVED CLOD CRUSHER

1845

This design is for forming the shaft upon which the cutters are fixed, in two separate parts which work parallel to each other but the one in advance of the other, and the chains or brackets by which these separate parts of the shaft are connected with the frame are formed with two centres and a central chair of this kind is also introduced at (C).

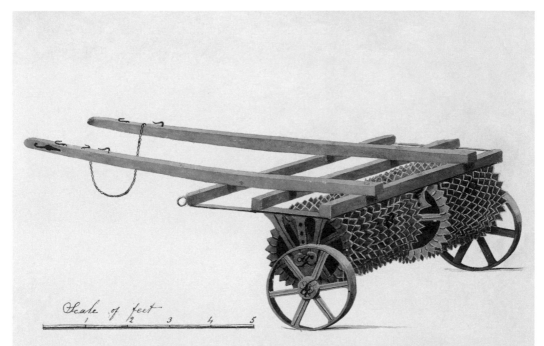

Scale of feet 1 2 3 4 5

Design for Improved Clod Crusher.
This Design is for forming the shaft upon which the cutters are fixed in two separate parts which work parallel to each other but the one in advance of the other, and the chairs or brackets by which these separate parts of the shaft are connected with the frame are formed with two centres as shewn at a and a central chair of this kind is also introduced at C The other parts shewn on the drawing are not new.

Useful Design
A Combined Lamp and Oil Can

John Murrell Jemmis, Birmingham   Proprietor

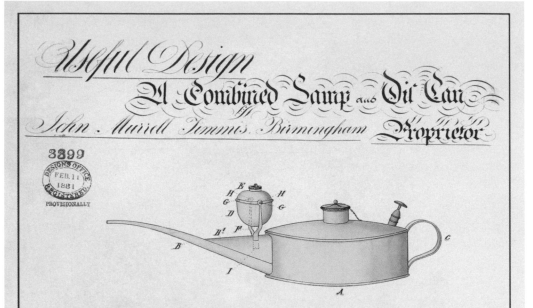

The **purpose of utility** to which the **shape or configuration** of the new parts of this design has reference is in combining a swinging lamp to an Oil can (chiefly employed by Engineers) so that when applied to its purpose no matter in what position the can may be placed the body of the lamp with its w light will assume a vertical position thus preventing an overflow of the oil.

The *Drawing* is illustrative of the same.
'A' is the body of the oil can with spout or pipe 'B' and handle 'C' 'D' is the body or reservoir for containing oil for lamp, 'E' is the burner or wick holder. 'F' is a Standard or support for carrying 'D' by means of the pins 'G' 'G' being securely connected to 'D' and passing through the holes 'H H' provided in 'F' thus forming a pivot.

The lamp in its entirety is temporarily affixed to the part 'B'' by means of the lower end of 'F' entering the tube 'I' so that the oil-can may be used either with or without the lamp.
Protection is sought for the **shape or configuration** of the parts marked 'f' 'g' 'h' 'i' which is original or new the remainder is old.

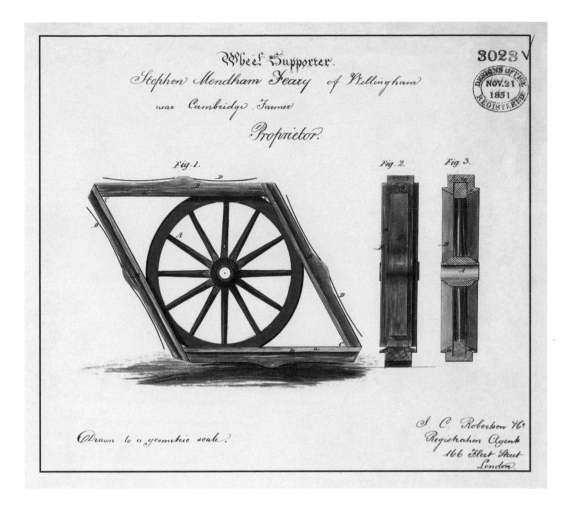

Wheel Supporter.

Stephen Mendham Feary of Willingham near Cambridge Farmer

Proprietor.

3023

DESIGNS OFFICE
NOV. 21
1851
REGISTERED

Fig. 1.   Fig. 2.   Fig. 3.

Drawn to a geometric scale.

J. C. Robertson & Co.
Registration Agents
166 Fleet Street
London.

OPPOSITE

A COMBINED LAMP AND OIL CAN*

1881

(A) *is the body of the oil can with spout or pipe* (B) *and handle* (C). (D) *is the body or reservoir for containing oil for the lamp,* (E) *is the burner or wick holder.* (F) *is a standard or support for carrying* (D) *by means of the pins* (GG) *being securely connected to* (D) *and passing through the holes* (HH) *provided in* (F) *thus forming a pivot. No matter in what position the can may be placed the body of the lamp with its light will assume a vertical position thus preventing an overflow of the oil.*

ABOVE

WHEEL SUPPORTER

1851

Fig. 1. side elevation • Fig. 2. end elevation
Fig. 3. cross section

(A) *is the wheel,* (BBBB) *are the four sides of the supporter which are joined endwise together by links of vulcanized caoutchouc or other suitable material* (CCCC) *which form joints so that as the wheel revolves the sides of the supporter are enabled successively to fall down and form rails for the wheel to roll upon. The purpose is the preventing of the wheels of ploughs carts and other machines from sinking into soft ground.*

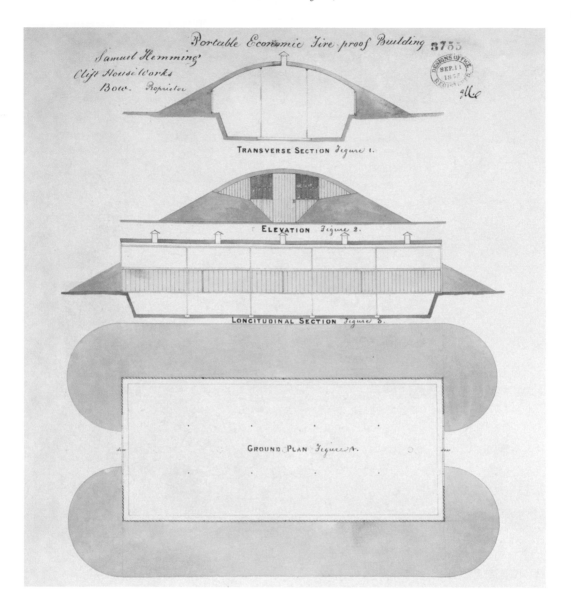

ABOVE

PORTABLE ECONOMIC FIRE-PROOF BUILDING
1855

Fig. 1. cross section of the Building underground
Fig. 2. End Elevation of the same ✦ *Fig. 3.* Longitudinal
Section ✦ *Fig. 4.* plan of the same

*The purposes of utility are for Dwelling Houses,
Barracks, Stables, Cattle Sheds, Stores, Cellars,
Dairy's and all other Buildings rendering them
Portable, Economical, Fire-proof and equalizing
the temperature of the same.*

OPPOSITE

NEW AND USEFUL DESIGN FOR A PORTABLE SHEEP HOUSE
1877

*The purposes of utility are the protection of sheep in
rainy or sunny weather, the depositing of their manure
when required, the prevention of injury to the hedges
and the saving of food. The sheephouse consists of a
framing (A) mounted on four wheels (B). The ends are
left open, or partly open so that free ingress and egress
may be obtained for the animals using it. (KK) are
axles cranked to admit of the animals passing beneath.*

A New and Useful Design
for a Portable Sheep House

James Buchanan
Campden
Gloucestershire—

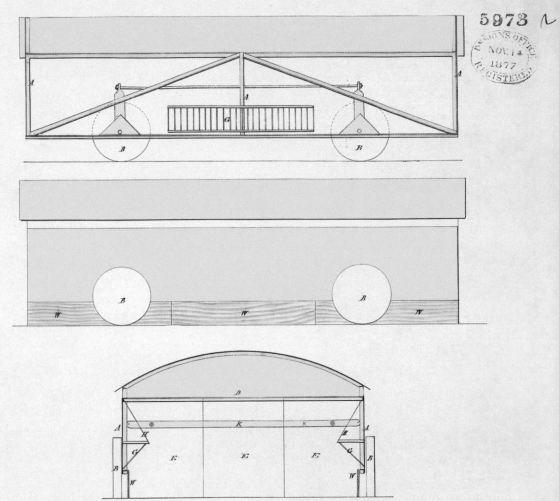

The purposes of utility to which the shape or configuration of this design have reference are the protection of sheep in dry or sunny weather the depositing of their manure where required, the prevention of injury to the hedges and the saving of food.—

The sheep house consists of a framing A mounted on four wheels B— The bottom of the framing A comes down to within about 16 inches from the ground and the height to the underside of the eaves is raised off at convenient distances by angle irons or rails to which the side plates are affixed. The side plates are by preference not carried the whole height but are terminated a few inches clear of the eaves thus leaving an air space for ventilation. The eaves are extended a few inches over each side of the house so that they may drip clear and act as a shelter for the air spaces in storms &c. The ends are left open, or partly open so that free ingress and egress may be obtained for the animals using it. By preference each end is partly closed in say from the underside of about one third down at D. A series of hooks or other mode of fastening is employed to fix the remainder of the end F, F, F, which is made loose in any required number of pieces so that they can be moved from one end to the other by the attendant as may be required by the state of the weather. From the bottom of the framing portable weather boards marked W. W. W. may be suspended so that in moving the house along the road they can be taken off. Another advantage is that long troughs can be put along each side of the house inside and the food can be put in from the outside. There are also two racks F, G inside properly stayed by bars H. H. so that hay or other food may be consumed inside. K, K are axles cranked to admit of the animals passing beneath.—

In wet weather a spaced floor may be drawn in below between the wheels for the sheep to lie on.—

The whole of this design is new in so far as regards the shape or configuration thereof.—

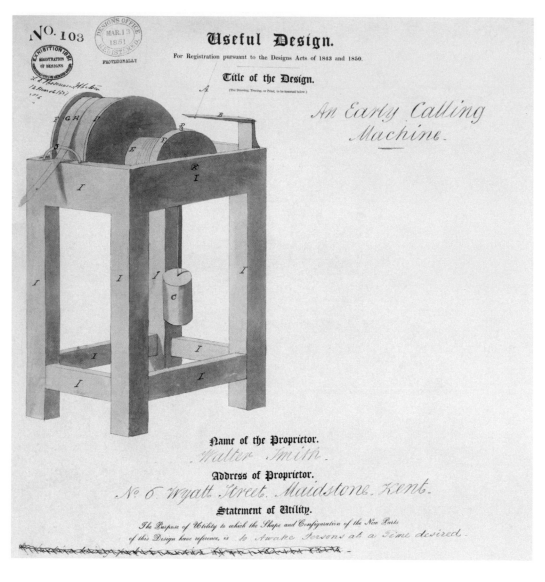

Useful Design.

For Registration pursuant to the Designs Acts of 1843 and 1850.

Title of the Design.

(The Drawing, Tracing, or Print, to be inserted below.)

An Early Calling Machine.

Name of the Proprietor.

Walter Smith.

Address of Proprietor.

No 6 Wyatt Street, Maidstone, Kent.

Statement of Utility.

The Purpose of Utility to which the Shape and Configuration of the New Parts of this Design have reference, is to Awake Persons at a Time desired.

ABOVE

USEFUL DESIGN: AN EARLY CALLING MACHINE*

1851

(A): *the String or Line attached to the clock;* (B): *the lever that is attached by a string to the clock and is drawn up at a set time;* (C): *the weight that runs down when the lever is lifted up;* (G): *the large Barrell or wheel to which a piece of tape or other material is attached;* (H): *the tape or other material that is attached to the wheel and also to the Person who is to be called. The purpose is to Awake Persons at a Time desired.*

OPPOSITE

USEFUL DESIGN: IMPROVED TELEKOUPHONON

1851

Fig. 1. side elevation · *Fig. 2.* front view of one end *Figs. 3., 5. & 7.* cross sections of pipe, mouthpiece and whistle · *Figs. 4. & 6.* front views

To give a signal from the end of pipe (A) *the piston* (P) *is forced in by hand which sounds the whistles and blows out the indicators* (N) *and* (J). *The person at the other end can see which tube the signal is coming from and indicates using the whistles that he is ready. The whistles are removed to converse with one another through the pipe.*

3046

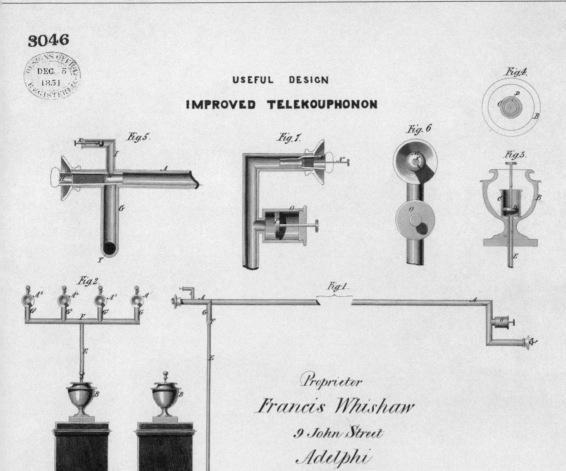

USEFUL DESIGN

IMPROVED TELEKOUPHONON

Fig.4.

Fig 5. *Fig. 7.* *Fig. 6* *Fig 3.*

Fig. 2. *Fig.1.*

Proprietor

Francis Whishaw

9 John Street

Adelphi

London

The purpose of utility to which the shape and configuration of the new parts of this design have reference is the communicating of visible and or audible signals between different rooms in the same building or other places at a distance from each other.

Figure 1 is a side elevation. Figure 2 is a front view of one end of the apparatus. A A¹ A² A³ are a series of speaking pipes of metal, gutta percha or other suitable material which extend from one room or station to several other rooms or stations. Only one of these pipes A is shewn in figure 1 and it is represented as broken in the centre to indicate that its length may be varied as required. The other pipes are similar to A. B is a vase containing a cylinder C and piston D as shewn in section in figure 3 and in plan in figure 4. A pipe E communicates from this cylinder to the main pipe F and the branches G G¹ G² G³ which are connected respectively to the pipes A A¹ A² A³. Figure 5 is a section on a larger scale shewing the end of the pipe A which terminates in a mouth-piece and contains a whistle H which is capable of being withdrawn and inserted at pleasure. G is the branch pipe already mentioned opposite to which is another branch pipe I which contains a loosely fitted piston and rod J which serves as an indicator and is limited in its motion by the cap K. The barrel of the whistle is provided with a lateral hole at I₁. In its present position the hole communicates with the branch I and closes the branch G but by turning it half round it closes I and opens G. The other extremity of the pipe A is shewn on a larger scale in elevation in figure 6 and in section in figure 7. It is formed with a mouth-piece in which is inserted a whistle H¹ the barrel of which contains a loosely fitted indicator piston and rod N. O is a cylinder communicating with the pipe A and containing a piston P.

The mode of using this apparatus is as follows. To give a signal from the last described end of the pipe A the piston P is forced in by hand and the air thus compressed immediately sounds the whistles H and H¹ and blows out the indicators N and J. The attention of the person at the opposite end being thus called he sees by the indicator J from which of the pipes the signal comes and he turns the whistle H and presses down the piston C which immediately blows the two whistles and signifies to the first person that he is ready. They then both remove the whistles and converse with one another through the speaking pipe. The second person when desiring to converse through either of the pipes A A¹ A² turns round the whistle of that pipe and depresses the piston C and thus sounds the whistles and blows out the indicators at both ends of that pipe. The attention of the person at the other end being thus called they each remove their whistles and converse through the pipe. In either case when the communication is completed the whistles are replaced and the indicators pushed in.

The parts of this design which are new and original as regards the shape and configuration thereof are the parts marked C, D, E, F, G, I, J, K, L, M, N, O, P and the whistle H as far as regards the lateral hole at I₁. The remainder of the design is not new.

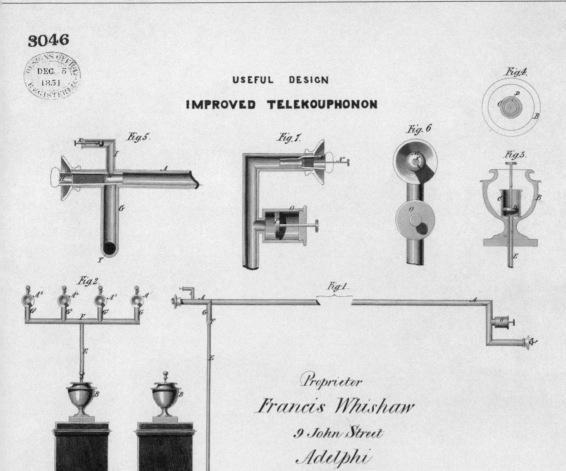

Charles Cowper
Patent Agent
20 Southampton Buildings
Chancery Lane

The Epanalepsian Advertizing Vehicle.

Provisionally Registered by James C. Wilson. C. E. Linday House Chea...

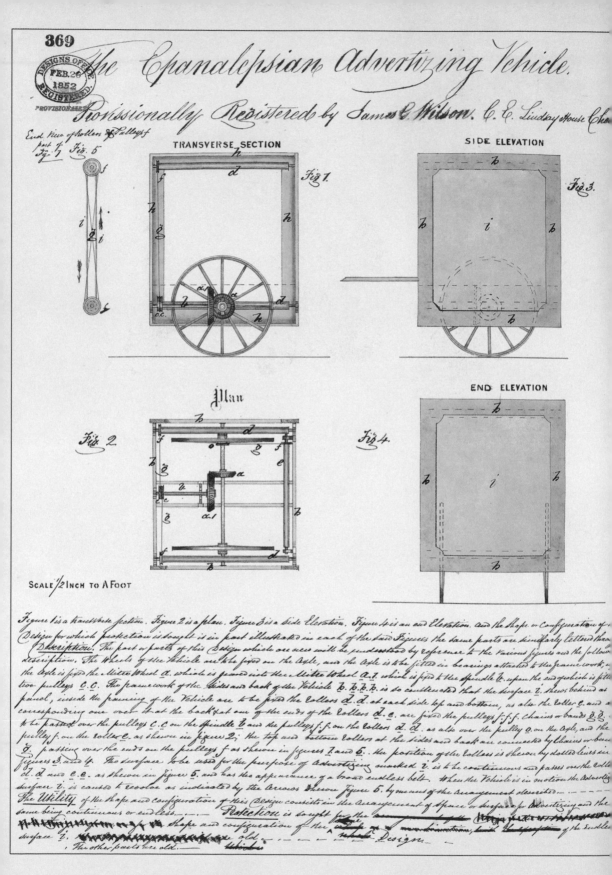

DESIGNS OFFICE / FEB. 26 / 1852 / REGISTERED · PROVISIONAL...

End View of Rollers & Pulleys
part of Fig. 5 Fig. 1

TRANSVERSE SECTION

Fig 1.

SIDE ELEVATION

Fig. 3.

Plan

Fig 2.

END ELEVATION

Fig 4.

SCALE 1/2 INCH TO A FOOT

Figure 1 is a transverse section. Figure 2 is a plan. Figure 3 is a Side Elevation. Figure 4 is an end Elevation. and the Shape or Configuration of the Design for which protection is sought is in part illustrated in each of the said Figures the same parts are similarly lettered thereon.

Description. The part or parts of this Design which are new will be understood by reference to the various figures and the following description. The Wheels of the Vehicle are to be fixed on the Axle, and the Axle is to be fitted in bearings attached to the frame work, on the axle is fixed the Mitre Wheel a. which is geared into the Mitre Wheel $a.1$ which is fixed to the Spindle b. upon the end whereof is fitted two pulleys $c.c$. The framework of the Sides and back of the Vehicle $b.b.b.b$. is so constructed that the surface i. shews behind as panel, inside the framing of the Vehicle are to be fixed the rollers $d.d$. at each side top and bottom, as also the roller e. and a corresponding one over it at the back & at one of the ends of the rollers $d.d.e$. are fixed the pulleys $f.f.f$. chains or bands $g.g$. to be passed over the pulleys $c.c$ on the Spindle b. and the pulleys $f.f$. on the rollers $d.d$. as also over the pulley a. on the Axle, and the pulley f. on the roller e. as shewn in figure 2; the top and bottom rollers at the sides and back are connected by Chains or bands g. passing over the ends on the pulleys f as shewn in figures 1 and 5. the position of the rollers is shewn by dotted lines in figures 3. and 4. The surface to be used for the purpose of advertizing marked i. is to be continuous and passes over the rollers $d.d$ and $e.e$. as shewn in figure 5. and has the appearance of a broad endless belt. When the Vehicle is in motion the Advertizing surface i. is caused to revolve as indicated by the arrows shewn figure 5. by means of the arrangement described.

The Utility of the Shape and configuration of this Design consists in the arrangement of Space or Surface for Advertizing and the same being continuous or endless. Protection is sought for the ~~~~~ Shape and configuration of the ~~~~~ Design. ~~~~~ of the endless surface i. ~~~~~ old ~~~~~ The other parts are old.

373

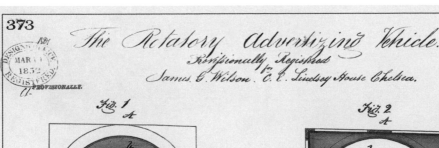

The Rotatory Advertizing Vehicle.

Provisionally Registered

James G. Wilson. C. E. Lindsey House Chelsea.

DESIGNS OFFICE
REGISTERED
MAR 1852
PROVISIONALLY

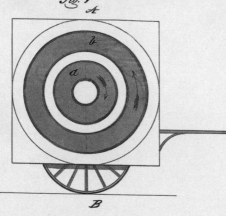

Fig. 1

A

B

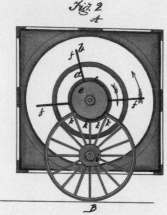

Fig. 2

A

B

Fig. 3

(a side view)

Figure 1. is an Elevation shewing outside.

Figure 2. is a Sectional side elevation shewing inside.

Figure 3. is a cross Sectional View in part taken through figures 1 & 2 (in part) at dotted lines A. B.

Description. a. b are two circular panels, the panel a. is attached to the socket and boss c, which fits on the Shaft d, the pulley c. is fitted on to the socket c, the panel b. is attached by the arms or rods f. f. to the socket g, which fits freely on the socket c, the pulley b. is fixed on the socket g. On to the boy or knave of the running Wheel of the Vehicle are fixed the two pulleys i. i. Chains or bands k. k are passed over the pulleys b. i and c. i. one being crossed to cause the pulleys b & c to revolve in different directions. Both sides of the Vehicle are similar to the half sectional View Fig 3. When the Vehicle is in motion the panels a. b. revolve in different directions as indicated by the arrows, by means of the connection of the pulleys b. i and c. i by the bands or chains k. k. — The Utility of the Shape and configuration of this Design consists in its attraction as an Advertizing Vehicle and its applicability to such Vehicles. — .. — ..

Protection is sought for the Shape and configuration of the Design —

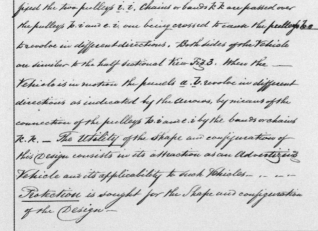

PREVIOUS LEFT

THE EPANALEPSIAN ADVERTIZING VEHICLE*

1852

Fig. 1. transverse section • *Fig. 2.* plan • *Fig. 3.* side elevation • *Fig. 4.* end elevation • *Fig. 5.* end view

Inside the framing of the vehicle are to be fixed rollers (dd); the surface to be used for the purpose of advertizing marked (i) is continuous and passes over the rollers (dd) and (ee) as shewn in Fig. 5. and has the appearance of a broad endless belt.

PREVIOUS RIGHT

THE ROTATORY ADVERTIZING VEHICLE*

1852

Fig. 1. side view elevation • *Fig. 2.* sectional side elevation shewing inside • *Fig. 3.* cross sectional view

Both sides of the vehicle are similar to the half sectional view of Fig. 3. When the vehicle is in motion the panels (ab) revolve in different directions as indicated by the arrows, by means of the connection of the pulleys (bi) and (ei) by the bands or chains (kk).

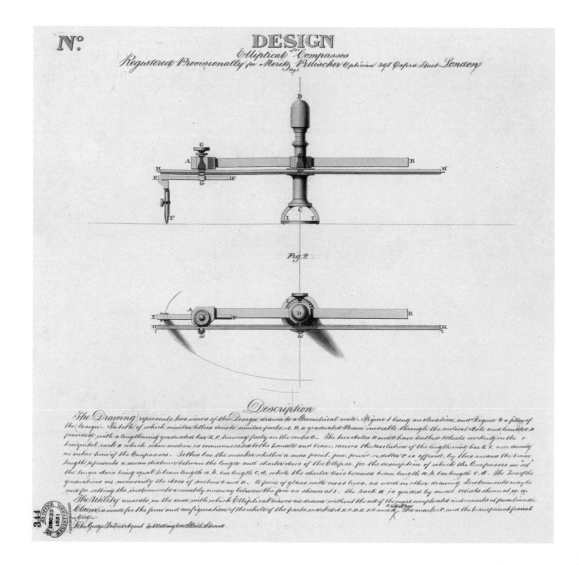

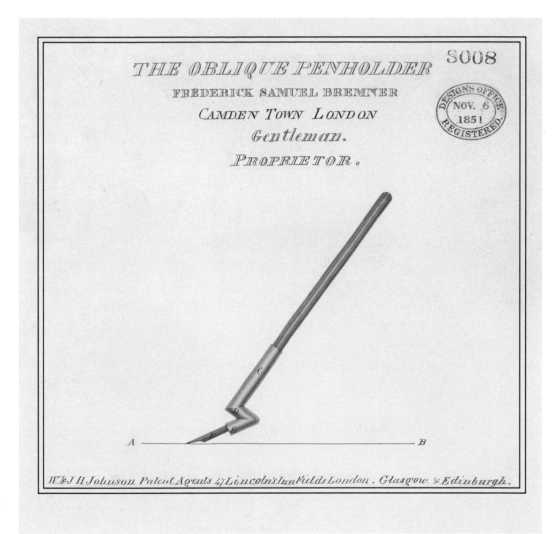

THE OBLIQUE PENHOLDER
FREDERICK SAMUEL BREMNER
CAMDEN TOWN LONDON
Gentleman.
PROPRIETOR.

8008

DESIGNS OFFICE
NOV. 6
1851
REGISTERED.

W & J H Johnson Patent Agents 47 Lincoln's Inn Fields London, Glasgow & Edinburgh.

OPPOSITE

DESIGN FOR ELLIPTICAL COMPASSES*

1851

Fig. 1. side elevation • *Fig. 2.* plan of the design

To the bar (EF) the marker whether a mere point, pen, pencil, or dotter (P) is affixed; the beam length represents a mean distance between the longer and shorter Axis of the Ellipse, for the description of which the Compasses are "set"; the utility consists in the ease with which Elliptical curves are drawn without the aid of the more complicated instruments at present in use.

ABOVE

THE OBLIQUE PENHOLDER

1851

Fig. 1. the drawing represents a side elevation

The upper part near the pen is bent or angled as delineated at (DE) in order to bring the termination (E), which receives the pen (F), to that acute angle with the line of the paper, which it is the object of the Design to secure. The purpose is the obtainment of superior facility in writing giving the steel pen numerous advantages now only attained by the Quill.

Design for a File for filing papers Bills &c. &c.
Provisionally Registered for Stephen Norris of New Peter Street Horseferry Road in the County of Middlesex.

562

FEB. 23 1854
DESIGNS OFFICE REGISTERED
PROVISIONALLY.

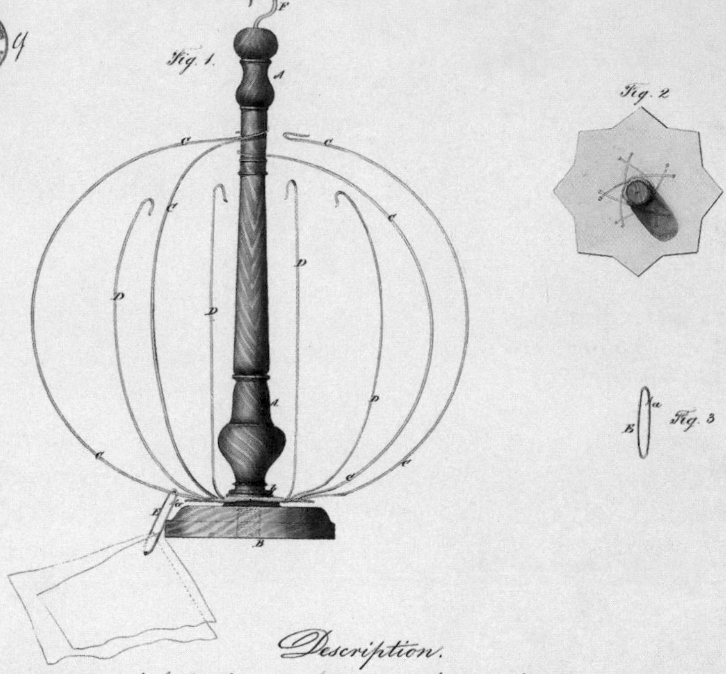

Fig. 1.

Fig. 2

Fig. 3

Description.

The purpose of utility to which the shape or configuration of this design has reference consists in its affording a more ready convenient and systematic mode of filing papers than heretofore. The Drawing exhibits three views of the design drawn to a geometrical scale of half the size or six inches to one foot — Fig. 1. is an elevation of the Design complete — Fig. 2. a bottom plan view thereof shewing the mode of arranging and securing the wires employed for filing the papers upon Fig. 3. shews a detached view of one of the parts hereinafter referred to — AA is a stand the lower part whereof has a screw formed thereon upon which is screwed the base B of the stand between which part and the part C of the stand A the bent wires CC and DD are securely held in proper position by arranging them in the manner exhibited at Fig. 2. The curved wires CC are more particularly intended for the reception of a series of flattened rings E (shewn at a) one of which is shewn at Fig. 3. so that by employing one of such said rings for filing the bills or other papers belonging to one person or firm such papers can thus be kept separate and distinct from those of other persons — The wires DD are intended for filing papers upon in the manner usually practised F is a hook by which to hang up the file — the upper ends of the wires CC are also formed hooked for connecting them to the stand A when necessary — The parts of this design which are not new or original as regards the shape or configuration thereof are all the parts except those marked A, B, C, D, E.

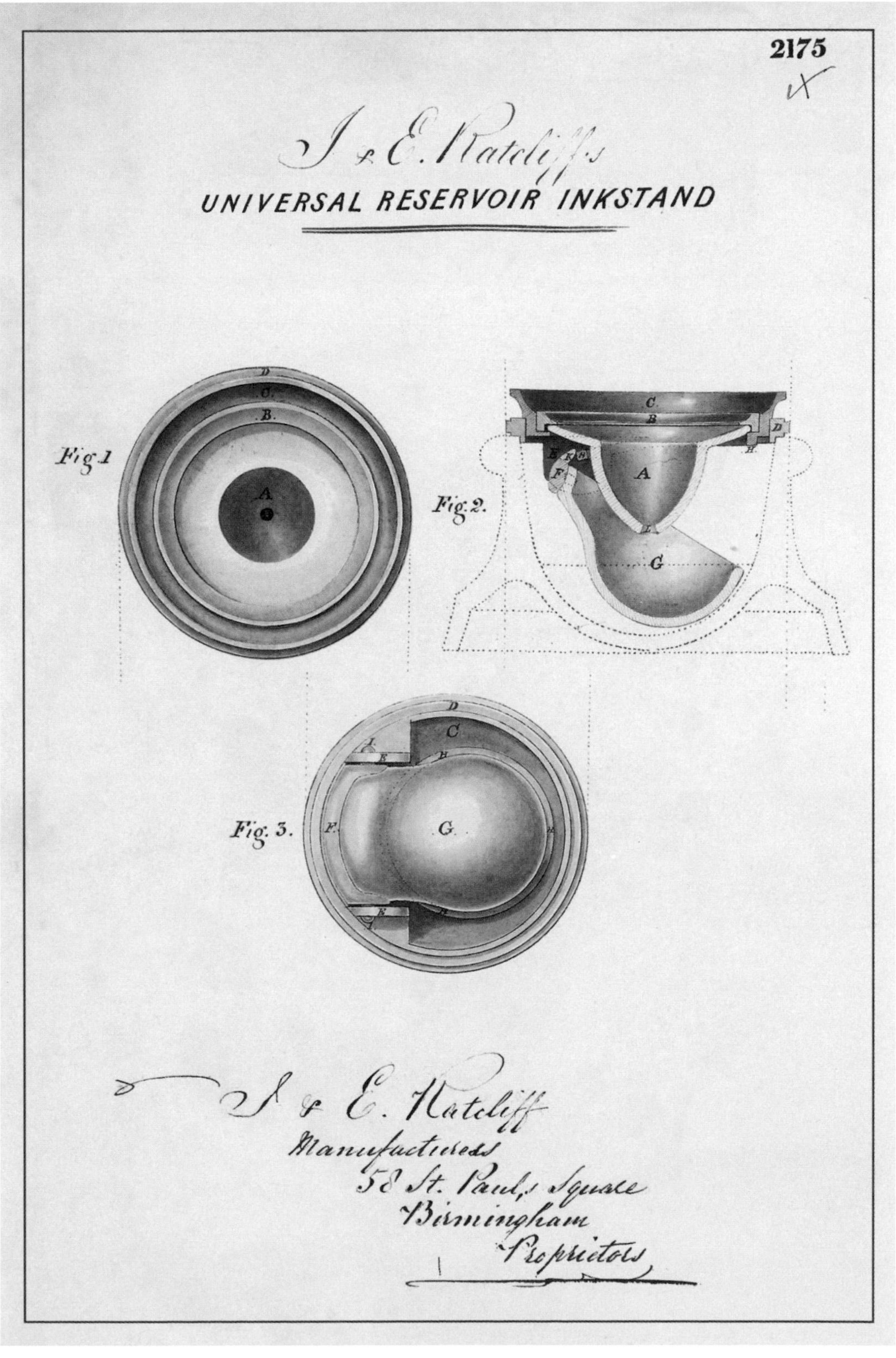

2175

UNIVERSAL RESERVOIR INKSTAND

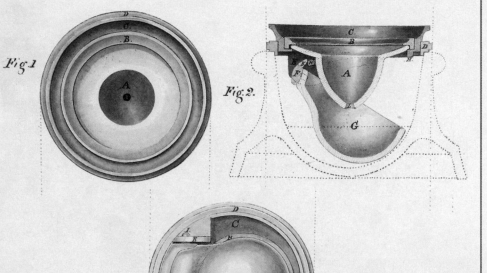

Fig. 1

Fig. 2.

Fig. 3.

J & E. Ratcliff
Manufacturers
58 St. Paul's Square
Birmingham
Proprietors

PREVIOUS LEFT

DESIGN FOR A FILE FOR FILING PAPERS, BILLS &c.*
1854

Fig. 1. elevation of the Design complete • *Fig. 2.* bottom plan view thereof shewing the mode of arranging and securing the wires employed for filing the papers upon *Fig. 3.* a detached view of one of the parts

The curved wires (CC) are intended for the reception of a series of flattened rings (E), so that by employing one of such said rings for filing, the bills or papers belonging to one person or firm can thus be kept separate and distinct from those of other persons.

BELOW

DESIGN FOR A SCHOOL ROOM*
1872

Fig. 1. plan of schoolroom with partitions open • *Fig. 2.* plan with partitions closed • *Fig. 3.* perspective view of Room forming centre of the cross

The purpose of utility is of enabling the Schoolmaster or Teacher to unite all the Divisions of the School or to isolate one class from another while supervising the whole.

PREVIOUS RIGHT

J. & E. RATCLIFF'S UNIVERSAL RESERVOIR INKSTAND
1850

Fig. 1. top view • *Fig. 2.* transverse section
Fig. 3. bottom view, or *Fig. 1.* reversed

(A) is the dipping cup. (B) a metal collar secured to (C) and which laps over on the cup keeping it in place. (D) is the outer rim which must be secured to the vessel that holds the ink; by turning the rim (C) in any direction the dipping cup will be filled or emptied as desired.

OPPOSITE

DESIGN FOR A FOLDING TRENCHER CAP
1850

Fig. 1. metal frame for the trencher when open • *Fig. 2.* metal frame when closed or folded • *Fig. 3.* cap complete when open for use • *Fig. 4.* the same when folded for convenience of placing same under the arm

In folding the cap, force is applied to the margin of the frame (aa) on both sides when the joints (b) are raised & the springs (cc) collapse from their extended length.

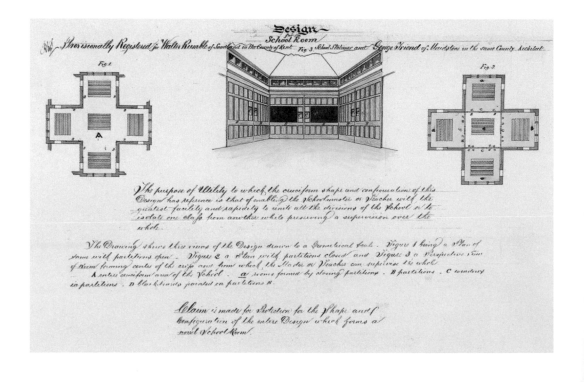

- DESIGN-FOR-A-FOLDING-TRENCHER-CAP -

Registered for Joseph Welch & John Margetson of No. 17 Cheapside London.

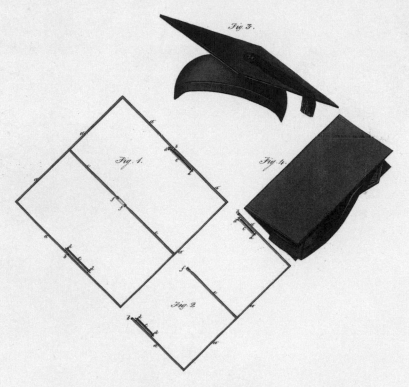

Fig. 3.

Fig. 1.

Fig. 4.

Fig. 2.

- DESCRIPTION -

The drawing exhibits four views drawn to a geometrical scale of three eights of the real size of the article. — Fig: 1 represents the naked metal frame for the trencher or top of the cap in its position when open for use, this frame is enclosed within two thicknesses of cloth or other material with which the cap is covered or made. — Fig. 2 represents the naked metal frame in its position when closed or folded. — Fig. 3. represents the cap complete in its position when open for use, and Fig. 4 represents the same when folded for convenience of placing same under the arm or for the general purpose of reducing the size of the cap in a very convenient manner admitting of being compressed perfectly close & flat. — The operation of folding the cap results from formation of the metal frame & the elasticity of the material composing the head piece. — Figs. 1 & 2 a.a. note the frame generally — b.b. are joints, — c.c. are strong helical springs of wire attached to the frame at points d.d. , — e.e. is a cross bar with joints f.f. — — In folding the cap, force is applied to the margin of the frame a.a. on both sides when the joints b are raised & the springs c.c. collapse from their extended length as in fig 1 & contract as shewn in fig. 2. which contraction is the power by which the cap is kept closed until the springs c.c are again forcibly extended, the cross bar serves to keep the frame in shape & preserve the covering level. The button in centre of fig 3 which holds down the tassel is provided with a ventilating valve as shewn which is opened or closed from within when required. —————————

The claim is for the whole of the parts contained in the figures 1. 2. 4. & the valve in fig 3 which are <u>New</u> the remaining portions are <u>old</u>.

Trim & Prince, Agents for Patents & Registration of Designs —
4 Trafalgar Square.

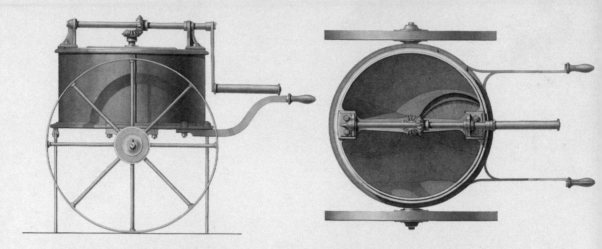

IMPROVED MACHINE FOR CUTTING TURNIPS

1841

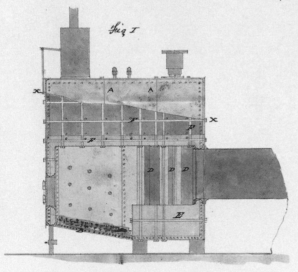

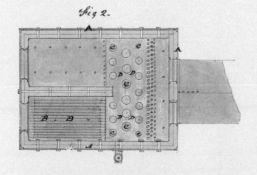

**DESIGN FOR A VERTICAL TUBULAR
FIREBOX BOILER**

1853

**A DESIGN FOR THE SHAPE OR CONFIGURATION
OF A BLOCK OF LEAD**

1858

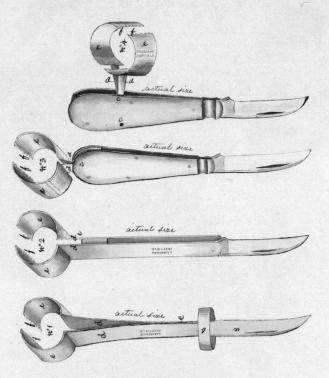

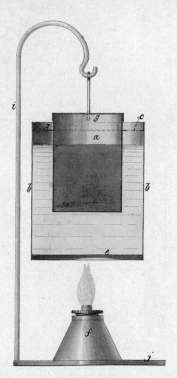

THE CASTRATING KNIFE

c. 1846

DESIGN FOR A GLUE POT AND STAND

1870

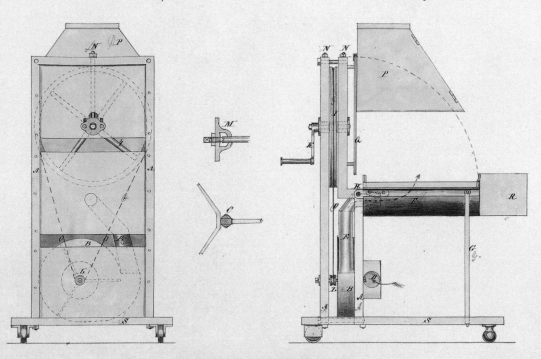

PORTABLE BLACKSMITH'S HEARTH

1848

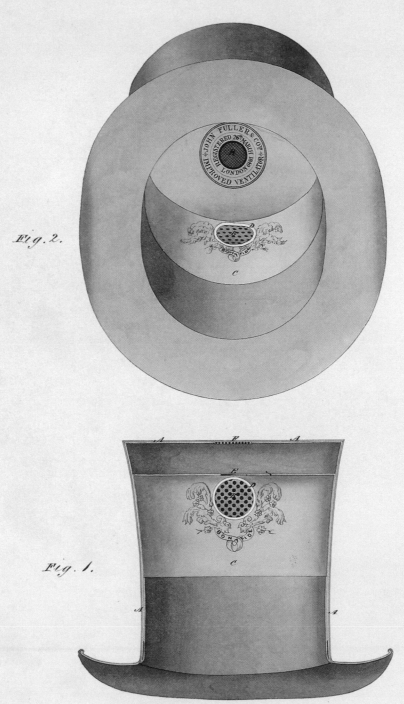

Fig.2.

Fig.1.

The ventilation is effected by the air passing through the perforated
holes thereby effectually carrying off the perspiration from the interior.

HIS & HERS

"YOU WILL BE ASTONISHED WITH THE QUALITY AND BEAUTIFUL COLOURS..."

◆ ◆ ◆

Advertisement for Lutas Leathley & Co.,
New Materials for Winter Dresses,

Pick Me Up

1891

ressing to impress in the nineteenth century meant wearing clothes that were appropriate to one's social station and conforming to a strict set of rules. Although fashions and etiquette changed over time, at any given moment advice books, magazines and journals clamoured to tell people what they should be wearing, where they should be wearing it, and at what time of day. Getting it wrong or taking an individualistic approach to dressing was to risk ridicule or social rejection. As people's level in society moved up or down, the way they dressed was expected to change accordingly. Every aspect of clothing gave other people information that enabled them to assess the wearer's place in society – or, importantly, their aspirations.

At the beginning of the nineteenth century most clothes were either home-made or made by independent tailors, dressmakers or hosiers – very few clothes were ready-made.[1] New technologies, which made the mass-production of clothing possible, led to major changes in the clothing industry. The most significant piece of new equipment was the sewing machine. Its use became widespread around 1860, and larger factories powered rows of sewing machines by steam, which was much more efficient than the treadle. As factories began to manufacture clothes on a larger scale, they began the widespread supply of ready-made clothing to shops. The department store emerged in the 1860s and 1870s, and with it coverage of fashion and clothing in the popular press expanded, along with increasingly sophisticated advertising. It was the beginning of the modern fashion industry.

Attitudes to both men's and women's clothing were double-edged. The rules, especially for women, were complex: for example, being 'very gaily dressed in the morning, or when walking down the streets' was 'vulgar', and 'to wear a

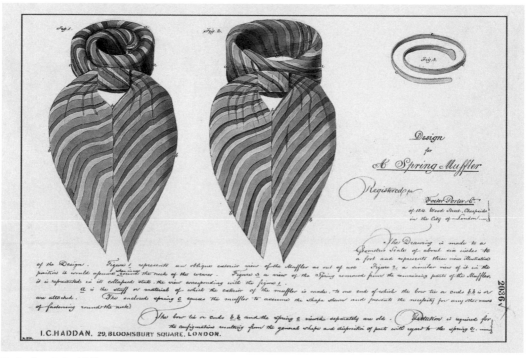

Design for a Spring Muffler, 1849

bonnet fit for a carriage, when one is not in one, is the extreme of bad taste'.[2] At the same time it was unseemly to divulge the slightest interest in one's own appearance. This was especially true for men, who were advised to wear muted colours and to avoid the sort of attention sought by the ostentatious upper-class 'dandy'. Between 1750 and 1850 men's dress changed radically, from powdered wigs, lace, knee breeches and stockings, to dark frock coats, subdued colours and top hats. Fashion journals emphasized the need for reserved understatement and relaxed effortlessness.

Fashions were created by those at the top of the social ladder, and were intended to reflect the wealth and status of the wearer. At the bottom of the ladder, the poorest just needed to cover up and keep warm. In the middle, people found themselves treading a fine line between conforming to expectations and being accused of 'aping their betters'. A woman writing about her 1860s childhood remembered going short of food because her father, a government clerk, was expected to wear 'nice black clothes and a silk hat', although he only received the same wages as 'an ordinary workman'.[3]

However, people with little money who made an effort to look fashionable were a frequent object of ridicule: 'We have seen the most diminutive bonnets, not bigger than saucers, ornamented with beads and flowers and lace, and backed up by ready-made "chignons" on the heads of girls who are only one degree removed from the poor house.'[4]

Not surprisingly, money-saving items such as shirt fronts (see p. 110), and collars and cuffs made from paper, rubber and celluloid were popular among clerks and shop assistants, who were expected to maintain a respectable appearance on very low wages. The demand for shirts rose as more men worked in clerical jobs, and the introduction of cotton shirts, instead of linen, made them more affordable. The quality

"IT IS NO UNUSUAL OCCURRENCE FOR A CUSTOMER TO ASK FOR A CERTAIN GARMENT OR A SPECIAL SHADE OF COLOUR, THAT HAS JUST BECOME THE 'GO' IN LONDON."

T. PATTERSON, 1893

and cleanliness of a man's shirt was frequently described in novels as an indication of character: Arnold Bennett, in his novel *The Old Wives' Tale*, describes Gerald Scales, as 'dressed with some distinction; good clothes, when put to the test, survived a change of fortune. Only his collar, large shaped front, and wristbands, which bore the ineffaceable signs of cheap laundering, reflected the shadow of impending disaster.'[5] The shirt front, or 'dicky', could hide a dirty shirt, or cover a shirt made in colours other than white. Striped shirts (see p. 110) were cheaper, and probably bought by poorer customers – they did not gain

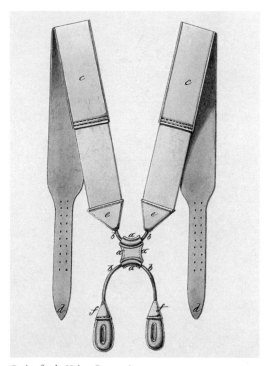

Design for the Unique Braces, 1851

Design for a Hat Cigar Holder, 1851

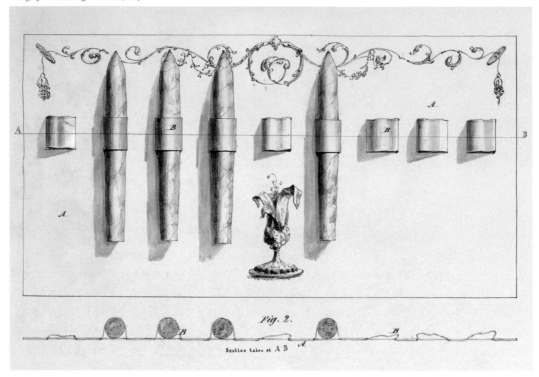

respectability among the upper classes until the turn of the century.[6]

Though men might have been advised not to let their interest in their appearance show, the market for men's clothing and accessories – such as umbrellas, cigar cutters, walking sticks and cigarette boxes – grew enormously as the century progressed. Merchants saw middle-class men as an untapped market, and advertised extensively to make conspicuous consumption for men acceptable. To do this successfully any feminine connotations associated with shopping had to be avoided, and images of sportsmen, soldiers or explorers were often used to sell products. Department stores, traditionally associated with women's pursuits, worked hard to gain the custom of middle-class men.[7]

At the turn of the century Harrods introduced a 'Gents' Club Room', with a large fireplace and comfortable armchairs, emulating the style of

exclusive West End gentlemen's clubs. Other department stores tried to tempt male customers with free shaves, cigars, newspapers and coffee.[8] Women were attracted by the addition of cafés, libraries and tea rooms.

Despite the exhortations to men not to show any interest in their clothing, fashion permeated men's clothing as well as women's – during the Boer War, for example, khaki fabrics appeared in the form of neckties, handkerchiefs and hats. It was particularly popular in items of men's sporting clothing.[9] Innovations were made to even mundane objects, and they were given exciting or pseudo-scientific names to make them sound more interesting. The 'Amphitrepolax Boot' (see p. 105) features a heel guard that not only allowed the wearer to swivel with ease, but had a name which made it sound positively exciting.

Throughout the nineteenth century no respectable person would go outside without wearing a hat, and for most of the Victorian period top hats were worn by middle-class men. They became a symbol of urban respectability. Early Victorian top hats were heavy, and the 'Bonafide Ventilating Hat' was one of several designs registered which attempted to tackle the problem of a build-up of steam, perspiration and hair-oil that resulted. The top hat was also unwieldy, a problem addressed by collapsible versions, such as the 'Elastic Dress and Opera Hat' (see p. 95), which used elastic, a newly invented product, to allow the hat to 'assume various forms or configurations'. 'Clark's Hat Suspender' (see p. 94) prevented the hat from being scuffed by feet while the owner was in church, allowing it to be suspended from the pew in front. A top hat could also be used to carry other items, including its own hat brush (see p. 115).

Elastic thread was enthusiastically adopted by the clothing industry and used in a range of

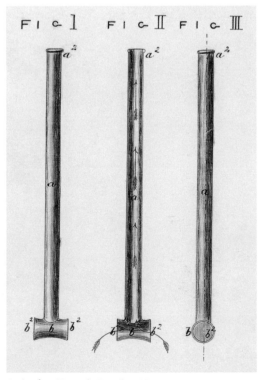

Design for a Moustache Protector, 1867

"EVERY MAN WITH A BEARD IS A MAN OF STRONGLY-MARKED INDIVIDUALITY."

ALEXANDER ROWLAND, *THE HUMAN HAIR*, 1814

products, including braces, used to hold up men's trousers throughout the nineteenth century. A vast array of braces was available, and many of the registered designs include elastic used in various ways, such as the 'Design for "Cantab" Braces'. There are also designs for elastic-topped 'drawers', or underpants, such as the 'extra-secure pantaloons' (see pp. 100–101). These are less common than braces, perhaps because of the greater risks associated with the perishing of the elastic, heightened by the energetic laundering of the time – they might have been less secure than they claimed.

One acceptable way in which a man could express himself through his appearance was in the cultivation of facial hair. This issue was widely written about, and passionate advocates of facial hair became known as the 'Beard and Moustache Movement'. Attitudes changed dramatically over the course of the century. In 1850 less than 10 per cent of men wore beards, although bushy sideburns, or 'mutton chops', were popular in the 1830s and 1840s. By 1870 about half of men wore full beards, and by the 1890s almost all men wore whiskers of some sort. This was quite a turnaround: in the 1840s wearing a beard was viewed with suspicion, as it was associated with political activism or an artistic temperament.[10] Charles Dickens's *Household Words* contained an article entitled 'Why Shave?' in which the writers ask: 'Why do we shave our beards? Why are we a bare-chinned people? [Facial hair] has various uses, physiological and mechanical. To take a physiological use first, we may point out the fact that the formation of hair is one method of extruding carbon from the system, and that the external hairs aid after their own way in the work that has to be done by the internal lungs.'[11]

By the turn of the century, men's interest in their appearance was becoming more acceptable, although it was still somewhat covert. Discussing how to choose colours, the magazine *Fashion* (1900) advised cautiously: 'Still, a sallow-faced man *might* just refrain from pink; and at all events, any man can properly refrain from such a relation in the adjacent colours of a coat flower and a cravat as produces what women call (to resort once more to the vocabulary of the adored and adorable sex) "a shriek."'[12]

Women's dress changed over the course of the nineteenth century, moving from the high-waisted, loose-fitting Empire line at the beginning of the century to a bell-shaped skirt with a fitted bodice and small waist in the mid-century, to the S-shape, popular at the end of the century. This silhouette required a full bust, a small waist and a bustle supporting a large amount of fabric at the back of a dress.

Achieving the required shape depended on the use of stays, known later in the century as corsets, which became an essential feature of a Victorian woman's life from puberty onwards. Not to wear them was to risk being considered a loose woman. It has been estimated that the average corset exerted a force of twenty-one pounds on the organs, although fashionable tight-lacing could increase that to eighty-eight pounds.[13]

A range of other scaffolding and upholstery was worn by women at different points in the century, including crinolines and the 'dress improver', or bustle. New methods of steel manufacture saw the introduction of the steel 'cage' crinoline, which gave a dress a circular shape while reducing the number of petticoats needed. Layers of underwear were worn by middle-class women, including a chemise, corset, camisole, petticoats and, with the introduction of the crinoline which tipped up easily, drawers. It has been estimated that while some Regency dresses weighed no more than a pound, a fashionable

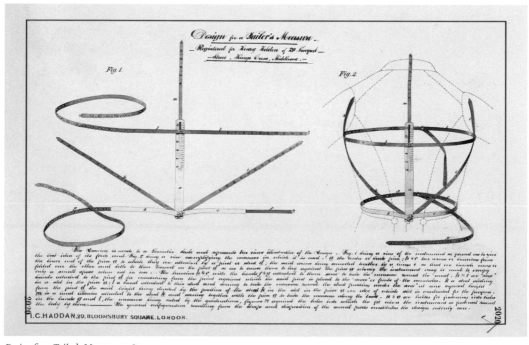

Design for a Tailor's Measure, c. 1849

Victorian woman could be wearing thirty-seven pounds of clothing.[14]

The ideal figure was an exaggerated hourglass shape – a potential source of anxiety for the flat-chested. Surviving dresses show that wadding was often placed in the linings of dresses to make the bust look larger, and rubber bust improvers could be bought to enhance the figure.[15] These were sometimes incorporated into the corset, as in the 'Corset with Expansible Busts', registered in 1881 (see p. 111). Such 'airwork' was also used to make inflatable crinolines and bustles.

Towards the end of the century the Rational Dress Society began to campaign against the clothing endured by women, which could restrict their movement and deform their bodies. There was a gradual move towards more comfortable clothing, but the wearing of corsets continued well into the twentieth century.

Attitudes towards men's dress also began to change, with some voices raised against its uniformity. In *The Picture of Dorian Gray* (1891), Oscar Wilde has Lord Henry Wotton complain: 'The costume of the nineteenth century is detestable. It is so sombre, so depressing. Sin is the only real colour-element left in modern life.'

"THE CORSET IS AN EVER-PRESENT MONITOR INDIRECTLY BIDDING ITS WEARER TO EXERCISE SELF-RESTRAINT; IT IS EVIDENCE OF A WELL-DISCIPLINED MIND AND WELL-REGULATED FEELINGS."

ADVERTISEMENT FOR A CORSET, 1878

Despite such protests, England was gaining a good reputation in the world of men's fashion. In a speech reported in the *Cutter's Gazette of Fashion* in 1893, a Mr T. Patterson celebrated the position of men's tailoring, by announcing: 'Fashions for gentlemen do not now originate across the channel, but in London....Nor are the provinces lagging behind so much as they used to'.[16]

As in all areas of Victorian life, achieving social acceptability was the main aim when choosing what to wear. Dressing appropriately was a duty, and as late as 1900 *Fashion* magazine asserted: 'To look well is part of the debt one owes to Society, since the seemliness of any assembly is the sum of the efforts of its units. Men as well as women owe something to Society.'[17]

[1] Sarah Levitt, *Victorians Unbuttoned*, London: George Allen & Unwin, 1986, p. 8.

[2] Ross Murray, *The Modern Householder*, 1872, pp. 372–74, quoted in Judith Flanders, *Inside the Victorian Home*, London and New York: W. W. Norton & Company, 2003, p. 440.

[3] Levitt, *op. cit.*, p. 10.

[4] *Ibid.*

[5] Arnold Bennett, *The Old Wives' Tale*, 1908, quoted in Levitt, *op. cit.*, pp. 56–57.

[6] Levitt, *op. cit.*, pp. 56–57.

[7] Brent Shannon, 'Refashioning men: Fashion, masculinity, and the cultivation of the male consumer in Britain, 1860–1914', *Victorian Studies*, 46(4), summer 2004, pp. 602–603.

[8] Shannon, *op. cit.*, pp. 611–12.

[9] *Ibid.*, p. 605.

[10] Christopher Oldstone-Moore, 'The Beard Movement in Victorian Britain' *Victorian Studies*, 48 (2005), 7–34, p. 8.

[11] Henry Morley and William Henry Wills, 'Why shave?' *Household Words* 13 (Aug. 1853): 560–63.

[12] Shannon, *op. cit.*, p. 614.

[13] Flanders, *op. cit.*, p. 309.

[14] Flanders, *op. cit.*, p. 306.

[15] Levitt, *op. cit.*, p. 39.

[16] Shannon, *op. cit.*, p. 597.

[17] *Ibid.*, p. 614.

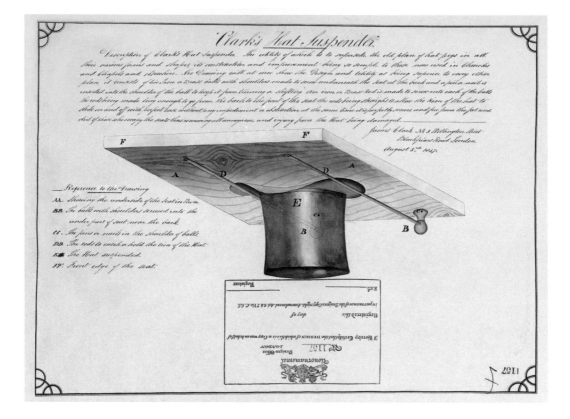

ABOVE

CLARK'S HAT SUSPENDER

1847

(AA): *underside of the seat in Pew &c;* (BB): *the balls with shoulders screwed into the under part of seat;* (CC): *the pins or rails in the shoulder of balls;* (DD): *the rods to catch or hold the rim of the Hat;* (EE): *the Hat suspended;* (FF): *front edge of seat. The utility is to supersede the old plan of hat pegs in all their various forms and shapes. The Hat is free from the feet and dirt of those who occupy the seats thus removing all annoyance and injury from the Hat being damaged.*

OPPOSITE ABOVE

DESIGN FOR AN ELASTIC DRESS AND OPERA HAT

1844

A Hat that will assume various forms or configurations, one only of which is shewn at (A), *which are essential when required to put the Hat in a small space: the elasticity or means employed for preserving its original form as shewn at* (B) *being effected without the aid of springs, such Hat being to all appearance similar to an ordinary Hat.*

OPPOSITE BELOW

THE DUPLEX HAT*

1878

Fig. 1. sectional view • *Fig. 2.* during conversion
Fig. 3. the hat when converted

By inverting the cup (C), *the supports* (fff) *and the top* (A) *being entirely hidden, a top hat becomes a low round topped hat and vice versa.*

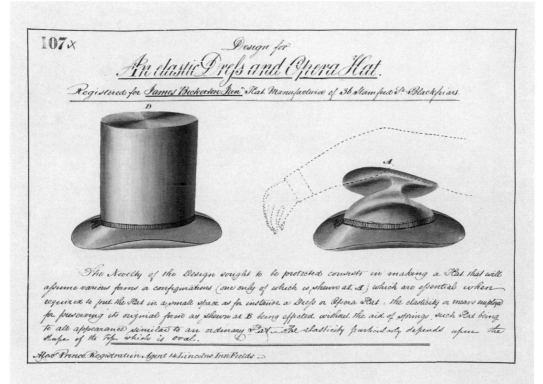

107 x

Design for

An elastic Dress and Opera Hat.

Registered for James Bickerton Junr Hat Manufacturer of 36 Stamford St. Blackfriars.

The Novelty of the Design sought to be protected consists in making a Hat that will assume various forms or configurations (one only of which is shewn at A) which are essential when required to put the Hat in a small space as for instance a Dress or Opera Hat. the elasticity or means employed for preserving its original form as shewn at B being effected. without the aid of springs such Hat being to all appearance similar to an ordinary Hat. The elasticity particularly depends upon the shape of the Tips which is oval.

Alex.^r Prince Registration Agent 14 Lincolns Inn Fields.

THE DUPLEX HAT.

Herbert Lintott of N.º 2 Souvenir Villas, Tavistock Road, Bedford -Park, Croydon, Surrey, and Charles Evelyn Smith of N.º 4 Welford Terrace, Brook Road, Upper Clapton Middlesex,

Fig N.º 1
Sectional View

scale 4 inches to the foot
Perspective

Fig N.º 2

Fig N.º 3

BELOW

**DESIGN FOR AN INSTRUMENT
FOR MEASURING PERSONS' HEADS**

1843

*The Design sought to be protected is represented by the
entire Drawing marked (1) which shows the Instrument
as applied to the head of a Person (see dotted lines).
The parts marked (A) are for the purpose of preserving
the shape of the lead whilst the material which forms the
Template is poured in: hats may thus be formed to suit
the exact shape of the head.*

OPPOSITE

PORTABLE APPARATUS FOR SHAPING HATS

1844

Fig. 1. plan view ⋅ *Fig. 2.* partial elevation
Fig. 3. vertical section through the line (AB)

(a): *a cylindrical vessel curved to suit the shape of the
hat; a valve (f) for the escape of steam; (g) an ordinary
lamp with a chimney extending through an opening
in the casing (h) fixed to the bottom of the reservoir for
the purpose of concentrating the heat from the lamp (g).
The brim of the hat becomes more uniformly softened.*

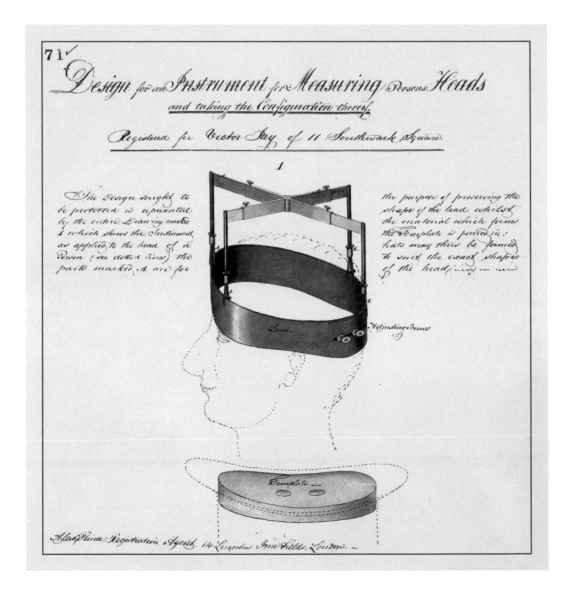

172

172

PORTABLE APPARATUS FOR SHAPING HATS

Registered for Henry Weir Collinson of Nº 14 Stamford St Blackfriars.

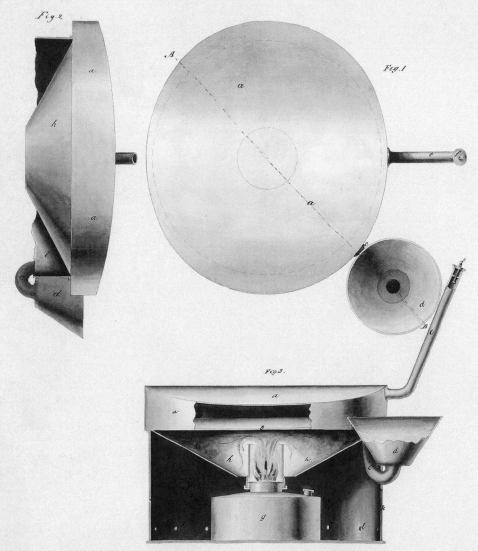

Fig.2

Fig.1

Fig.3

The Novelty of the Design sought to be protected and represented by the drawing (which is to a scale of 6 inches to a foot) consists in constructing a Portable apparatus of the shape in configuration wherein to be employed during the process of hat shaping: by this apparatus the brim of the hat becomes more thoroughly and uniformly softened throughout which is operated in shaping it, the leather or lining of the hat is not injured the crown does not go out of shape, the heat being entirely confined to the brim of the Hat/neither does it destroy the brightness of the material of which the external part of the hat is composed and is in all respects a safer cheaper more convenient and effective method than that hitherto employed for the purpose. The Fig 1 of the drawing represents a plan view of the apparatus Fig 2 a partial elevation thereof. Fig 3 a vertical section through the line A.B. a a cylindrical vessel the upper part of which is curved to suit the shape of the hat, the bottom b of this vessel is made flat as shewn, c a pipe fixed to one part of the vessel a for the purpose of charging the same with water, the outer end d of this pipe is enlarged in order that it may contain a greater quantity of water for supplying the reservoir as the water therein evaporates c a pipe situate at the upper part of the reservoir a and furnished with a valve f at the upper extremity for the escape of steam g an ordinary lamp furnished with a chimney extending through an opening in the inverted conical casing h fixed to the bottom of the reservoir a for the purpose of concentrating the rays of heat from the lamp g which rests upon the cylindrical casing i the upper part of which supports the reservoir a. this case is constructed with a door or opening k as also perforations l l for the admission of air.

Alex. Prince, Office for Patents of Inventions and Registration of Designs, 14 Lincolns InnFields.

1345

Registered
(Provisionally)

VOLUNTEER REVERSIBLE TROWSERS,

Michael Mendelssohn,

58 Millbank Street, Parliament Street, London, Tailor,

PROPRIETOR.

DESIGNS OFFICE
APR 28
1862
REGISTERED

PROVISIONALLY

The purpose of Utility to which the shape or configuration of this Design has reference is, to render a pair of Trowsers reversible, so that the inside may be worn outwards, if desired, by occupying less space than two ordinary pairs of Trowsers, is suitable for Military men, Tourists, and others.

The accompanying Drawing represents a pair of Trowsers, the inside being turned outwards, and is drawn to a scale of two and a half inches to the foot. A is the inside lining, of blue, or other colored cloth; stripes of cloth B,B, of a red, yellow, or other suitable color, being attached in the usual manner, or not at option. C,C, are the buttons, corresponding in size and position to the buttons D,D, of the exterior trowsers E, made of green or other colored cloth as desired. In

the fly F, between the inside and outside cloth is a piece of lining material G, formed with button holes H,H, by which the fly is fastened when the trowsers are worn either outwards or inwards. I, I, are straps for tightening the trowsers and are placed outside when the inside is worn outwards by passing them through slits J,J, formed in the material.

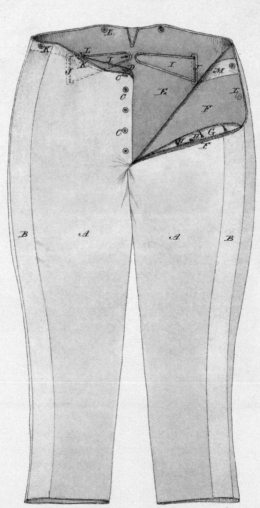

The brace buttons K,K, have also corresponding buttons L, attached to the material. The fly F, being folded down shews the stripe M, of the exterior trowsers E.

The parts of this Design which are not new or original as regards the shape or configuration thereof, are all the parts taken separately but the parts A, B,B, C,C, F, G, H,H, J,J, and K,K, as here combined form a new design.

OPPOSITE
VOLUNTEER REVERSIBLE TROWSERS*
1862

(A) *is the inside lining, of blue, or other colored cloth, stripes of cloth (BB) of a red, yellow, or other suitable color; (CC) are the buttons, corresponding in size and position to the buttons (DD) of the exterior trowsers (E). The purpose is to render a pair of trowsers reversible, so suitable for Military men, Tourists and others.*

BELOW
THE TROUSER ALLIANCE
1855

Fig. 1. interior view of waistcoat • *Fig. 2.* section view

The tabs have button holes (aa) which fit over the back buttons of the trowsers and so serve to keep them up.

OVERLEAF
DESIGN FOR DRAWERS OR PANTALOONS
1860

Fig. 1. front view • *Fig. 2.* side view • *Fig. 3.* back view

The purposes are the easy method by which they are placed upon or over the hips and secured thereon, the great support they afford to the back and stomach of the wearer, and the means by which they are prevented slipping down. The band (e) passes round the loins over the cords (bb) and whalebone (cc) and when the ends thereof are drawn through the buckles, causes the whalebone and cord to fit into the small of the back thereby affording great support and comfort to the wearer.

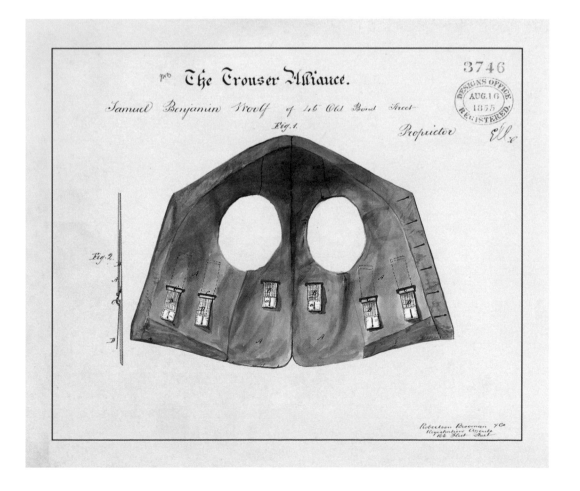

DESIGN for DR

Registered for Henry Cutler of

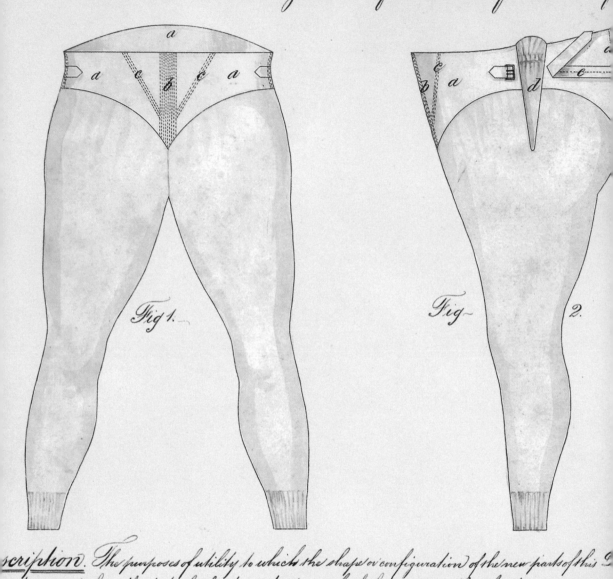

Fig 1.

Fig 2.

scription. The purposes of utility to which the shape or configuration of the new parts of this D

eat support they afford to the back and stomach of the wearer. Thirdly dispensing with

The drawing exhibits three views of the Design drawn to a proper geometrical scale Fig

parts appear at each of the figures respectively. It will be seen that a band _a. a._ is p

_nd_ is brought down to a point, rows of cord _b. b._ are here inserted, and by the side of which are

ich a gussett piece _d._ of soft material is inserted having a piece of elastic webbing run t

_s_ the band close around the loins and hips after which they are secured in their plac

_ds_ thereof are drawn through the buckles, causes the whalebone and cord to fit into the

The parts of this Design which are new and original as far as regards the sh

Prince & C° &c... by Patent... d Registration of D

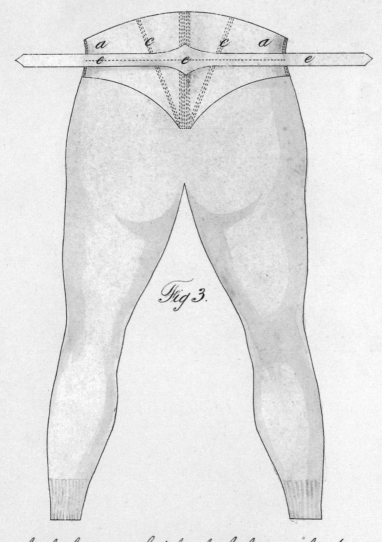

Fig 3.

DESIGNS OFFICE REGISTERED. DEC. 14 1860

4316

reference as firstly the easy method by which they are placed upon or over the hips and
stening to the trousers, and lastly the means by which they are prevented slipping d
a front view Fig. 2 a side view and Fig 3 a back view similar letters of reference den
attached to the upper part of the drawers and formed narrower at the sides than at the from
whalebone c c, for the purpose of keeping the band a a, flat against the body, an of
he top to allow of the top of the drawers being extended for putting on and when pulle
kles and a narrow band e, as shown this band e, passes round the loins over the com
f of the back thereby affording great support and comfort to the wearer.
d configuration thereof are those marked a, b, c, d & e for which Protection is

Trafalgar Square Charing Cross London

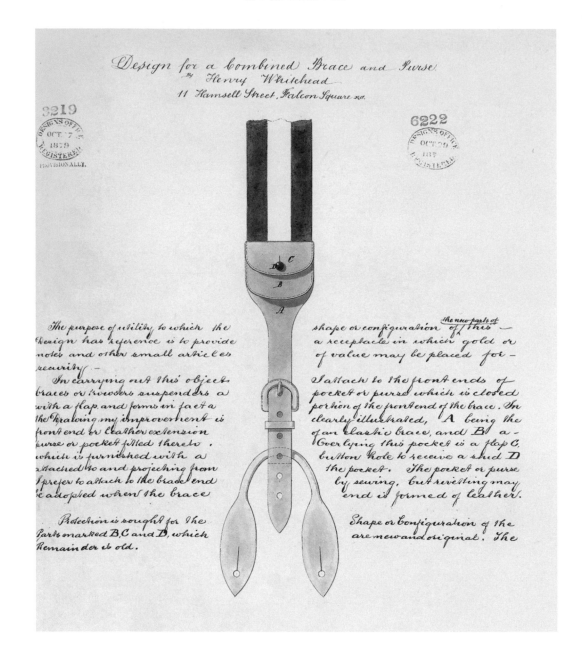

Design for a Combined Brace and Purse
by Henry Whitehead
11 Hamsell Street, Falcon Square &c.

3219

6222

The purpose of utility to which the Design has reference is to provide notes and other small articles security. —

In carrying out this object braces or trowsers suspenders a with a flap, and forms in fact a the drawing my improvement is front end or leather extension purse or pocket fitted thereto. which is furnished with a attached to and projecting from I prefer to attach to the brace end be adopted when the brace

Protection is sought for the Parts marked B, C and D, which Remainder is old.

shape or configuration *the new parts of* this — a receptacle in which gold or of value may be placed for —

I attach to the front ends of pocket or purse which is closed portion of the front end of the brace. In clearly illustrated, A being the of an elastic brace, and B a — Overlying this pocket is a flap C, button hole to receive a stud D the pocket. The pocket or purse by sewing, but rivetting may end is formed of leather.

Shape or configuration of the are new and original. The

ABOVE

DESIGN FOR A COMBINED BRACE AND PURSE
1879

Overlying the pocket (B) is a flap (C) which is furnished with a button hole to receive a stud (D) attached to and projecting from the pocket. The purpose is to provide a receptacle in which gold or notes and other small articles of value may be placed for security.

OPPOSITE

DESIGN OF AN IMPROVED COMBINED GLOVE AND PURSE*
1861

The purpose consists in securing to the wearer a convenience of withdrawing or depositing money unattainable by the articles in a separate state. The part colored violet is fastened to the glove by sewing or stitching.

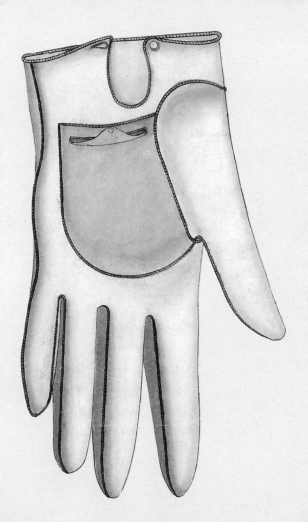

Nᵒ 1257

"Design
of an Improved Combined Glove and Purse
———— Registered by ————

Henry Sumner of Liverpool in the County of Lancaster, Architect.

The purpose of Utility to which the Shape or Configuration of the new part of this Design has reference consists in securing to the wearer a convenience of withdrawing or depositing money unattainable by the articles in a separate state.

The glove drawing which is drawn to a Geometrical Scale represents a front view of the combined Glove and Purse. The part coloured violet which is made of the same material as the glove and fastened to the same by sewing or stitching, shews the shape and configuration and position in which the purse is placed.

The whole of this Design is old except the part coloured violet.

BELOW

DESIGN FOR SPRING SOLES FOR BOOTS AND SHOES

1845

Fig. 1. plan view of the under side of a boot or shoe
Fig. 2. the outer sole when detached from *Fig. 1.* and in an inverted position

A flat spring of thin metal (A) (shewn in dotted lines in Fig. 1.) is rivetted or otherwise fastened to the outer sole (B), being for the purpose of preventing the toes of boots or shoes from turning upwards.

OPPOSITE

THE AMPHITREPOLAX BOOT*

1868

On the ordinary Sole and Lift of the Boot is fitted a circular piece of hard Leather (a, Fig. 3.) the Edge of which is Bevelled, the Heel turns on this as on a Pivot. Upon this a ring of Leather (b, Fig. 3.) fits closely. Over this is screwed a circular plate of Brass (c, Fig. 4.) this holds the ring (b, Figs. 3. & 4.) on securely and at the same time allows it to turn freely. The purpose is the great amount of extra wear gained by a Rotary Heel, which may be turned a complete revolution; hence, always ensuring a perfectly Flat and Even-worn Heel.

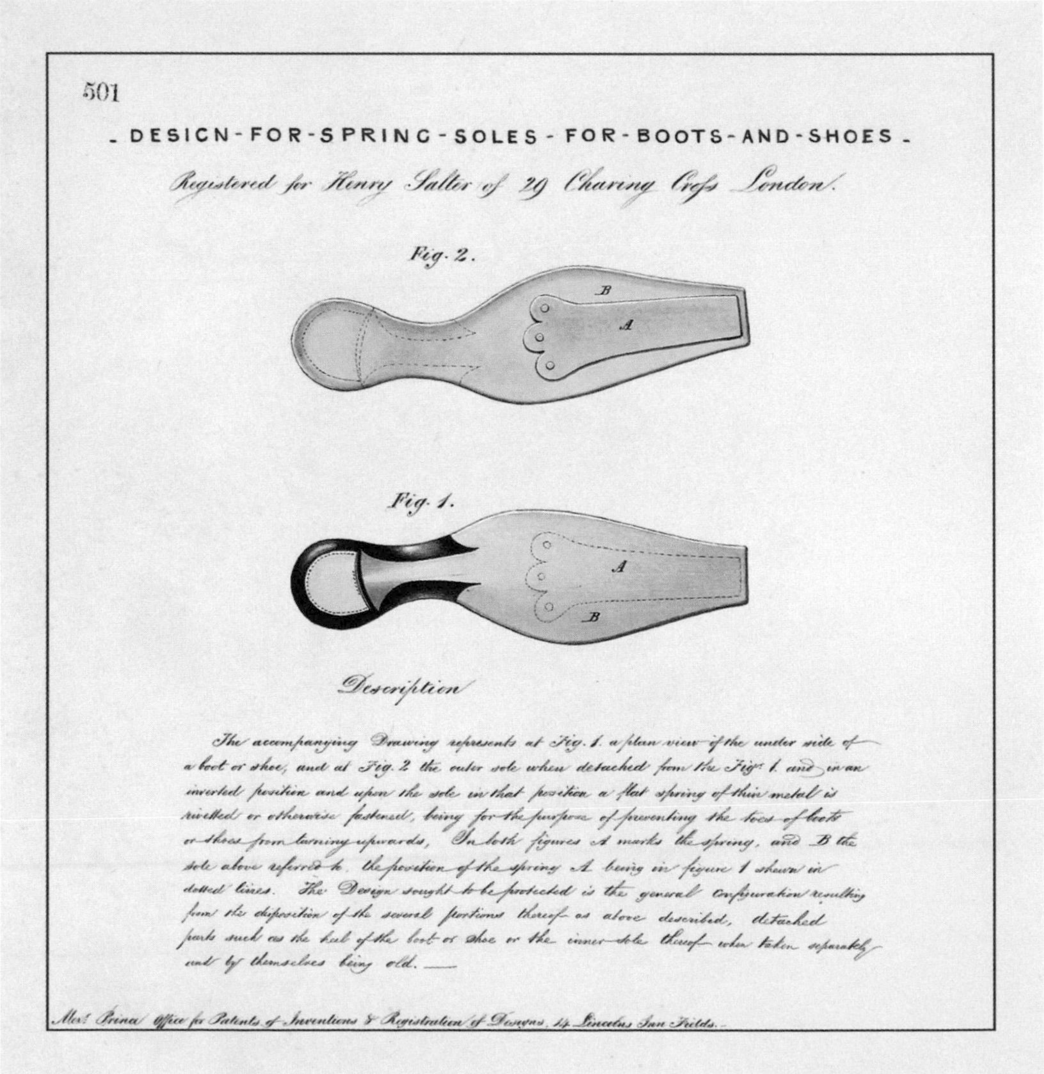

501

‑ DESIGN ‑ FOR ‑ SPRING ‑ SOLES ‑ FOR ‑ BOOTS ‑ AND ‑ SHOES ‑

Registered for Henry Salter of 29 Charing Cross London.

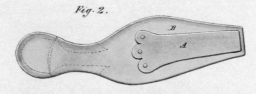

Fig. 2.

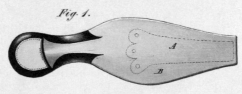

Fig. 1.

Description

The accompanying Drawing represents at Fig. 1. a plan view of the under side of a boot or shoe; and at Fig. 2. the outer sole when detached from the Fig. 1 and in an inverted position and upon the sole in that position a flat spring of thin metal is rivetted or otherwise fastened, being for the purpose of preventing the toes of boots or shoes from turning upwards. In both figures A marks the spring, and B the sole above referred to. the position of the spring A being in figure 1 shewn in dotted lines. The Design sought to be protected is the general configuration resulting from the disposition of the several portions thereof as above described, detached parts such as the heel of the boot or shoe or the inner sole thereof when taken separately and by themselves being old. —

Mess. Prince office for Patents of Inventions & Registration of Designs. 14 Lincoln's Inn Fields.

THE AMPHITREPOLAX BOOT.

1892

DESIGNS OFFICE
DEC.4
1868
REGISTERED

PROVISIONALLY

CHARLES ISAAC SWIFT.
99 HIGH STREET, CAMDEN TOWN.

FIG. 1. ELEVATION SHEWING HEEL IN SECTION.

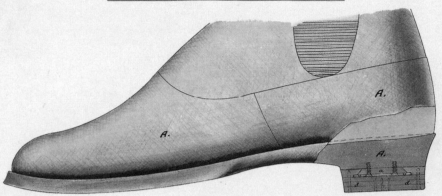

FIG. 2. PLAN WITH COMPLETE HEEL.

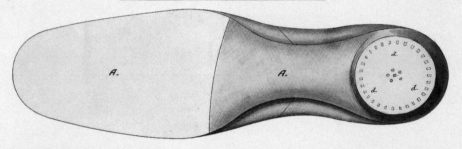

FIG. 3. PLAN WITH BRASS COVER PLATE REMOVED.

FIG. 4. PLAN SHEWING BRASS COVER PLATE.

FIG. 5. SECTION WITH LOWER HEEL REMOVED.

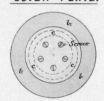

The purpose of Utility to which the Shape or Configuration of (the New Parts of) this Design has reference is the great amount of extra Wear gained by a Rotary Heel; which may be turned from the smallest part of to a complete revolution; hence, always ensuring a perfectly Flat and Even worn Heel.

Also in there not being any Hollow in the Bottom of the Heel into which Dirt may accumulate, and, furthermore the comparative little trouble required to set the Heel.

Description. On the ordinary Sole & Lift of the Boot is fitted a circular piece of hard Leather (a. Fig. 3), the Edge of which is Bevelled; the Heel turns on this as on a Pivot. Upon this a ring of Leather (b. Fig. 3), of the same outer diameter as the Heel and with its inner Edge bevelled, fits closely. Over this is screwed a circular plate of Brass (c. Fig. 4), the diameter of which is about 1/4 of an inch larger than that of the Pivot (a. Fig. 3), this holds the ring (b. Figs. 3 & 4) on securely and at the same time allows it to turn freely. Upon this Ring (b. Figs. 3 & 4), is built in the ordinary manner the remaining portion (d. Figs. 1 & 2), which will revolve with it freely round the Pivot. Note. The Drawings are full size.

The Parts of this Design which are not New or original as regards the Shape or Configuration thereof, are those marked. **A. A.**

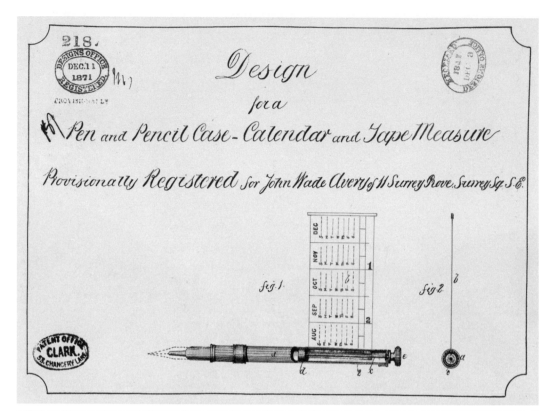

218

DESIGNS OFFICE
DEC 11
1871
REGISTERED

PROVISIONALLY

Design

for a

Pen and Pencil Case - Calendar and Tape Measure

Provisionally Registered for John Wade Avery of 11 Surrey Grove, Surrey Sq. S.E.

fig. 1.

fig. 2.

PATENT OFFICE
CLARK.
53. CHANCERY LANE.

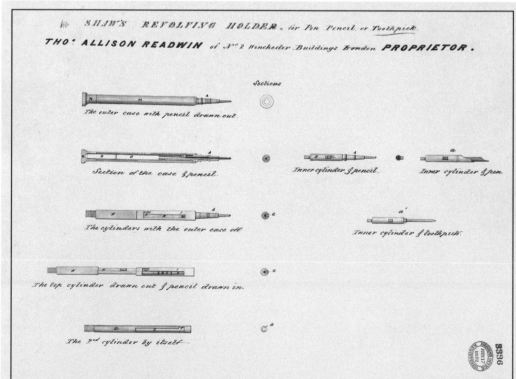

SHAW'S REVOLVING HOLDER - for Pen Pencil, or Toothpick.

THOS ALLISON READWIN of No 2 Winchester Buildings London PROPRIETOR.

Sections

The outer case with pencil drawn out.

Section of the case & pencil.   Inner cylinder & pencil.   Inner cylinder & pen.

The cylinders with the outer case off.   Inner cylinder & toothpick.

The top cylinder drawn out & pencil drawn in.

The 3rd cylinder by itself.

8896

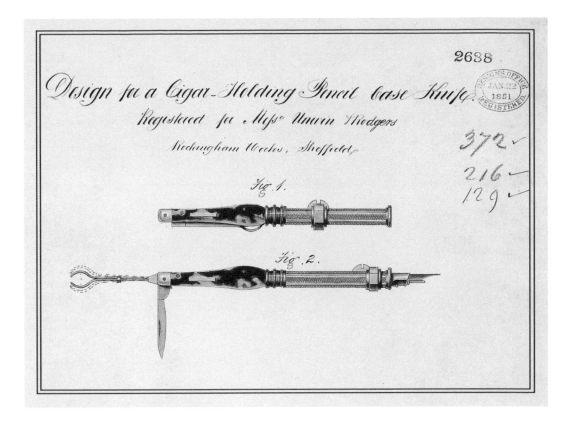

OPPOSITE ABOVE

DESIGN FOR A PEN AND PENCIL CASE-CALENDAR AND TAPE MEASURE*

1871

Fig. 1. the case ◆ *Fig. 2.* transverse section of the case

(a) *shows an ordinary pen and pencil case, containing a combined 6 inch measuring tape and calendar* (b) *coiled up on a spindle* (c) *having a head* (d) *turning within the case* (a), *the spindle being rotated by a button* (e).

OPPOSITE BELOW

SHAW'S REVOLVING HOLDER FOR PEN, PENCIL, OR TOOTHPICK

1852

Fig. 1. the outer case with pencil drawn out ◆ *Fig. 2.* section of the case & pencil ◆ *Fig. 3.* the cylinders with the outer case off ◆ *Fig. 4.* the top cylinder drawn out & pencil drawn in ◆ *Fig. 5.* the 2nd cylinder by itself *Fig. 6.* Inner cylinder & pencil; (a): Inner cylinder & pen; (a'): Inner cylinder & toothpick

ABOVE

DESIGN FOR A CIGAR-HOLDING PENCIL CASE KNIFE

1851

Fig. 1. the instrument with the Cigar Holder and pencil Case enclosed within the case ◆ *Fig. 2.* the same with those articles extended or partially so

The parts individually being well known do not require to be described, the novelty for which protection is sought is the form and configuration of the design consisting of the Cigar Holder in conjunction with the pencil case Knife.

OPPOSITE ABOVE
DESIGN FOR A SMOKING PIPE
1875

Fig. 1. the pipe when open for cleaning the interior bowl and tube • *Fig. 2.* the pipe when closed

Fig (aa) *is the bowl of the pipe,* (bb) *the stem and* (c) *the binding tube and mouth piece. When it is desired to cleanse the interior of the pipe the mouth piece and binding tube* (c) *are withdrawn at which time the pipe can be opened so as to swing on the hinge* (d) *and expose the interior surfaces in which position they are readily cleaned.*

BELOW
PROVISIONAL USEFUL DESIGN: CIGAR TUBE*
1872

Fig. 1. the cigar tube in elevation • *Fig. 2.* se&ion view

The purpose is the combination of these light weighted and different coloured bodies, meerschaum, lobster shell, and amber, forming a cigar tube of extreme lightness.

OPPOSITE BELOW LEFT
PROVISIONALLY REGISTERED PIPE CANE*
1852

Fig. 1. top of Cane with Elastic Ind. Rubber Tube attached to stem of pipe, with mouth piece at the other end • *Fig. 2.* external appearance of *Fig. 1.* *Fig. 3.* Tube stowed away in the chamber

The purpose is to carry the pipe & Tobacco without giving their disagreeable odour to the clothes & to conceal the pipe when smoking.

OPPOSITE BELOW RIGHT
PROVISIONALLY REGISTERED CIGAR CANE*
1852

Fig. 1. Aperture to extra& one cigar at once, the rest following in succession on inverting the cane. *Fig. 2.* external appearance of *Fig. 1.*

The purpose is to obviate the inconvenience of carrying in the pocket the cumbrous cigar boxes now in use.

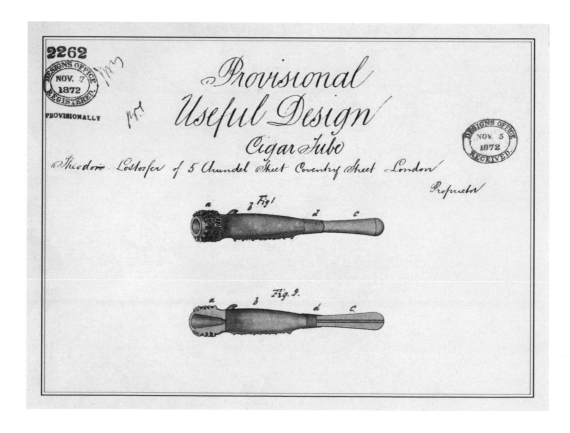

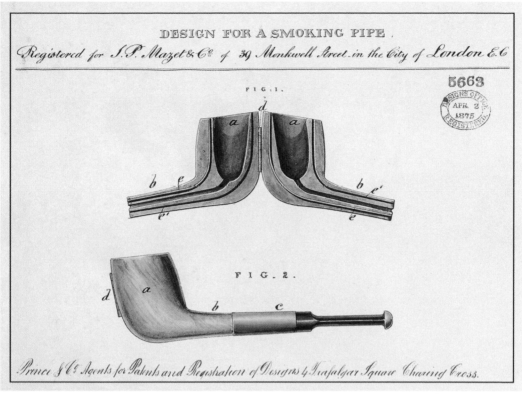

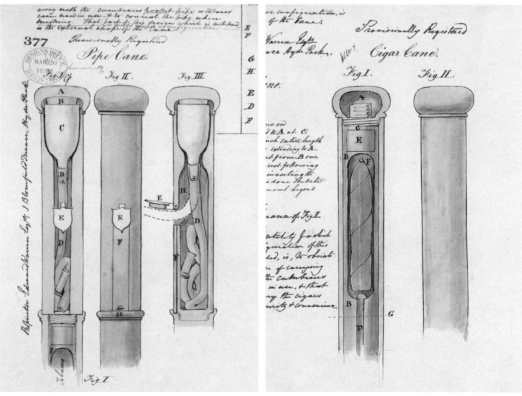

New Uniform The Front

Figure 1

Thomas Richard Barlow
143 Tooley Street
Southwark

Provisionally

The purpose of Utility to which the
shape or configuration of this design
has reference is its easy adjustment
to the figure and its close resemblance
to the Shirt also the impossibility
of its becoming deranged through
exertion
Figure 1 Shows the Front entire
Fig 2 the Front when on
Fig 3 Back of same
The whole of this design is new in so far as
regard the shape or configuration thereof

OPPOSITE

THE NEW UNIFORM FRONT

1858

Fig. 1. the front entire ⬥ *Fig. 2.* the Front when on
Fig. 3. Back of same

The purpose of utility to which the shape or configuration
of this design has reference is its easy adjustment to the
figure and its close resemblance to the shirt — also the
impossibility of its becoming deranged through exertion.

BELOW

DESIGN FOR A CORSET WITH EXPANSIBLE BUSTS

1881

Fig. 1. front view of a corset with expansible busts in
position ⬥ *Fig. 2.* inside view of the corset spread out

(aa) *is a corset which is made in the usual manner;* (bb)
are pockets or receptacles secured externally to the corset
by sewing and intended to receive the expansible busts
(cc). *The busts consist of india rubber or other air proof*
bags which are made of a form to represent as nearly as
possible when distended the shape of the human breasts
and they are provided at the back with a short tube (d)
fitted with a suitable mouth piece whereby the busts may
be expanded as required when the corset is on the body.

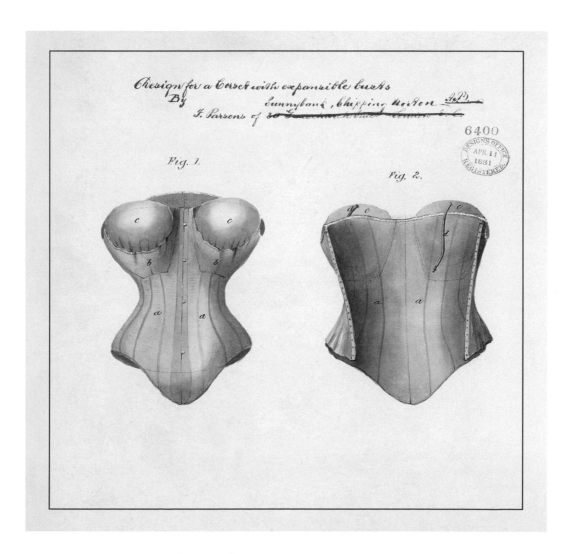

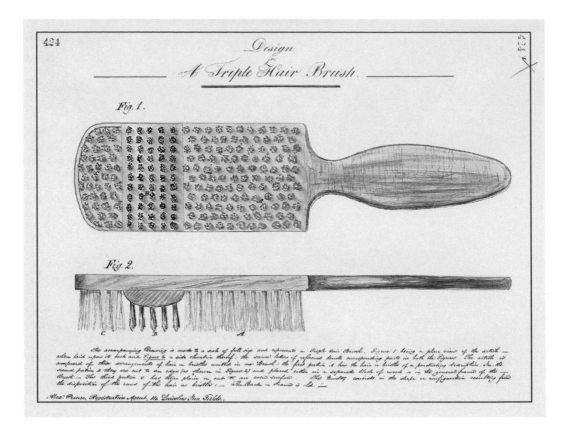

A TRIPLE HAIR BRUSH

1845

Fig. 1. plan view of the article when laid upon its back

Fig. 2. side elevation thereof

The article is composed of three arrangements of hair or bristles united in one Brush, the first portion (A) has the hair or bristles of a penetrating description. In the second portion (B) they are cut to an edge (as shewn in Fig. 2.) and placed either in a separate block of wood or in the general frame of the Brush. The third portion (C) has them plain or cut to an even surface.

PORTABLE ROTARY HAIR BRUSHING MACHINE

1864

The portion of the machine marked blue to be made of metal, either brass or iron. The portion marked brown to be made of wood. The large wheel by which velocity and power are gained is worked by the handle (K) and is connected with the small wheel (F) by a band of india rubber & by which it communicates the speed. Such a brush may be applied for the purpose of Hair brushing or any other purpose to which such a brush may be applied, viz flesh or clothes brushing, obtaining a greater velocity for the brush than has heretofore been obtained by such hand machines.

No. Title of the Design
Portable Rotary Hair Brushing Machine

Names of Proprietors.

James Beckett
Lambs Buildings. Stephens Green West. Dublin

·and·

Nathaniel Lewis Griffin
17 Suffolk Street Dublin

4659

DESIGNS OFFICE
SEP. 27
1884
REGISTERED

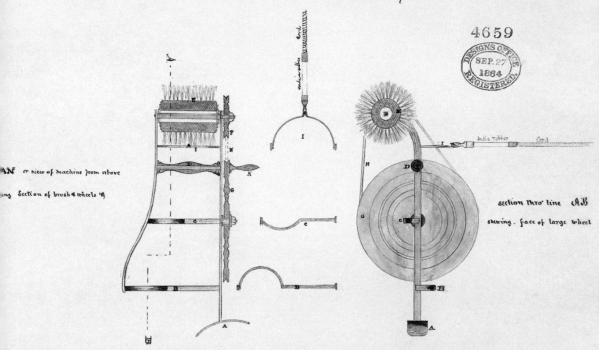

PLAN or view of machine from above
showing Section of brush & wheels &

section thro' line A.B
showing. face of large wheel

scale ¼ inch to one inch

Statement of Utility

The purpose of utility to which the shape or configuration of the new parts of this design has reference —— is. that by this machine a ready method is obtained whereby a rotary brush can be applied for the purpose of Hair brushing or any other purpose to which such a brush may be applied. Viz flesh or Clothes brushing. and at the same time be both portable and effective — The shape or Configuration enabling the person using it to keep it perfectly steady while using, and obtaining greater velocity for the brush than has been heretofore obtained by such hand machines at the same time having perfect personal control over its movements.

Description

The portion of the machine marked blue —— to be made of metal Either brass or iron	A Breast plate to steady the machine
The portion marked Brown —— to be made of wood	B Cross Stay to pass over the left arm do
The large wheel by which velocity and power are gained is worked by the handle K and is Connected with the small wheel F by a band of india rubber H by which it communicates the speed	C Cross stay to pass under the left wrist do
	D Handle to be grasped by the left hand. do
The Brush works on the same axle as the small wheel and receives all its velocity. which is three times as great as that of the large wheel, the small one being ⅓ the diameter of the large one.	E Brush working on a axle
	F Small wheel working on same axle as brush
	G Large wheel worked by handle
The machine is rendered steady for hair brushing by the hook marked I which hangs from a Cord to the Ceiling of the room or any other support, attached to the Cord is a piece of indiarubber by which means the brush can be raised or lowered to the top or lower part of the head	H Band or belt from large to small wheel
	I Hook to hang machine while working

The parts of this design which are not new or Original as regards the shape or configuration are those coloured Brown

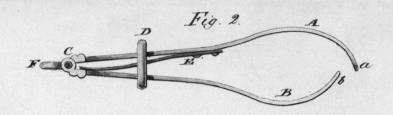

DESIGN FOR AN INSTRUMENT FOR HOLDING UP LADIES' DRESSES

1846

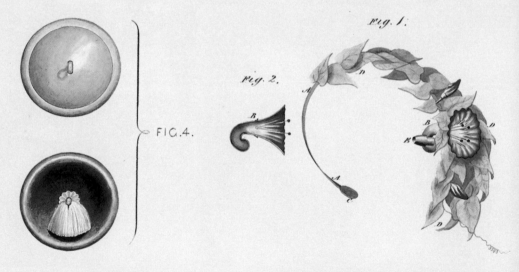

**DESIGN FOR AN IMPROVED ECONOMIC
BUTTON FOR LADIESWEAR**

1852

DESIGN FOR THE MIMOSA OR FLOWER CORNET

1849

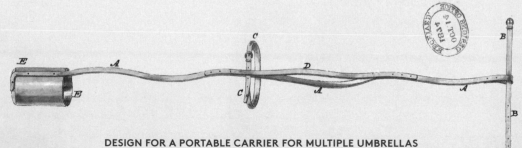

DESIGN FOR A PORTABLE CARRIER FOR MULTIPLE UMBRELLAS

1874

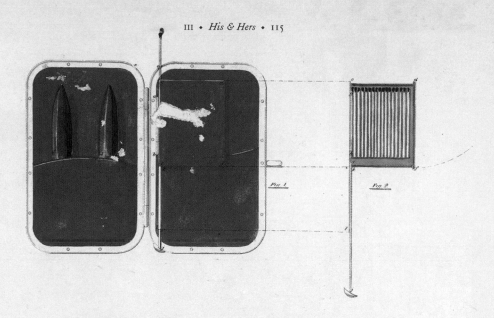

DESIGN FOR A CIGAR CASE WITH SELF LIGHTING MATCHES
1852

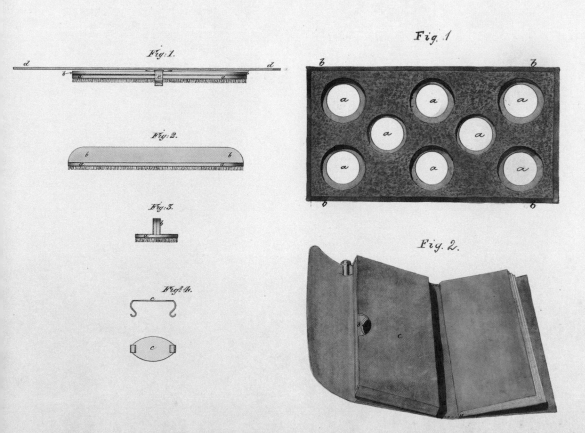

DESIGN FOR HAT BRUSH TO BE CARRIED INSIDE A HAT *1869*

DESIGN FOR A PORTE MONNAIE
1860

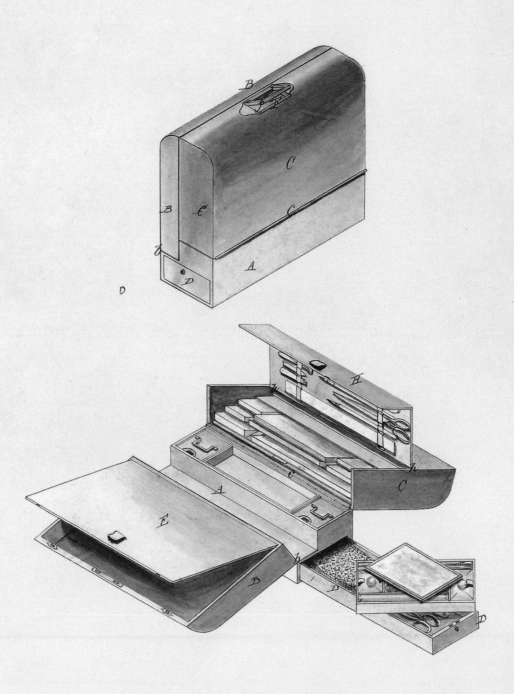

A compendious and portable travelling case serving both as a writing
case and despatch box and as a dressing case or lady's work box.

OUT & ABOUT

"THE PASSION FOR LOCOMOTION IS A SIGN OF THE TIMES..."

• • •

Newspaper article on railway
and steamboat holiday excursions,
The Morning Chronicle
1856

ne of the defining features of the nineteenth century was an increase in travel. At the beginning of the century most people remained close to home, rarely travelling farther than was necessary to get to work, to go shopping or to socialize. Those who could afford it might use coaches for longer journeys, pulled by teams of horses that were exchanged about every ten miles. Coaches were expensive and uncomfortable, and travelled at an average of no more than ten miles an hour. By the end of the century, not only could people travel between the major cities with ease, but it seemed that the whole world was within reach. The British Empire was expanding and it was an age of international exploration and adventure. Every aspect of travel created opportunities for inventors, from ways to keep warm on train journeys (see p. 125) to methods of cleaning the gold found during the rush to the world's gold fields (see p. 131).

As technological advances brought new forms of transport, patterns of life changed. Suburban housing grew up along omnibus, railway and tram routes. People began to travel from the suburbs to work in the cities, burdening the already overcrowded city roads. Railways, in particular, transformed the Victorian economy and society, bringing new opportunities for commerce and travel around the world. At home, day trips to the countryside were now easy for city dwellers, and seaside towns flourished as trips to the coast became a popular and affordable recreation.

However, the construction of railways also had a social cost, and thousands of people were displaced as their homes and communities were demolished to make way for the lines, which could not be adapted for gradients or curves. Dickens describes the building of a railway through Camden Town in London: 'Houses were knocked down; streets broken through and stopped; deep pits and trenches dug in the ground; enormous heaps of earth and clay thrown up; buildings that were undermined and shaking, propped up by great beams of wood...In short, the yet unfinished and unopened Railroad was in progress; and, from the very core of all this dire disorder, trailed smoothly away, upon its mighty course of civilization and improvement.'[1]

Steam locomotives were developed at the beginning of the century to haul coal in mining areas, but the age of the steam train really began in 1830 with the opening of the Liverpool and Manchester Railway. This was the first line intended for passenger use as well as freight. There were less than 100 miles of railway line in Britain in 1830; by 1852 this had increased to around 6,600, and by the time Queen Victoria died in 1901 there were almost 19,000 miles of track.[2]

The social classes were segregated on the railways as on other forms of public transport. Railway trains had three classes of travel, as well as cheap 'workmen's trains' which enabled labourers get to work in the cities. There were other cheap schemes operating earlier in the day before most people wanted to travel. Many train companies had

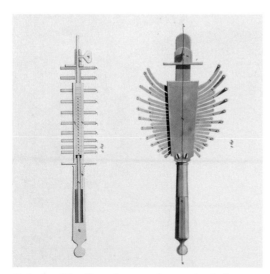

Design for a Plantoform or instrument for measuring the feet of Horses for facilitating Shoeing, 1850

Design for An improved Pole and Bolster for Railway and other Trucks, 1853

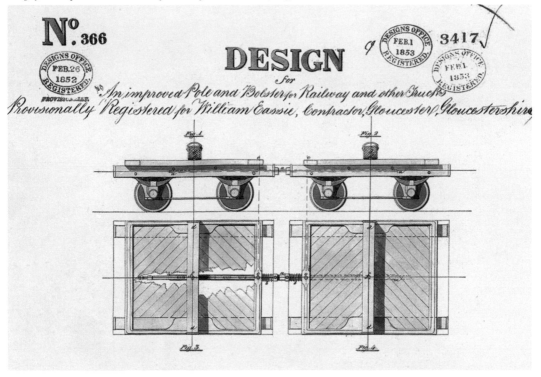

offered cheap fares from the 1860s, and the Cheap Trains Act in 1883 made this compulsory. This meant that the less wealthy could now move out to the suburbs, as well as the middle classes.

As railway travel became commonplace, journeys grew more comfortable. The trains had gas lighting, and the added comforts of luncheon baskets, railway blankets and foot-warmers (see p. 125, 140). Some of these were filled with acetate of soda, which melted at 200 degrees Fahrenheit and in the process of recrystallizing remained hot for about twenty hours.[3]

Telegraph wires were run alongside the railway tracks. These were originally used for railway business, but the usefulness of the telegraph was soon seized on, and telegraph communications spread across the globe. Isambard Kingdom Brunel's steam ship *The Great Eastern* played a large part in laying thousands of miles of transatlantic telegraph cable. Charles Dickens

believed that the telegraph was 'of all our modern wonders…the most wonderful'.[4]

Despite the growth of the railways, within the cities the horse was still relied on for most forms of transport – in fact the horse population was at its highest in the golden age of the steam railway.[5] Victorian society remained dependent on horses until the advent of the motor car in the 1880s, and the electrification of trams, which was not widespread until the turn of the century.

"A SPECTATOR OBSERVING THEIR APPROACH, CAN SCARCELY DIVEST HIMSELF OF THE IDEA, THAT [TRAINS] ARE NOT ENLARGING AND INCREASING IN SIZE RATHER THAN MOVING."[1]

REV EDWARD STANLEY, *BLACKWOOD'S MAGAZINE*, 1830

There was a thriving market for horse-related equipment: the Great Exhibition of 1851 had a section for 'leather, saddlery and harness' as well as a whole gallery devoted to carriages. The newly affluent Victorian middle classes aspired to own one of these sophisticated vehicles, and now that the components were mass-produced they were more affordable. Varieties included Broughams, Victorias, sociables and sulkys, to name but a few.[6]

Many more people hired four-wheeled carriages or Hansom cabs, a two-wheeled vehicle that was light and manoeuvrable through busy city streets. Horse-drawn omnibuses, too, were a popular form of travel, aimed at the middle rather than the working classes. They began service at eight in the morning, when labourers had already started work, and the fares cost more than the third class fare on a train. The driver and conductor often operated their own screening system, slowing down rather than stopping if they saw only poorly dressed people waiting.[7]

People, mostly men, also rode on top of omnibuses, climbing an iron ladder to reach the roof. Although rather middle-class, the omnibuses were still far from salubrious. As the journalist George Sala described: 'The rumbling, the jumbling, the jolting, and the concussions – the lurking ague in the straw when it is wet, and the peculiar omnibus fleas that lurk in it when it is dry, make the interior of one of these vehicles a place of terror and discomfort.'[8]

Horse-drawn trams pulled carriages along fixed tracks, and an extensive tramway system grew up in many Victorian towns and cities, extending out into the suburbs. This was a cheap form of transport with special concessionary fares, making it popular with the working classes.

The huge amount of traffic meant that London, in particular, suffered increasingly from traffic jams. Horse-drawn carriages and omnibuses, and horse-drawn wagons carrying materials to workshops and finished goods to stores, clogged

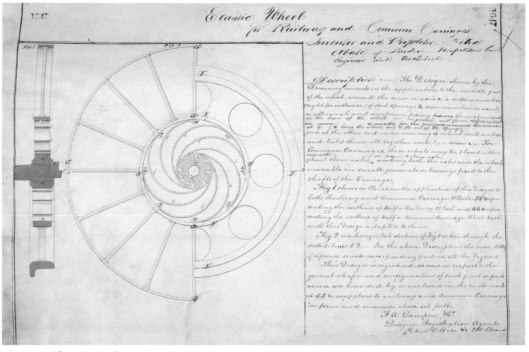

Elastic Wheel for Railway and Common Carriages, 1847

Design for a Marine Steam Propeller, 1845

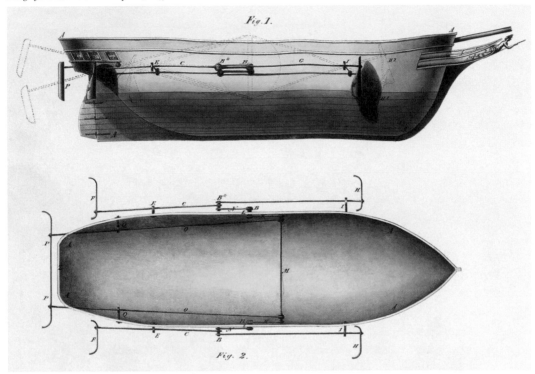

up the city. Pedestrians dodged between these vehicles in streets covered with horse manure.[9] It was estimated that in the middle of the century a train could get from London Bridge Station to the city of Brighton in about fifty minutes, less time than it took to go by road from London Bridge to Paddington (about five miles).[10]

To help tackle the problem of congestion, London began to develop its underground rail system in the 1880s. The early underground trains emitted dense coal smoke, creating health risks and problems of visibility, so that ventilation openings into the London streets had to be built at intervals. This problem was solved when the lines were electrified, beginning in 1890.

A non-polluting form of transport gained huge popularity in the nineteenth century – the bicycle. It went through several incarnations, beginning with the 'hobby horse' or 'dandy horse', essentially a bicycle without pedals, propelled by the feet. It became a craze with young upper-class men but proved short-lived, as frequent collisions with pedestrians caused more and more boroughs to ban its use. Quadricycles and tricycles became popular – Queen Victoria owned several tricycles – but it was the early bicycles, known as velocipedes, that brought cycling into the mainstream. Early examples were known as 'boneshakers' because of the effects of their wooden wheels with tyres made of iron. By 1870 there were at least fifty English manufacturers who followed the lead

"AS AERIAL NAVIGATION IS NOT YET AN ACCOMPLISHED FACT, THE ONLY ALTERNATIVE LEFT TO US IS TO BURROW THROUGH THE EARTH LIKE RABBITS."

BUILDING A TWO-PENNY TUBE, *THE LONDON MAGAZINE*, 1902

of the French Michaux brothers and manufactured iron-tyred bicycles.[11] In the 1870s the 'ordinary', or 'penny farthing' became popular. The front wheel was larger, increasing speed; the pedals were still fixed to the front wheel.

The 'safety bicycle', with pneumatic tyres and a chain and sprocket to drive the rear wheel, was introduced in the 1880s. In the 1870s a bicycle cost between £12 and £25; by 1894 they could be bought for £4.50, making them affordable and earning the bicycle a reputation as 'the working man's friend'.[12] Frances Willard, a leader of the women's social reform movement, agreed: 'Tens of thousands who could never afford to own, feed and stable a horse, had by this bright invention enjoyed the swiftness of motion which is perhaps the most fascinating feature of material life.'[13]

The Victorians measured all forms of mechanical power in terms of 'horse power', and when the motor car was first manufactured at the end of the century it was referred to as a 'horseless carriage'. The Daimler Company extolled the virtues of their vehicles by comparing them (with great optimism as to reliability) to horses: 'There are no saddles to be rented, no feed, no trouble about the horse being out of order or sick.'[14] The motor car also had advantages over bicycles, particularly, it seems, for women less intrepid than Frances Willard. The *Illustrated London News* considered that '"Horseless Carriages" promise to be a great institution for ladies with plenty of pluck to go out and about alone who can steer themselves, but with not enough vital force to propel a bicycle.'[15]

"LOOKING AFTER A MOTOR CAR IS CHILD'S PLAY COMPARED TO LOOKING AFTER A HORSE."

CHAIRMAN OF THE DAIMLER COMPANY, 1897

The British were not only travelling further within their own nation: they had also spread English rule to large parts of the world. By the time of the 1897 Diamond Jubilee celebrating the sixtieth year of Queen Victoria's reign, her Empire contained one quarter of the world's population. England's overseas possessions supplied raw materials for industry and new commodities were imported. There was great economic mobility: educated men from the new and expanding middle classes emigrated to countries across the Empire to improve their job prospects and enjoy a standard of living unimaginable at home.

The nineteenth century was also a great age of exploration. Explorers, like soldiers, were lauded in the newspapers, and boys' magazines, in particular, thrilled their readers with stories of courage, adventure and derring-do. These explorers had a range of motivations: religious, commercial, or the hope of making their fortune.[16]

Religious societies financed expeditions to countries such as China and Africa to spread Christianity. The explorer David Livingstone believed that his duty was 'to go forward into the dark interior' of Africa to spread Christianity, collect information that would be used to suppress the slave trade, and to make maps for the Royal Geographical Society.[17] Not everyone shared his motives: England joined what became known as 'the scramble for Africa' to keep the continent, its raw materials and trade routes from being dominated by France, Belgium and Germany.

Explorers also headed to the Arctic in search of a potentially valuable trade route, the Northwest Passage, a sea route connecting the North Atlantic and Pacific Oceans. One of the best-known of these explorers was Captain Sir John Franklin. On his final voyage Franklin, along with 128 of his men, was lost. Many subsequent expeditions were launched to try to find them, one of which was led by Commander Robert McClure and his crew in

HMS *Investigator*. Although they did not find Franklin, McClure's expedition was the first to discover and transit the Northwest Passage, by ship and sledge. Explorers like Franklin and McClure became national heroes, and their exploits were widely reported in the press. The date of registration of the 'Aerial Machine adapted for the Artic Regions' (see pp. 136–37) suggests that its inventor may have felt he had found an innovative solution to conquering the Northwest Passage – although the first truly successful airship was not built until 1896.

The hope of making a fortune motivated those who headed for North America, Australia and South Africa in search of gold. People from around the world, of all social classes, joined the gold rush. Between 1852 and 1860, for example, more than 290,000 people arrived in Victoria, Australia, looking for gold. As ever, inventors were quick to spot an opportunity, as the designs for gold-washing machines and a gold-digger's dwelling (see pp. 130–31) demonstrate. These immigrants often experienced great hardships, losing their savings and even their health. 'Canvas towns' of tents sprang up near gold fields as hotels and lodging houses became full. Although some amazing discoveries were made in the gold fields, not many people made the fortunes of their dreams.

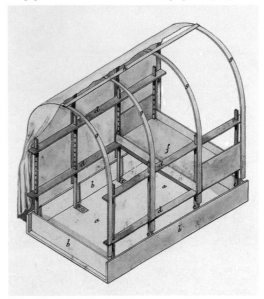

Design for a Universal Portable Tent or Sleeping Cabin, 1852

By 1850 the new transport systems reached most parts of the country. As the century progressed, people became more mobile, and no longer expected to remain near the place that they were born. Communications sped across the country and the world, transforming traditional ways of life and heralding a new era in which communications would become ever quicker and easier, and the world would seem ever smaller.

[1] Charles Dickens, *Dombey and Son*, London: Bradbury and Evans, 1858, p.40.

[2] Michael J. Freeman, *Railways and the Victorian Imagination*, New Haven: Yale University Press, 1999, p. 4.

[3] Judith Flanders, *Inside the Victorian Home*, London and New York: W. W. Norton & Company, 2003, p. 407.

[4] Charles Dickens, 'Wings of wire', *Household Words: A Weekly Journal*, vol. 2, New York: G. P. Putnam, 1851, p. 241.

[5] Michael J. Freeman and Derek H. Aldcroft (eds), *Transport in Victorian Britain*, Manchester and New York: Manchester University Press, 1988, p. 15.

[6] Asa Briggs, *Victorian Things*, London: Penguin, 1988, p. 415.

[7] Flanders, *op. cit.*, pp. 403–404.

[8] *Ibid.*, p. 406.

[9] Herbert Sussman, *Victorian Technology: Invention, Innovation, and the Rise of the Machine*, Oxford: Praeger, 2009, p. 122.

[10] Flanders, *op. cit.*, p. 408.

[11] Briggs, *op. cit.*, pp. 418–19.

[12] *Ibid.*, p. 420.

[13] Frances Willard, *A Wheel Within a Wheel: How I Learned to Ride the Bicycle*, Illinois: Women's Temperance Publishing Company, 1895.

[14] Briggs, *op. cit.*, p. 415.

[15] *Illustrated London News*, 9 May 1896.

[16] Sally Mitchell, *Daily Life in Victorian England*, Westport, Conn: Greenwood Press, 2009, p. 273.

[17] *Ibid.*, p. 274.

BELOW

DESIGN FOR THE PILLOW CAP
FOR TRAVELLERS

1860

Fig. 1. front view • *Fig. 2.* section

The body of the cap (aa) is formed as usual. The rim (bb) is composed of an annular airtight bag provided with a nozzle or valve (c) through which it may be inflated so as to form an annular air cushion round the head. The purpose is to form a soft pillow or cushion round the head, so that the same may rest easily against the back or side of the carriage or other place and thus afford additional ease to the wearer when sleeping or otherwise.

OPPOSITE

DESIGN FOR A RAILWAY RUG
OR CARRIAGE WRAPPER

1856

Fig. 1. the strap, wrapper and two pieces of the fabric for the feet • *Fig. 2.* the covering for the upper part of the foot • *Fig. 3.* a sole piece lined with fur and sewn to openings made in the wrapper • *Fig. 4.* the wrapper in use.

(aa) are two coverings for the feet, these project from the surface of the wrapper and each of them is formed by joining two pieces of the fabric similar in shape to (b) to form the covering for the upper part of the foot and a sole piece (c), these are lined with fur and sewn to openings made in the wrapper. (d) is a strap for fastening the wrapper around the neck when required to be worn temporarily as a cloak. The object is that of more effectively protecting the feet from cold, and permitting greater freedom of motion than the ordinary wrapper admits of.

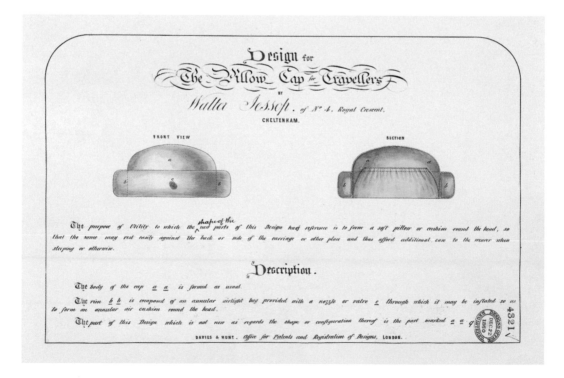

Design for a Railway Rug or Carriage Wrapper

Registered for Mess.rs H. J. & D. Nicoll

of Regent St. and Cornhill London.

3883

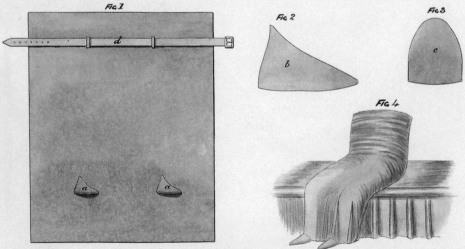

Fig 1   Fig 2   Fig 3   Fig 4

The above drawing which is made to a geometrical scale represents a design for an Improved Railway Rug or Carriage Wrapper. The object of utility to which the new parts of this design has reference is that of more effectually protecting the feet from cold, and permitting greater freedom of motion than the ordinary wrapper admits of — a,a, Fig 1, are two coverings for the feet, these project from the surface of the wrapper and each of them is formed by joining two pieces of the fabric similar in shape to b Fig 2, to form the covering for the upper part of the foot, and a sole piece c, Fig 3, these are lined with fur and sewn to openings made in the wrapper. — d, is a strap for fastening the wrapper around the neck when required to be worn temporarily as a cloak. The Sketch Fig 4, represents the wrapper in use.

Protection is sought for the parts marked a,a, Fig 4 (formed by joining two upper pieces b, and one lower piece c, together) as being new, the other parts are old.

NEW AND USEFUL DESIGN

COMBINED WALKING-STICK AND RAILWAY-CARRIAGE DOOR-KEY.

WILLIAM AGNEW POPE.
42 CANNON STREET, E.C.
PROPRIETOR

The purpose of utility to which the shape or configuration of the new part of this Design has reference is rendering the handle of a Walking Stick capable of being used as a key for opening Railway Carriage doors.

The above drawing represents the upper part of a Walking Stick constructed in accordance with this Design.

The crutch or handle A of the stick is formed with a projection B of a polygonal shape adapted to the key hole of the doors of Railway Carriages.

Protection is sought for the shape or configuration of the parts marked A. B. which are new and original. The remainder is old.

NEW AND USEFUL DESIGN FOR A

COMBINED UMBRELLA HANDLE AND RAILWAY CARRIAGE DOOR KEY

WILLIAM AGNEW POPE
42 Cannon Street, E.C.
PROPRIETOR

The purpose of utility to which the shape or configuration of the new parts of this design has reference is rendering the handle of an umbrella capable of being used as a key for opening Railway Carriage doors.

The above drawing represents the upper part of an umbrella having the handle constructed in accordance with this design.

The crutch or handle A of the umbrella is formed with a projection B of a polygonal shape suited to the key hole of the doors of railway carriages.

Protection is sought for the shape or configuration of the parts marked A. B which are new and original. The remainder is old.

2895

DESIGNS OFFICE
JULY 31
1851
REGISTERED

Design for an improved Travelling Label

Registered for Messrs Cox and Wilson Oxford Works Oldbury Oxfordshire

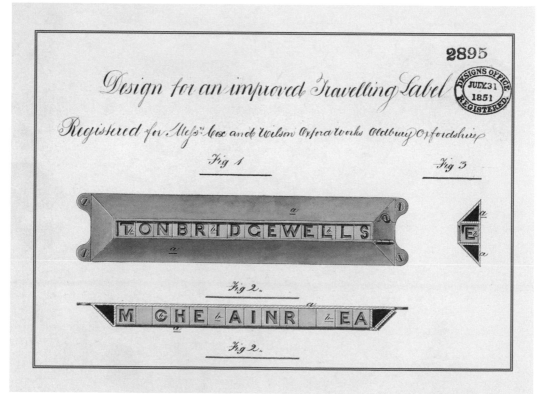

Fig 1   Fig 3

Fig 2.

Fig 2.

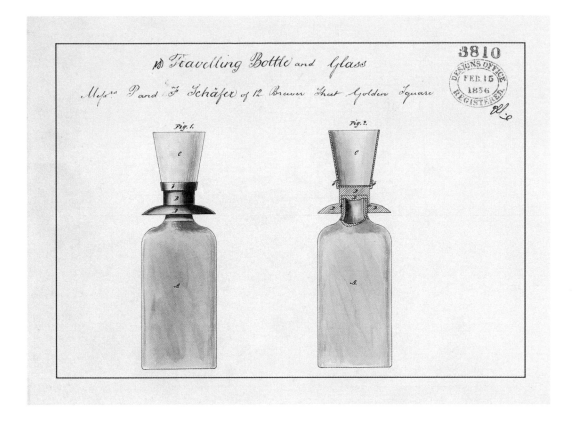

Travelling Bottle and Glass

Messrs P and F Schäfer of 12 Brewer Street Golden Square

3810

DESIGNS OFFICE
FEB. 15
1856
REGISTERED

Fig. 1.   Fig. 2.

OPPOSITE ABOVE LEFT

COMBINED WALKING STICK AND RAILWAY-CARRIAGE DOOR-KEY*

1880

The crutch or handle (A) of the stick is formed with a projection (B) of a polygonal shape suited to the key holes of the doors of Railway Carriages. The purpose is rendering the handle of a walking stick capable of being used as a key for opening Railway Carriage doors.

OPPOSITE ABOVE RIGHT

COMBINED UMBRELLA HANDLE AND RAILWAY CARRIAGE DOOR KEY*

1880

The crutch or handle (A) of the umbrella is formed with a projection (B) of a polygonal shape suited to the key holes of the doors of Railway Carriages. Protection is sought for the shape or configuration of the parts marked (AB) which are new and original. The purpose is rendering the handle of an umbrella capable of being used as a key for opening Railway Carriage Doors.

ABOVE

TRAVELLING BOTTLE AND GLASS

1856

Fig. 1. external elevation • *Fig. 2.* elevation in section

(A) is the bottle the neck of which is encased in metal and has a screw (aa) cut on it. (BB) is the stopper which is screw threaded and being flat at bottom and of the shape represented in the drawing when removed acts as a stand for the glass. (CC) is the glass which is imbedded in cement or otherwise secured in the socket (b).

OPPOSITE BELOW

DESIGN FOR AN IMPROVED TRAVELLING LABEL

1851

Fig. 1. front view of the Label • *Fig. 2.* longitudinal view • *Fig. 3.* transverse section

One end of the case (a) is made moveable or to open with facility for the purpose of removing the Cubes from and replacing them within the case.

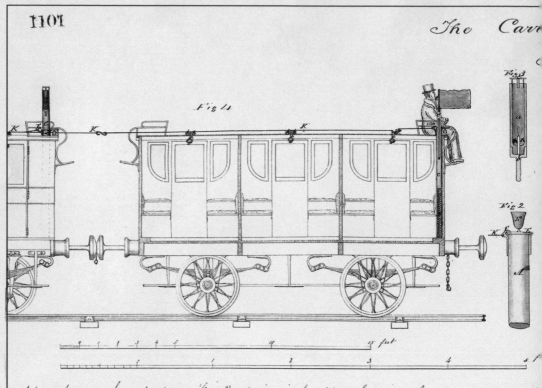

1107

The Carr

apparatus can be actuated.—Fig 2 A view in elevation shewing the apparatus as et
tube or burner, to form an illuminated signal or telegraph to be used instead
a the glass tube or burner, b metal socket and screw for screwing it into th
blowing out the candle, lamp or other apparatus for lighting, d, d perfo
Fig 4 exemplifies in longitudinal section the application of the apparatus
The tube A being fixed in the corner of the carriage close to the guard or co
which secures the cover is attached the wire, chain or rod (K) having the b
passed through the roofs of the carriage and pendant inside; is continued
other smaller wires chains or rods (L) with handles (L) and communica
regard to the first two carriages of a train.

It is evident that any person
wire chain or rod (K) and put the apparatus or carriage Telegraph
figuration thereof are all the parts if separately considered but what to
on carriage telegraphs as shewn by Figures 1,2,3 and before describe

Telegraph

...etor. Frederick Richard Louis Koepp of No.14 Chadwell Street, County of Middlesex, Gentleman

Description. — The drawings exemplify a Design for an apparatus whereby the persons inside Railway Carriages can communicate with the Guards or conductors in the outside thereof; in cases of accident and necessity for stoppage of the train, such apparatus being also advantageously applicable to other Carriages besides those travelling in railways, as Omnibuses, for the purposes of warning their conductors when to stop the vehicle for passengers to alight, or otherwise. The same parts are denoted in all the Figs by corresponding letters of reference. — Fig 1 Views in longitudinal section shewing the construction of this apparatus, composed of a tube A in the lower part of which is placed a spring B, and on the top thereof a staff or standard C, with a small flag-staff carrying a flag screwed thereto as shown. To the tube (A) is fixed a pin D, which passes through a slit in the staff or standard (C) and prevents it from piling too far out of the tube when in action, as shewn. E a hinged cap, having a spring catch F for keeping the apparatus shut-up when not in action (as shewn by fig 2), with an inverted bell (E) placed atop thereof. To this cap (E) is affixed a wire, chain or rod I, having a bell crank lever K from which is pendant a smaller wire, chain or rod L having a handle L' by which the shut up and not in action — Fig 3 Longitudinal section of a glass staff and flag before mentioned by trains travelling in the dark standard C-c cover to prevent a downward current of wind from ... the glass tube or burner to supply air to support combustion configuration or arrangement before stated to railway carriage seat or in other convenient position, to the spring catch Ik' 1 lever fk' attached, with the shorter wire, chain or rod Li and ring... the whole train, passing over rollers or pulleys KK and having other such apparatus or carriage Telegraphs (C') as shewn with

carriage by pulling down the handles (Li) will actuate the

are not new or original in respect to the shape and con new is the general shape and configuration of an apparatus

F. W. Campin & Co
Designs Registry Agents
210 Strand

PREVIOUS PAGE

THE CARRIAGE TELEGRAPH

1847

Fig. 1. views in longitudinal section • *Fig. 2.* view in elevation • *Fig. 3.* longitudinal section of a glass tube or burner • *Fig. 4.* the flag in use

Persons inside Railway Carriages can communicate with the Guards or conductors in the outside thereof by pulling down the handles, which actuate the wire chain or rod.

BELOW

DESIGN FOR A GOLD DIGGER'S DWELLING

1853

A Chest, Dwelling or Cart for Emigrants and others. The body is made in separate parts screwed to each other by pins and sockets. Below the flooring are secret places for depositing valuable property. (l) is a shelf for stowing things or may be used as a sleeping place for children.

OPPOSITE

J. SYMONDS AND CO'S GOLD WASHING CRADLE

1852

Fig. 1. side elevation • *Fig. 2.* plan of this cradle
Fig. 3. longitudinal section of one recess •
Fig. 4. a cross section of recess

(A) is a hopper for receiving the matter to be operated upon. (BB') two sieves of different sized meshes of which (B) is the coarser. The lower part of the hopper opens into the serpentine channel (C) at the point (C') formed by the curvilinear pieces (DD) in the manner shewn in Fig. 2. Fig. 3. is a longitudinal section of one of the recesses (E), in which heavier particles will settle; Fig. 4. is a cross section. The purpose is the greater facility for cleansing and separating by the aid of a liquid agent matters mixed or held in combination the heavier particles thereof being separated and retained by their superior gravity.

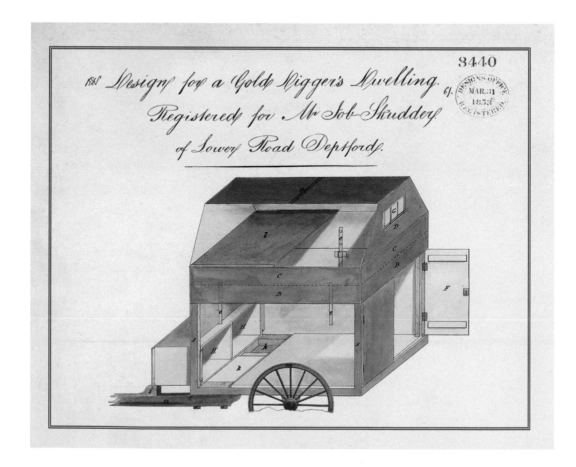

№ J. Symonds and Cos Gold washing Cradle.

John Symonds of the Circus Minories

Manufacturer.

Proprietor.

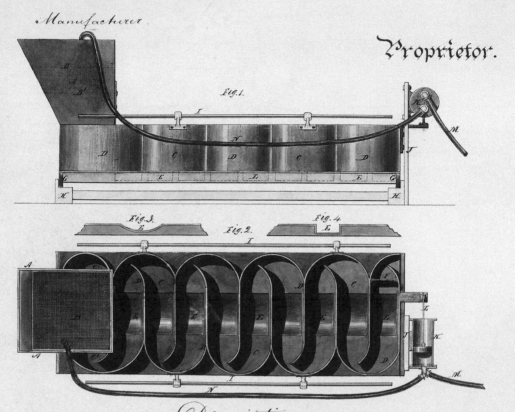

Fig.1.

Fig.3.   Fig.4.

Fig.2.

Description

FIGURE 1 of the above drawings is a side elevation and Figure 2 a plan of this Cradle A is a hopper for receiving the matter to be operated upon B B' two sieves of different sized meshes of which B is the coarser. The lower part of the hopper opens into the serpentine channel C at the point C' formed by the curvilinear pieces D D in the manner shewn in Figure 2. In the bottom of the channel C are a number of hollow recesses E E in the spaces formed by the pieces D D for intercepting the heavier particles of such mixed matter which by their specific gravity will settle in these recesses or collectors while the lighter portions of such matter under process of cleansing or parting will pass on through and from one end to the other of the machine — when after such heavier particles have subsided the residue is allowed to escape through the sluice F. Figure 3 is a longitudinal section of one of these recesses E: and Figure 4 a cross section, F is the sluice, G G are the rockers and H the rocking frame, I I are two handles for working the machine. J is a standard fixed to the rocking frame H which serves to support the pump K which is worked by a rod L attached to the washer, M is the induction pipe and N the eduction pipe.

THE purpose of utility to which the shape or configuration of the new parts of this design has reference is the greater facility for cleansing and separating by the aid of a liquid agent matters mixed or held in combination the heavier particles thereof being separated and retained by their superior gravity.

THE parts of this design which are not new or original in so far as regards the shape and configuration thereof are all the parts excepting those marked C. D. E. F. J. K. L. M. and N.

J. C. Robertson & Co
Registration Agents
166 Fleet Street

Drawn to a geometric scale

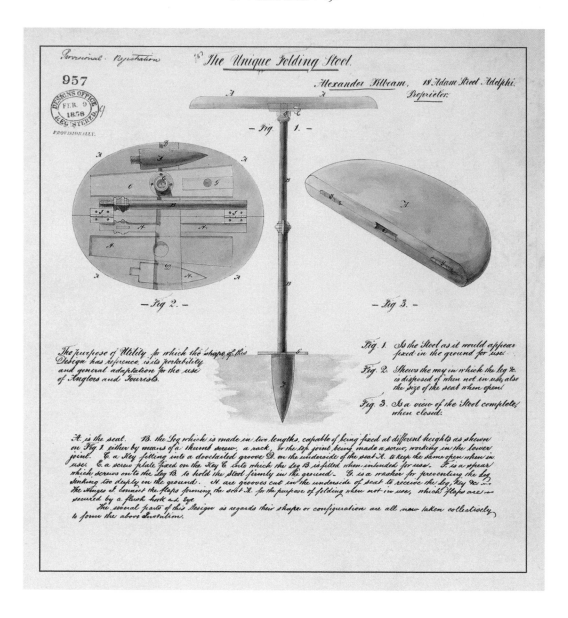

THE UNIQUE FOLDING STOOL*

1858

Fig. 1. stool fixed in the ground for use • *Fig. 2.* Leg disposed of when not in use • *Fig. 3.* stool closed

(A) *is the seat,* (B) *the Leg capable of being fixed at different heights,* (F) *a spear which screws on to the Leg to hold the stool firmly in the ground. The purpose is its portability and general adaptation for the use of Anglers and Tourists.*

DESIGN FOR A PORTABLE COOKING APPARATUS

1845

Fig. 1. vertical section • *Fig. 2.* horizontal plan

(AA) *is a cylindrical vessel open at its upper end and then receiving a second vessel* (BB) *of conical shape. In the interstitial spaces left by the arrangement of two conical boilers* (FF) *are set vertical ovens of triangular form* (GGG) *in which meats or matters to be baked are placed as shewn in Fig. 1.*

478

- DESIGN · FOR · A · PORTABLE · COOKING · APPARATUS.

Registered for Henry Madden of N.º 14 George Street Adelphi London.

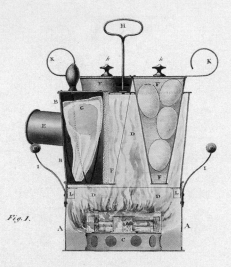

Fig. 1.

Fig. 2.

Description

The Design sought to be protected is the configuration of the Cooking Apparatus shewn in the Drawing in a view of vertical section Fig 1 and a view of horizontal plan Fig 2. the Parts being drawn to a scale of One half the linear dimensions of the apparatus made for use and the parts respectively marked in both Figs with the same letters of reference: A A is a cylindrical vessel of metal open at its upper end and their receiving a second vessel B B of conical shape which fits into it resting upon supporting pieces L L. in the vessel, A A is put a fire dish or frame C in which the usual Patent fire-work is burned the flame and heat from which ascends through the machine as shewn at D D D the generated Smoke passing off by a chimney E in and passing through the lid of the vessel B B B B are inserted conical metal boilers F F and in the interstitial spaces left by the arrangement of the conical boilers F F are set vertical ovens of triangular form G G G in which meats or matters to be baked are placed as shewn in Figure 1 – H is the lifting handle of the vessel B B B B – I I lifting handles of the lower vessel A A –, K K and k k large and small handles of the conical vessel F F – The entire configuration of the apparatus taken collectively is new

478

Alex.ʳ Prince Office for Patents & Registration of Designs. 14. Lincolns Inn Fields.

The Combination "Pack Saddle" Boxes & Bedstead

Bowring, Arundel & Co. Outfitters &c. 118½ Fenchurch Street, London, E.C.

6648

DESIGNS OFFICE
MAR. 20
1883
REGISTERED

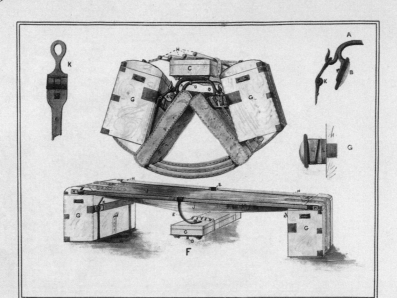

Statement of Utility

The purpose of Utility to which the shape or Configuration of this Design has reference is:— That by the construction of two irons of the shape of an arch connecting two side-boards to which are attached two pads, forming the base of the Saddle, the pressure upon the back of a Pony, Mule, or Horse, is relieved and is calculated to give the greatest strength, with the minimum of weight these irons being slightly flattened at the top, and a perforation made in each to receive a stub afford a bearing for carrying a box on the top of the saddle, for the conveyance of guns, Fishing Rods, and scientific Instruments, requiring care.— Two other Boxes are also hung upon the aforesaid irons on either side of the Saddle for the conveyance of Clothing Provisions &c the three Boxes when detatched and placed upon the ground forming a most complete Portable Bedstead.

Description

The sketch above is a representation of a Pack-Saddle and three Boxes together, with four poles neccessary to the formation of a Portable Bedstead, the whole making a complete travelling equipment for Explorers, Sportsmen, Tourists, Military Officers, &c in countries where the only means of transport is by the use of Pack Ponies Mules, or Horses the detailed particulars being as follows.— The arch shape irons A attached to the side boards B together with the pads form the Saddle, the irons A being flattened upon the top of the arch are perforated with a hole in the centre and afford a bearing for carrying a Box C to the bottom of which at each end is a wooden bearer with an iron stub D. Another important feature is the mode of attaching the two side Boxes G to the saddle by the means of jinged ring irons K, this allowing them always to hang fairly against the animals sides, and at any angle there are furthermore two leather covered pads L attached to the Boxes G with corresponding pads on the side boards B to prevent holes being worn in the boxes through the friction of the ironwork on the Saddle; The Bedstead F is formed by the combined use of the two sideboxes G and the box C on the top of which are affixed by the means of thumb screws or studs peculiarly shaped iron bearers E which are used to form a centre support and four wooden poles H being supported by the means of iron bracket rings I fixed at each side of the Boxes G the canvas sacking J being stretched upon the wooden poles H and fastened to the Boxes G by the use of Straps and Buckles

The whole of this Design is New so far as regards the Shape or Configuration thereof, Protection is sought for the Whole Design with all its integral parts.

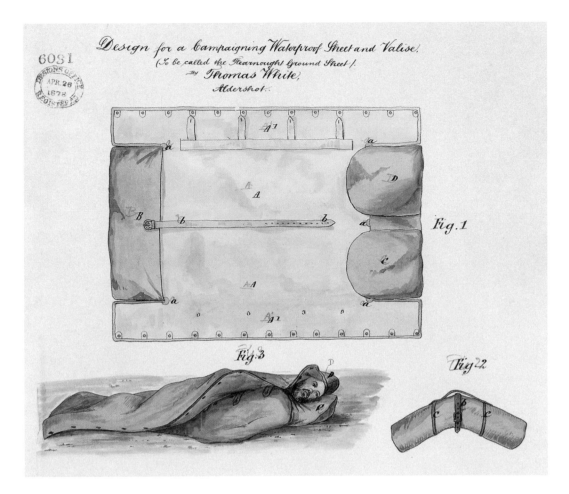

Design for a Campaigning Waterproof Sheet and Valise.
(To be called the Fearnought Ground Sheet.)
By Thomas White.
Aldershot.

6081

DESIGNS OFFICE
APR 26
1878
REGISTERED

Fig. 1.

Fig. 3

Fig. 2.

ABOVE

DESIGN FOR A CAMPAIGNING WATERPROOF SHEET AND VALISE

1878

Fig. 1. ground sheet laid out flat • *Fig. 2.* rolled up
Fig. 3. forming a covering for a recumbent soldier

*The pockets (B, C & D) of a sheet of waterproof cloth
(AA) are intended to contain the requisites for a soldier
or other person camping out.*

OPPOSITE

THE COMBINATION "PACK SADDLE" BOXES & BEDSTEAD

1883

*Complete travelling equipment for Explorers, Sportsmen,
Military Officers &c, in countries where the only means
of transport is by the use of Pack Ponies, Mules, or Horses.*

OVERLEAF

DESIGN FOR A FLYING OR AERIAL MACHINE ADAPTED FOR THE ARTIC REGIONS*

1855

Fig. 1. side elevation • *Fig. 2.* a transverse and vertical
section through the line (AB) at *Fig. 1.*

*The machine is propelled through the air by the rotary
movement of the wheels (D & E) acting against the
external air and at the same time forcing it through the
pipes (G & H). The centre part of the wheels is formed
hollow to contain gas for lightening the weight of such
wheels, motion being imparted thereto through the
Agency of ordinary 'treadles' (K). The guard plates
(d & e) are shod with metal to allow the machine to
be propelled upon the ice. (W) is a suspended room
of sufficient size to hold beds for about three persons.
(X) is an elastic pipe for supplying atmospheric air
to said room.*

Design for A Flying or Aerial Machine adapted for the Artic Regions

Provisionally. Registered for Arthur Kinsella, of Kilkenny, Ireland.

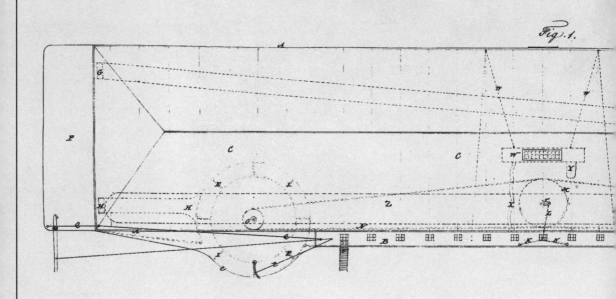

Fig. 1.

Description.

The purpose of Utility, to which the shape or configuration of this Design has reference, is the facility with which the machine can be raised and lowered and guided in and through the air, without the aid of Ballast or the escape of gas as heretofore practised in Aerial Machines. The Design is exhibited drawn to geometrical scale and exhibits two views thereof. Fig. 1. is a side elevation thereof and Fig. 2. a transverse and vertical section through the line AB at Fig. 1. AA is a shell or casing of light wood twisted cane, or rope covered with oiled silk, B a gallery connected and secured thereto by standing rigging C, D and E are propelling wheels or fans each revolving in a case F built in and forming part of the casing AA. There are pipes G and H extending from the top of one of the aforesaid cases and the side of the other as exhibited one end of each of such said pipes being open to the case to which it is fixed and the other end opens to the atmosphere at the stern or rear end of the machine, the centre part of the wheels D and E is formed hollow to contain gas for lightening the weight of said wheels, and the floats or vanes I fit as near as may be the case in which they rotate, motion being imparted thereto through the Agency of ordinary "treadles" K a connecting rod L Fly, wheel M and straps or bands N passing over said Fly wheel and a pulley O fixed upon the hollow axes of the wheels D and E, P is a rudder to each side of which tiller ropes Q are attached and extend into the aforesaid gallery to enable the persons thereto alter the direction of

Prince and Compy. Agents for Patents and Registration of Designs – 4. Trafalgar Square, London.

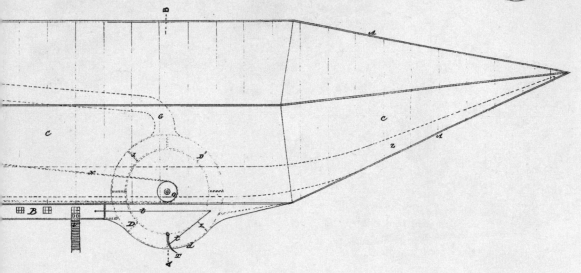

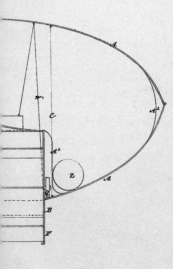

motion of the machine from right to left and vice versâ. The guard plates _d_ and _e_
are shod with metal to enable the machine to be propelled upon the ice. T T are grappling
irons two at each side of the machine which may be raised up by means of ropes _t t_
when not required for use. U U are gangways two at each side of the machine for affording
access to the gallery. The treadles K are connected by a rod I to a crank Y on the Fly
wheel shaft, said treadles being employed for imparting motion to the propelling wheels
or fans D and E. W is a suspended room of sufficient size to hold beds for about three persons
and capable of being raised and lowered by the ropes _w w_. X is an elastic pipe for supplying
atmospheric air to said room, and Y is a bag through which persons enter the aforesaid room
when lowered — the end of said bag being tied before raising the room. Within the case A A a
flexible airtight bag or case made of rope and silk fits as near as may be, said bag being employed
to contain gas with which it is inflated, when the machine is required for use. Within this bag or
case are placed two flexible pipes marked Z at Fig. 2 and shewn by dotted lines at Fig. 1
extending from stem to stern of the machine as shewn. The pipes Z are furnished with the means
of opening or closing a communication with one or other or both of the fans D and E, said pipes
being employed for raising and lowering the machine at will — that is to say by compressing atmospheric
air therein, the machine will descend and by allowing the air to escape therefrom the machine will ascend.
The machine is propelled through the air by the rotary movement of the wheels D and E acting against the
external air and at the same time forcing it through the pipes G and H and the exit of the air at the
rear end or stem of the machine pressing against the external atmospheric air serves as a buoyant
for the compressed air to push against and thus effect the desired horizontal movement of the machine.
The parts of this design which are new or original as said the in a confirmation thereof are all the parts.

BELOW

LUNETTE PARASOL OR UMBRELLA

1844

Fig. 1. elevation of this parasol or umbrella
Fig. 2. plan • *Fig. 3.* section of one of the eyesights

(AAA) are eyesights inserted in the covering – one, two, three or more of these may be used according to fancy or convenience. (E) is the glass, (G) a narrow metal rim perforated with holes by means of which it is sewn into place.

OPPOSITE

HEARSE

1849

Fig. 1. longitudinal section of the hearse • *Fig. 2.* back end elevation

(AA) is the carriage body, (BB) the seat for the mourners; it is placed longitudinally in the middle of the carriage so that the passengers sit back to back. The box forming the seat is made perfectly air tight inside of the carriage by a covering of lead or gutta percha. It descends a little deeper than the floor and forms a chamber (C) of sufficient size to hold one or two coffins.

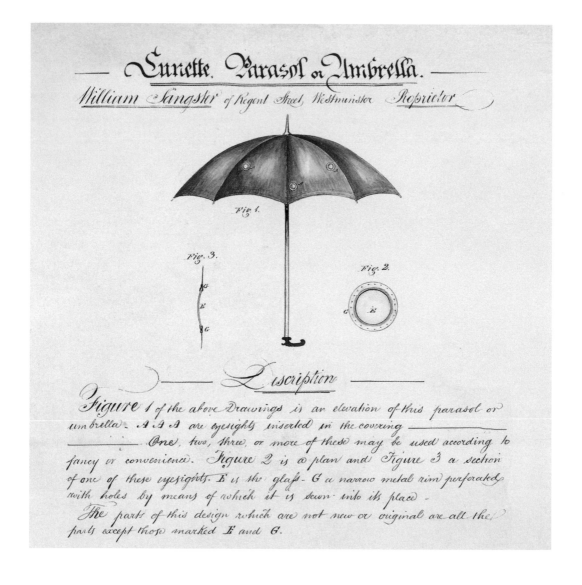

Hearse

Charles Edward Butler of 31 Farringdon Street
Furnishing Undertaker   Proprietor

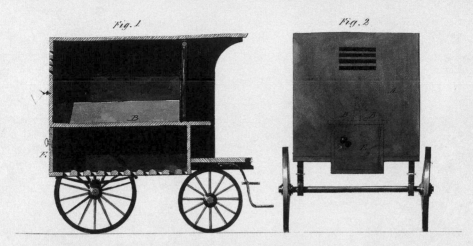

Fig. 1   Fig. 2

Description

Figure 1 is a longitudinal section of this hearse
Figure 2 is a back end elevation A A is the Carriage
body — B B the seat for the mourners; it is placed
longitudinally in the middle of the carriage so that the
passengers sit back to back. The box forming the seat
is made perfectly air tight inside of the carriage by a
covering of lead or gutta percha. It descends a little
deeper than the floor and forms a chamber C of sufficient
size to hold one or two coffins. The chamber C has
openings D D in the bottom to allow of a free circulation
of air and thus afford protection to the mourners from
any injury — E is the door of the chamber.

This design is registered as new in so far as
respects the shape and configuration of the parts
marked B C D and E.

J C Robertson & Co
Registration Agents
166 Fleet Street

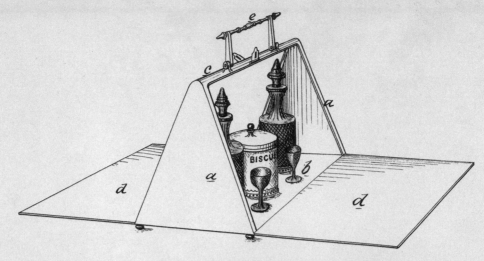

DESIGN FOR A LUNCHEON CASKET

1878

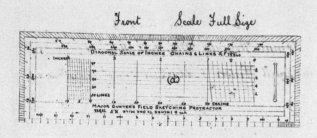

**DESIGN FOR MAJOR GUNTER'S FIELD
SKETCHING PROTRACTOR**

1883

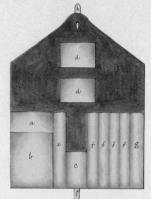

**DESIGN FOR MAJOR GUNTER'S FIELD
SKETCHING HOLDALL**

1883

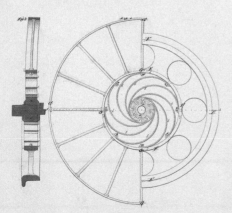

**ELASTIC WHEEL FOR RAILWAY AND
COMMON CARRIAGES**

1847

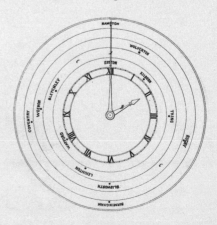

**DESIGN FOR BENNETT'S LOCOMOTIVE
REGULATOR**

1853

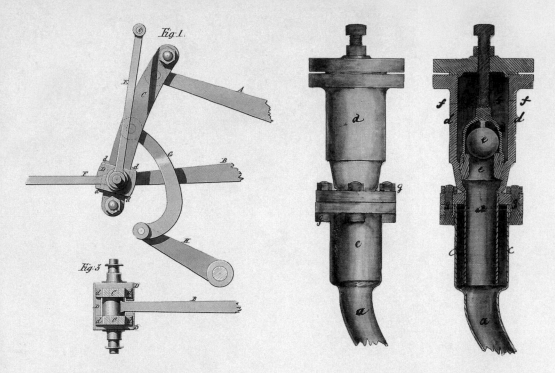

**DESIGN FOR AN IMPROVED LINK-MOTION
FOR STEAM ENGINES**

1853

**DESIGN FOR A CLACK BOX FEED PIPE
FOR LOCOMOTIVES**

1853

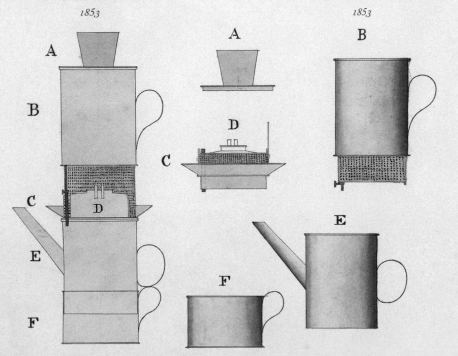

DESIGN FOR "THE IMIGRANT'S COMPANION"

1853

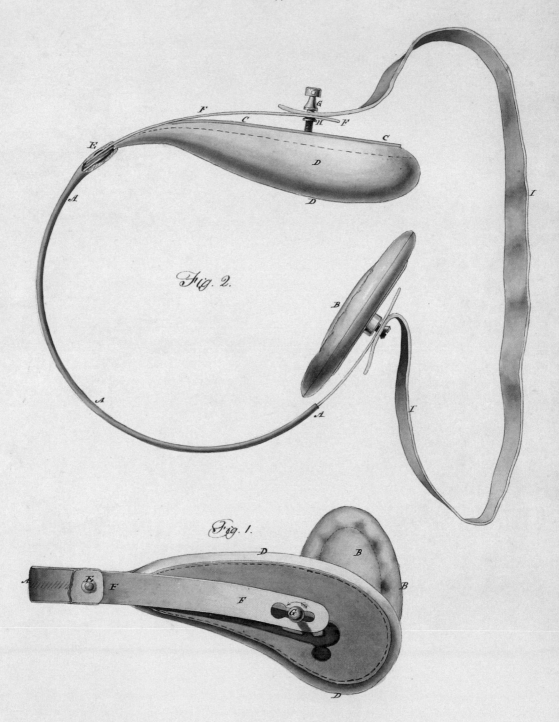

A curved piece of steel at one end of which a back pad is attached by a screw;
when it is required to increase the pressure it will be necessary to turn the pin.

V

PREVENTATIVES & PANACEAS

"IMPART NEW LIFE AND VIGOUR TO THE DEBILITATED CONSTITUTION..."

• • •

Advertisement for Harness's Electropathic Belt
by The Medical Battery Co. Ltd,
Pick Me Up
1891

he Victorians were obsessed with health. This manifested itself not only in a well-founded fear of contagious disease, but also in crazes for various 'systems' of medicine – including homeopathy, mesmerism and hydropathy (the 'water cure') – as well as different forms of diet and exercise.

Throughout the nineteenth century immense energy was devoted to scientific research into health and medicine, but at the same time traditional beliefs about medicine and how the body worked persisted. New devices such as the stethoscope, ophthalmoscope and thermometer allowed an unprecedented insight into the internal workings of the body, and work was being carried out to try to understand the major diseases and how they were spread. Between 1800 and 1870 more than seventy special hospitals were founded, including the London Fever Hospital and the Kensington Children's Hospital.[1]

But alongside this activity, old systems of medicine continued. Bloodletting was still widely practised, with leeches and scarificators (see p. 152) a popular method. An excess of blood was believed to be responsible for many conditions, and leeches were used to treat everything from headaches to prostate problems. When used internally (leeches might also be used to treat tonsillitis, for example), a piece of string would be tied to them to ensure they couldn't be swallowed or otherwise go astray. Over-use of leeches (there are contemporary references to a 'mania' for leeches[2]) resulted in a shortage which, along with some understandable squeamishness, led to the development of artificial leeches (see p. 150).

A number of important drugs were introduced in the nineteenth century, including morphine, quinine, atropine, codeine and iodine; yet some were used in ways that now seem surprising to say the least. Preparations containing opium derivatives were especially popular. Laudanum, a combination of opium and alcohol, was freely available to buy and used for a range of ailments from insomnia to cholera – William Gladstone used it to settle his nerves before making parliamentary speeches.[3] Godfrey's Cordial was a combination of opium, treacle, water and spices, used to calm fractious infants. Calomel (mercury[1] chloride, or mercurous chloride) was used for various purposes: as a purgative, as a treatment for syphilis, and for teething babies.

These remedies were at the 'respectable' end of the spectrum. The complete lack of regulation of medical practitioners for most of the nineteenth century meant that anybody could hang up a sign and begin practising as a physician, surgeon or apothecary, treating patients and concocting 'remedies'. Although the Medical Act of 1858 created the General Council for Medical Education and Registration (now the General Medical Council), it was not until the Medical Act Amendment Act of 1886 that it became illegal to set up in practice without the appropriate qualifications.

Those in search of dental care also entered risky and uncertain territory, as the designs for the toothless (see pp. 158–59) suggest. There was no

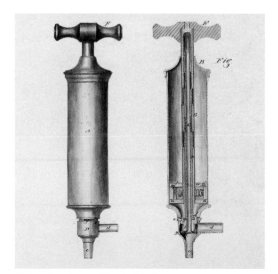

Design for an Improved Surgical Syringe, 1844

Design for a Graduated Medical Galvanic Machine, c. 1846

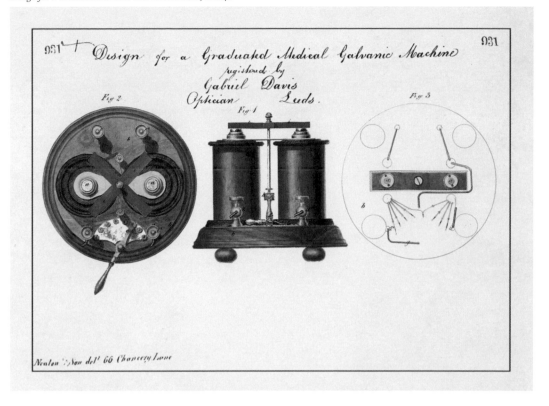

regulation of dentistry until the second half of the nineteenth century, and even then it was patchy. In the 1840s attempts at regulation began to be made, but both Parliament and the public at large were slow to show interest. Dental work was usually carried out as a lucrative sideline, mostly by tradesmen such as blacksmiths. There was no code of ethics, and unscrupulous advertisements claimed miraculous abilities for these dentists at temptingly low fees to draw in the unsuspecting sufferer. Removal of teeth was the main remedy for toothache: a contemporary definition of a dentist was 'one who cleans and extracts teeth'.[4] A life with few if any teeth was the outcome for many.

Eye care, too, was unregulated for most of the century. There seems to have been reluctance among the Victorians to wear glasses: as late as 1900 a writer in the *Optical Journal* said that: 'wearing spectacles out of doors is always

"A MAN MUST DESTROY A HAT-FULL OF EYES, BEFORE HE CAN BECOME A GOOD OPERATING OCULIST."

PROFESSOR ANTONIO SCARPA, QUOTED IN 1822

a disfigurement'.[5] Fortunately, as the century progressed, the extraction of cataracts became one of the major improvements in the prevention or cure of blindness.

The causes of sight problems were not understood: age-related sight loss was attributed to learning to read too early, sleeping in overheated and unventilated rooms, lack of exercise and even bending forwards when reading. The invention of the ophthalmoscope, an instrument for examining the inner structure of the eye, allowed a much greater understanding of eye disease.[6]

Although spectacles had existed in various forms for centuries, most people did not wear glasses prescribed for their needs, and the poor, if they wore glasses at all, tended to buy them very cheaply from market stalls or travelling salesmen. It was not until the introduction of the National Health Service in 1948 that appropriate glasses became available to everyone.

The Victorians could be grateful that as the century progressed they could benefit from the introduction of anaesthesia. Before the 1840s most patients had to endure excruciating pain if they needed surgery. This meant that most operations were limited to those that were relatively simple, such as pulling teeth or setting fractures, or life-saving, such as amputations or the removal of tumours. The first recorded use of ether in Britain was in December 1846, when it was administered by an English dentist, James Robinson, for the removal of a tooth. The physician John Snow visited Robinson to see the process for himself. A few days later the first surgical anaesthetic with ether was used during surgery by the renowned surgeon Robert Liston.

John Snow went on to become a pioneer in the use of anaesthesia, administering chloroform to Queen Victoria for the birth of her eighth and ninth children in 1853 and 1857.

The inhaler on p. 153 was registered in May 1847 and mentions ether (aether), so its inventor, a surgeon called William John Bowden, was clearly up-to-date with the latest medical developments. Unfortunately ether had a number of drawbacks. There was no way of controlling the amount that

"DR SNOW ADMINISTERED THAT BLESSED CHLOROFORM, AND THE EFFECT WAS SOOTHING AND DELIGHTFUL BEYOND MEASURE."

QUEEN VICTORIA, JOURNALS, 22 APRIL 1853

Design for a Portable Regulating Ether Inhaler, c. 1847

a person inhaled: if they had too little they might wake up during the operation in great pain, but if they inhaled too much they might not wake up at all. Ether is also highly flammable – a single spark in the operating room could result in an explosion. Ether was largely replaced by chloroform, although it remained popular for recreational use.

Existing medical practice was totally unequal to the devastating series of epidemics of contagious diseases that afflicted nineteenth-century Britain. These included influenza, cholera, typhus, typhoid, smallpox and scarlet fever. Tuberculosis (consumption) was rife: between 1838 and 1840, for example, it was responsible for about a quarter of all deaths. In 1841 the Registrar General reported that while mean life expectancy in Surrey was forty-five, it was only thirty-seven in London and twenty-six in Liverpool. The average age of 'labourers, mechanics, and servants, etc' at time of death was only fifteen.[7]

The terror created by contagious diseases dominated the nineteenth century. Their spread was exacerbated by industrialization and the movement of people from the countryside to the cities, where they lived in overcrowded, unsanitary conditions.

Mortality figures for crowded city areas could be as much as twice those for less crowded middle-class areas. For most of the century the way these diseases were spread was a mystery, and the treatments administered were often hideously misguided in the light of what we know today.

Panic followed the outbreak of cholera in 1831. This was followed by three more outbreaks, in 1848–49, 1853–54 and 1866–67. It was a completely new disease in Britain – until the nineteenth century it was unknown outside India. It spread around the globe as a result of increasing population movements resulting largely from military and commercial activity, and its symptoms were appalling. Victims suffered such severe diarrhoea and vomiting that rapid dehydration caused their skin to become a blue-grey colour – the disease was sometimes referred to as the 'blue terror'. Not surprisingly they experienced insatiable thirst, and suffered agonizing cramps throughout the whole body – they could be dead within a few days or sometimes hours.

The treatments for cholera were many and ineffective, and must have increased the suffering of the victims. They included laudanum, which may have helped the stomach spasms, but this was usually combined with calomel, a powerful laxative which, it was thought, would help to get the cholera 'poison' out of the system. A report 'on the advantage of copious bleeding in inflammatory diseases' described a case of cholera treated by transfusion, by small and repeated doses of calomel, and by injections of strong liquid ammonia in the 'collapse' stage of the disease.[8] Some supposed cures or preventatives look like 'quack' products (and some were), but they make more sense when understood in the light of contemporary beliefs about how the body worked. The cholera belt (see below) seems like the most unlikely protection. However, it was believed that a chilled body could cause disease, and that keeping the stomach and abdomen warm could protect against bowel complaints. It was also thought to protect against miasma.

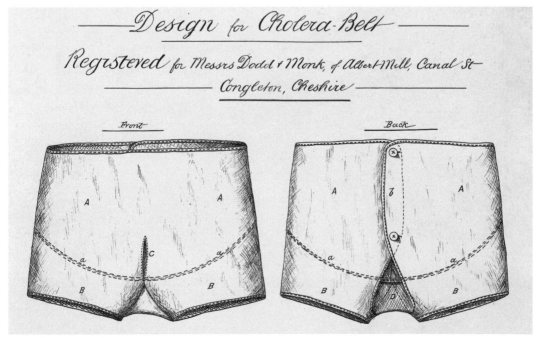

Design for a Cholera Belt, 1882

The apparently random nature in which cholera spread added to the sense of panic. People believed that it was transmitted through bad air – miasma or effluvia coming from sewage pipes, cesspools, polluted rivers, graveyards, or even from the air around a cholera victim. In 1854 an outbreak of cholera in Broad Street, Soho, killed around 500 people in ten days within a very small area. John Snow, in pioneering work, traced the source of the epidemic to water from a single well, contaminated by sewage from the cesspool of a house next to it. A baby in the house had cholera, and its mother had thrown the water used to wash its nappies into the cesspool. The Public Health Act of 1848 set up local boards to ensure that all new homes had proper drainage and clean water supplies.[9]

Venereal disease was considered the province of surgeons, and a report in 1846 stated that nearly half the surgical outpatients at St Bartholomew's Hospital in London had venereal complaints.[10] In the 1860s it was reported that one in three patients in the army was afflicted with venereal disease, and one in eleven in the navy. Contemporary estimates suggested that at least 10 per cent of the population of large cities was infected with syphilis, and it is thought to have been particularly prevalent among middle- and upper-class men and the transient working poor.

Until the early twentieth century the primary treatment for syphilis was mercury in various forms (including calomel), ointments, steam baths, pills and fumigation (see this page). Its effects were horrific. In 1858 the American physician Nathan Knepfler described how mercury treatment destroyed the parts of the body it touched, so that the lips, the cheeks and even the upper and lower jaw bones could rot away, and parts of the tongue and palate could be lost. As the author laments, 'This happens when mercury performs *a cure!*'[11]

Given the constant threat of disease, it is perhaps not surprising that the Victorians became so preoccupied with their health. A culture of invalidism grew up, particularly among the more affluent classes, with a proliferation of vague ailments that doctors were able to do little about. The term 'hypochondria' was often used to describe this state, and referred not to imagined illnesses but to a chronic disease of the whole person, involving both physical and psychological depression. Sufferers included the philosopher and essayist Thomas Carlyle, whose correspondence, throughout his long life (he lived to be eighty-five), is filled with descriptions of the 'grinding misery of ill-health' – he is 'sick with sleeplessness, quite nervous, *bilius*, splenetic, and all the rest of it'. Other well-known Victorians, including John Ruskin, Charles Darwin and George Eliot, suffered similarly. Many cures were tried, and a brisk business in panaceas grew up. These included 'the Golden Pill of Life and Beauty', Parr's Life Pill and the Gamboge Pill, promoted as the 'universal medicine'.[12]

The nineteenth century saw the transformation of medicine from traditional practices to a regulated, scientific discipline. At the beginning of the century it could be difficult to distinguish an unqualified 'quack' doctor from a skilled

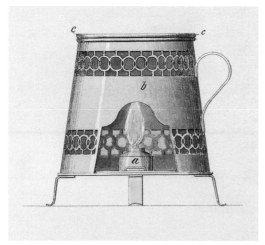

Design for a Fumigating Apparatus to Cure Syphilis, 1857

Design for a Mill for Grinding Drugs and Groceries, 1843

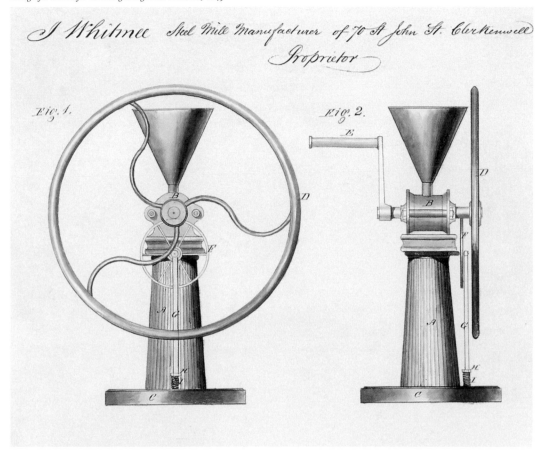

practitioner; by the end of the century medicine was regulated in much the same way as it is today. Breakthroughs had been made in understanding how disease was transmitted. The bacteria that caused cholera, tuberculosis and syphilis were identified, paving the way for effective treatments. A century of scientific endeavour and demands for greater regulation provided the foundation for future breakthroughs in the battle against contagious diseases and a cleaner, safer environment.

[1] Bruce Haley, *The Healthy Body and Victorian Culture*, Cambridge, Mass. and London: Harvard University Press, 1978, p. 5.

[2] Robert G. W. Kirk and Neil Pemberton, 'Re-imagining bleeders: The medical leech in the nineteenth century bloodletting encounter', *Medical History*, 55, 2011, pp. 355–60.

[3] Matthew Sweet, *Inventing the Victorians*, London: Faber and Faber, 2001, p. 98

[4] N. David Richards, 'Dentistry in England in the 1840s: The first indications of a movement towards professionalization', *Medical History*, 12(2), April 1968, pp. 137–52.

[5] Asa Briggs, *Victorian Things*, London: Penguin Books, 1988, p. 115.

[6] Briggs, *ibid.*, p. 107.

[7] Haley, *op. cit.*, p. 8.

[8] Haley, *op. cit.*, p. 10.

[9] Mary Wilson Carpenter, *Health, Medicine and Society in Victorian England*, Oxford: Praeger, 2010, pp. 45–49.

[10] *Ibid.*, p. 72.

[11] *Ibid.*, p. 82.

[12] Haley, *op. cit.*, pp. 12–14.

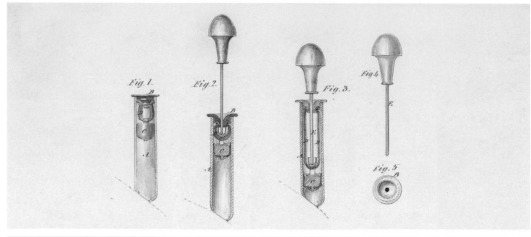

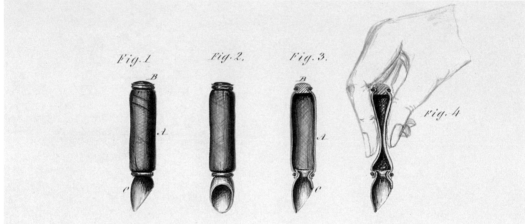

ABOVE, TOP & BOTTOM
ARTIFICIAL LEECHES
1848

TOP
Figs. 1., 2., 3. & 4 horizontal views • *Fig. 5* aerial view

The piston (C) and the disc (B) are connected together by a band of India Rubber.

BOTTOM
Fig. 1. side view • *Fig. 2.* front view • *Figs. 3. & 4.* sectional views shewing the manner of operation

On releasing the instrument from the pressure of the fingers, the tendency of the elastic cylinder to expand and resume its original form produces a sucking action which continues until it is filled more or less with blood.

OPPOSITE
IMPROVEMENTS IN THE SHAPE OR CONFIGURATION OF MECHANICAL OR ARTIFICIAL LEECHES AND THE LANCET USED THEREWITH
1848

Figs. 1. & 2. cross section of artificial leeches without improvement • *Figs. 3. & 4.* cross section of straight or partly curved tube with ring or collar • *Fig. 5.* bolt or pin of the Piston

The tube is so formed as to have a ring or collar (mm) of a greater diameter than the tube, so as to afford a hold or purchase for the fingers of the Operator. The facility of operating is increased and the danger of breaking the Leech or Lancet in the application thereof is avoided or lessened.

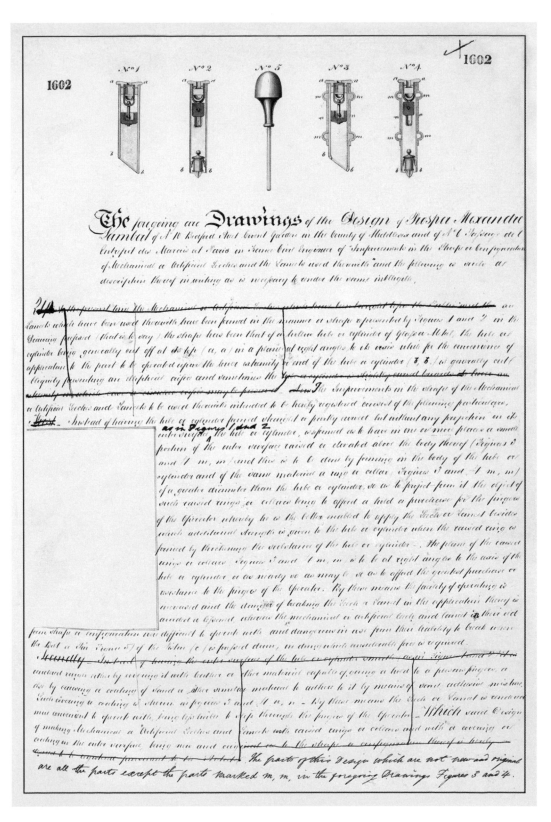

— Improved Scarificator. —

Fred Joraux Weiss of the Strand Surgical Instrument Maker Proprietor.

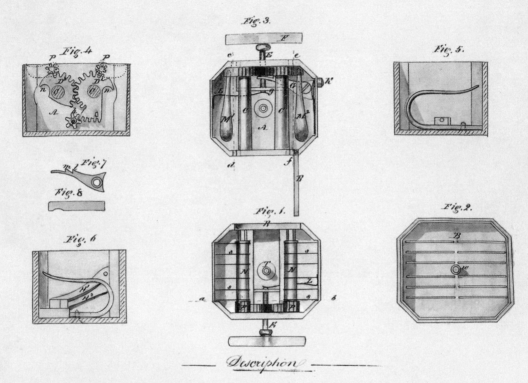

Fig. 3.

Fig. 4.   Fig. 5.

Fig. 7.

Fig. 8.

Fig. 6.   Fig. 1.   Fig. 2.

— Description —

Fig 1 is a top plan of this instrument with the lid (Fig 2) off. Fig 3 is another top plan with the scarifiers as well as lid removed. Fig 4 is a sectional elevation on the line a b. Fig 5 a sectional elevation on the line c d of Fig 3 and Figure 6 a sectional elevation on the line e f of Fig 3.

A is the box or case. B (fig 2) the lid. C C are two noses to which are attached at one end the bothed segments D¹ D². K is a third axis which is passed through one of the sides of the box between the segments D¹ D² and supported at its inner extremity by a bridge g raised in the bottom of the box through an orifice in which it is free to move to and fro. This axis there is affixed a pinion b which takes into the tail of the segment D¹ (see fig 4). F is a thumb piece by which the axis K is moved. G is a detent of the form shown separately in the top and side views Figs 7 & 8 which is screwed fast at one end to a stud in one of the four corners of the box and at the other is free end grips the axis K² bears at that end slightly curved for this purpose. To this detent there are two teeth i n which project sidewards and are successively acted upon by a small pin v which projects from the face of the segment D¹. — H¹ H² are two springs which press respectively against the two ends of the crutch for tail of the detent. K is a pin moved from the outside by which the detent can be pushed inwards to a small extent L is a spring which presses against the inner end of the axis K when it projects from the bridge g. M¹ M² are two strong doubled up springs, the upper or free ends of which are inserted under the hooked ends n n of the segments D¹ D². N N are two axes to which the scarifiers S S S S are attached & which have at one end two pinions P P which work respectively into the segments D¹ D². R is a bar which turns on a hinge at one end and when brought over near ends of the axes N N secures them in their places as shown in Fig 1 when it is desired to lift these axes out for the purpose of cleaning or sharpening the scarifiers this bar is drawn back as shewn in Fig 3. T is a screw threaded pin which takes into the pipe w of the lid B (fig 2) and by which the box and lid are firmly secured together.

The parts of this design which are new in respect of the form and configuration thereof are all the parts except those marked C F G H H² K L & g.

H. Robertson & Co
Registration Agents
166 Fleet Street
London

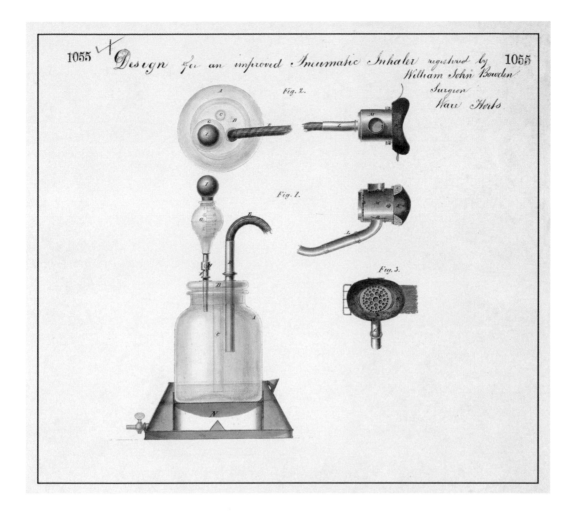

OPPOSITE

IMPROVED SCARIFICATOR

1845

Fig. 1. top plan of the instrument • *Fig. 2.* the lid
Fig. 3. top plan with the scarifiers as well as lid removed
Fig. 4. sectional elevation on the line (ab) • *Fig. 5.*
section elevation on the line (cd) of *Fig. 3.* & *Fig. 6.*
Fig. 6. sectional elevation on the line (ef) of *Fig. 3.*
Figs. 7 & 8. Detail of the detent (G)

The teeth (lm) *are acted upon by a small pin* (v) *which
projects from the face of the segment* (D'). *A vacuum
is created with a cup and the lancets or scarifiers sprung
through the skin. The cup is reapplied so that the blood
flows into it.*

ABOVE

DESIGN FOR AN IMPROVED PNEUMATIC INHALER

1847

Fig. 1. novel form of apparatus in elevation; the mouth
piece being in section to shew the valves • *Fig. 2.*
plan view • *Fig. 3.* a buckle and strap to fasten the
mouthpiece to the Patient's head

(AA) *is a jar furnished with an air tight stopper* (B)
*in which three openings are made one for the insertion
of a pendant air tube* (C) *another for the insertion of a
tube* (D) *connected to the elastic tubing* (E) *which leads
to the Patient and the third for the insertion of a tube*
(F) *which supports a glass vessel* (G) *containing the
æther or other spirit.*

Continuous Stream En

Registered for Joseph Gray & Henry

The drawing exhibits several views of the 2 Design draw
side elevation of the design shown partly in section. Fig. 2 a side view of the of the upper part
are employed to denote corresponding parts in so far as such parts appear or can be seen at each of the
duced by the addition of certain new parts to a single action operative fountain syringe of
addition of parts a single action syringe is rendered considerably more simple and equally
use and employed to produce a continuous stream. I will now proceed to describe the arra
the configuration whereof is denoted by lines of red color) within which the syringe
which is so disposed within the reservoir B as to leave a space between the said plate
purpose hereafter mentioned. It will be seen upon referring to Fig 3 which exhibits
that there is a hole's formed therein through which passes the lower extremity of the pip
to the syringe as exhibited. It will further be seen upon referring to Figs 1 and 2
is affixed a pipe F, the lower end whereof is closely connected to the syringe and the
therein. E a pipe connected to the reservoir B a little below the false bottom or plate C
enable said pipe when out of use to be folded against the reservoir. The opera
Having charged the reservoir B through the part K with water the operator raises the
of the air contained in the reservoir will pass through the pipe E into the syringe and
lower part of the syringe thus as the operator presses down the handle H the chamber a will be
at each stroke and during the filling of said chamber with water the air contained therein be
exert its elastic force upon the surface of the water in the chamber thereby maintaining a continuous
during the time that the handle of the syringe is being pulled up.

The Claim is for the general configuration of those parts of the design mar
New and for which protection is sought; the remaining portions are *Old.*

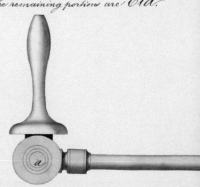

Green & Prince, Agents for Patents &

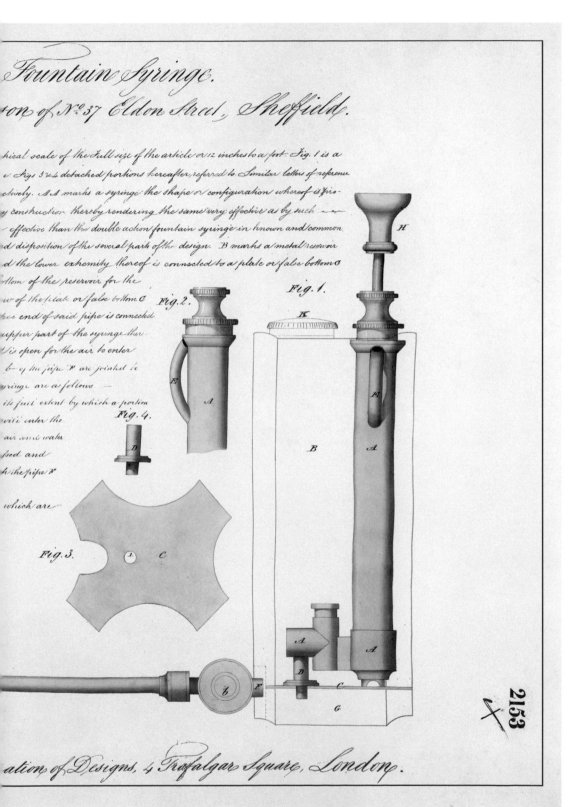

Fountain Syringe.

...on of Nº 37 Eldon Street, Sheffield.

...hical scale of the full size of the article or 12 inches to a foot. Fig. 1 is a
...e Figs 3 & 4 detached portions hereafter referred to. Similar letters of reference
...ctively. A A marks a syringe the shape or configuration whereof is pro-
...y construction thereby rendering the same very effective as by such ...
... effective than the double action fountain syringe in known and common
...d disposition of the several parts of the design. B marks a metal reservoir
...d the lower extremity thereof is connected to a plate or false bottom C
...ttom of the reservoir for the
...w of the plate or false bottom C
...er end of said pipe is connected
...upper part of the syringe there ...
...'is open for the air to enter
...b... of the pipe F are jointed to
...yringe are as follows —
...its full extent by which a portion
...will enter the
...air and water
...sed and
...the pipe F

...which are

Fig. 2.

Fig. 4.

Fig. 3.

Fig. 1.

2153

PREVIOUS PAGES

CONTINUOUS STREAM ENEMA FOUNTAIN SYRINGE

1850

Fig. 1. side elevation of the design shewn partly in section • *Fig. 2.* side view of the upper part of the syringe • *Figs. 3. & 4.* detached portions

Having charged the reservoir (B) *through the part* (K) *with water the operator raises the handle* (H) *to its full extent as the operator presses down the handle the chamber* (G) *will be charged with air and water at each stroke and during the filling of said chamber with water the air contained therein becomes compressed and exerts its elastic force upon the surface of the water thereby maintaining a continuous stream.*

BELOW

PESSARY FOR PROLAPSUS UTERI

1847

A new configuration of an Instrument intended for the support of Prolapsus or Procidentia Uteri.

OPPOSITE ABOVE

DESIGN FOR THE "PESSARY" FOR THE RELIEF OF "PROLAPSUS UTERI" OR "PROLAPSUS ANI"

1847

A vulcanized India Rubber bag (a) *made air tight which is to be inflated within the vagina by means of a tube* (b) *of sufficient length to allow the patient to inflate the bag —* (c) *a stop cock for allowing the air to escape.*

OPPOSITE BELOW

DESIGN FOR A TRUSS

1846

Fig. 1. the truss in perspective • *Fig. 2.* the design in perspective • *Fig. 3.* transverse and vertical section

(AA) *marks a piece of copper covered with chamois leather or other soft substance,* (BB) *marks pieces of brass or pads. It will appear evident that as the part* (A) *is adjusted more or less tight to the body by means of the buckle* (E); *the part* (A) *being of copper will readily adapt itself to the form of that part of the body.*

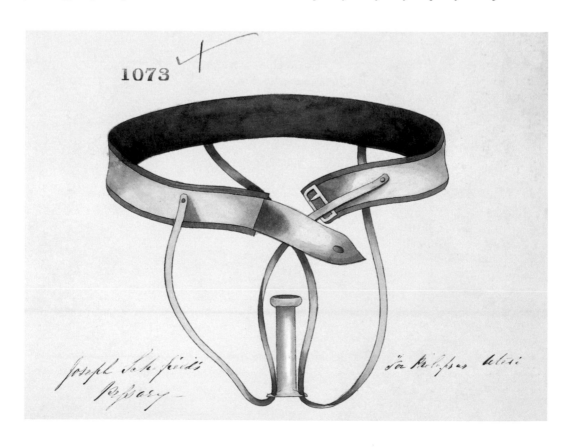

1073

Joseph Schofield's
Pessary —

For Prolapsus Uteri

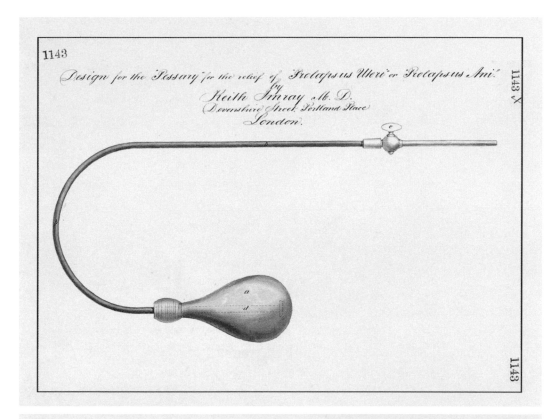

1143

Design for the Pessary for the relief of Prolapsus Uteri or Prolapsus Ani by Keith Imray M. D. Devonshire Street, Portland Place London.

∨ 1143

1143

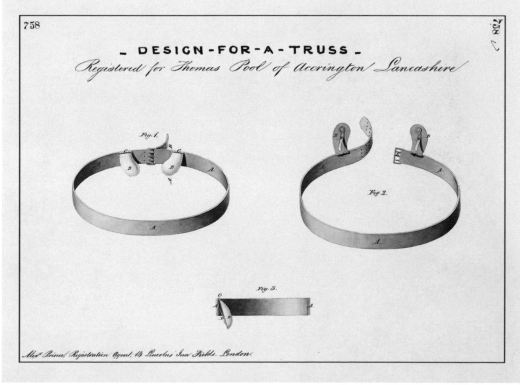

758

758 ⌄

_ DESIGN-FOR-A-TRUSS _

Registered for Thomas Pool of Accrington Lancashire

Alexr Prince Registration Agent, 14 Lincolns Inn Fields, London.

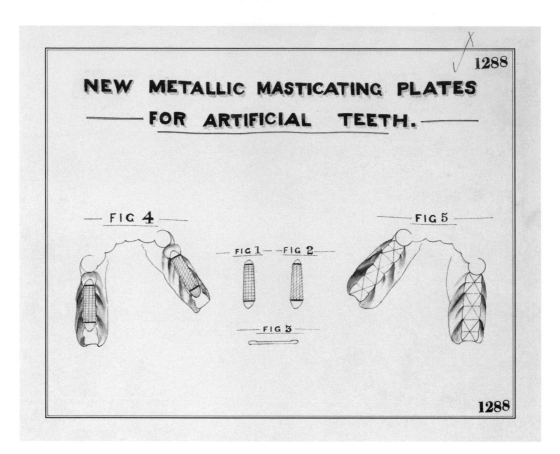

NEW METALLIC MASTICATING PLATES — FOR ARTIFICIAL TEETH. —

FIG 4

FIG 5

FIG 1 — FIG 2

FIG 3

1288

1288

NEW METALLIC MASTICATING PLATES FOR ARTIFICIAL TEETH

1847

The two Plates are intended for and possess the two following important objects in Dentistry, giving greater durability to the Ivory Side Blocks as hitherto used and considerably increased powers of Mastication. The Plates may be of Gold, Platina, Silver, Palladium or such alloy of metals as may be found most desirable. It is proposed as shewn in Fig. 4. to insert or countersink on the top of each Ivory Block a Masticating Plate as shewn in Figs. 1., 2. & 5. Fig. 5. shews the Ivory Side Blocks as now used without Plates.

AN IMPROVED MASTICATING KNIFE AND FORK

1851

(A) and (B) *in the drawing represent back and side views of the masticating knife;* (C) and (D) *being back and side views of the fork;* (e) *represents the form or configuration of a Blade of which there are five more or less. The mode of using the masticating knife and fork is simply by placing the blades of the same between the prongs of the fork and drawing the same through by which means the food is cut into pieces sufficiently small for mastication. The purpose of utility is to enable persons who have lost their teeth and are unable to masticate their food to cut the same into small pieces.*

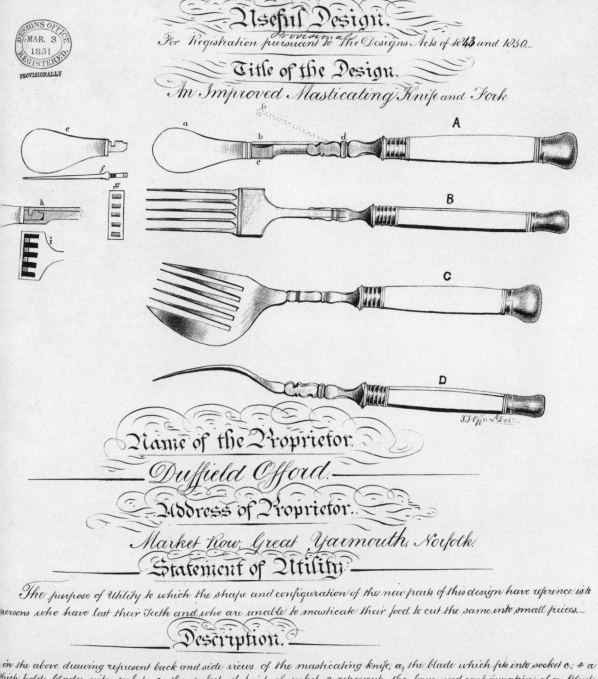

Useful Design.

For Registration pursuant to the Designs Acts of 1843 *provisionally* and 1850.

Title of the Design.

An Improved Masticating Knife and Fork

A

B

C

D

Name of the Proprietor.

Duffield Offord.

Address of Proprietor.

Market Row, Great Yarmouth, Norfolk.

Statement of Utility.

The purpose of Utility to which the shape and configuration of the new parts of this design have reference is to persons who have lost their Teeth and who are unable to masticate their food to cut the same into small pieces.

Description.

in the above drawing represent back and side views of the masticating knife, a, the blade which fits into socket c; & b which holds blades into sockets, c the socket, d joint of socket e represents the form and configuration of a Blade there are five more or less), f back of blade e, g front view of socket, h section shewing Blade in socket, i top socket.

D represent the form and configuration of the fork being back and side views of the same

The mode of using the masticating knife and fork is simply by placing the blades of the same between the two of the fork and drawing the same through by which means the food is cut into pieces sufficiently small for mastication.

Statement of Old Parts.

The parts of this Design which are not new or original as regards shape and configuration thereof are the handles of the knife and fork.

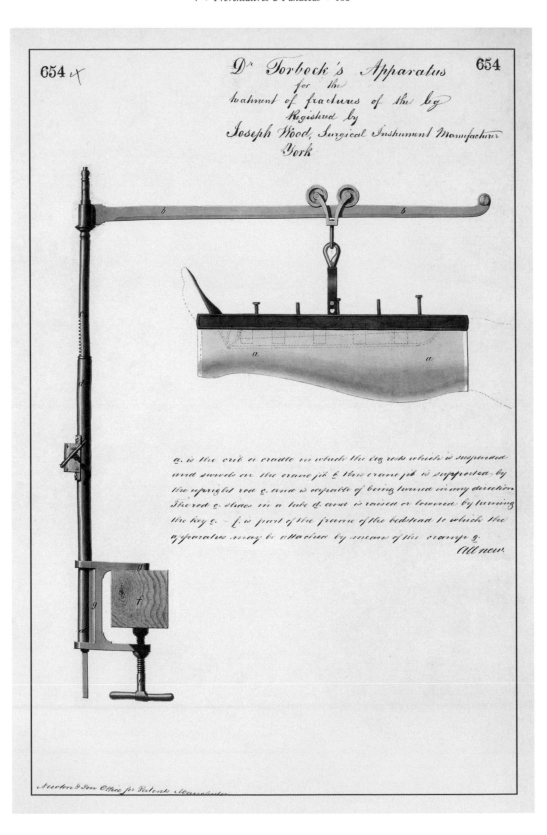

654 ✗

D[r] Torbock's Apparatus
for the
treatment of fractures of the leg
Registered by
Joseph Wood, Surgical Instrument Manufacturer
York

654

a. is the crib or cradle in which the leg rests which is suspended and swivels on the crane jib b. this crane jib is supported by the upright rod c. and is capable of being turned in any direction. The rod c. slides in a tube d. and is raised or lowered by turning the key e. — f. is part of the frame of the bedstead to which the apparatus may be attached by means of the cramp g.

All new.

Newton & Son Office for Patents Manchester

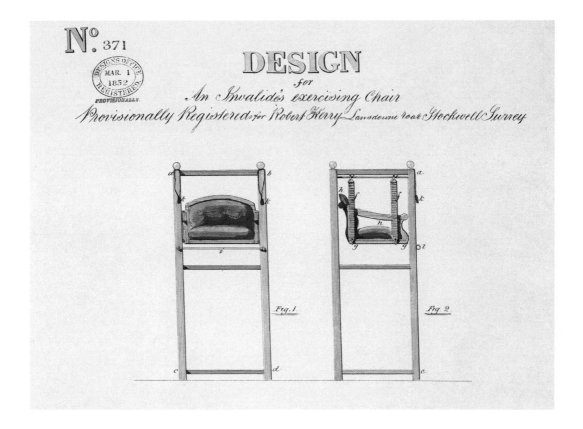

№ 371

DESIGN

for

An Invalide's exercising Chair

Provisionally Registered for Robert Kerry—Lansdowne road Stockwell Surrey

DESIGNS OFFICE
MAR. 1
1852
REGISTERED
PROVISIONALLY.

Fig. 1.   *Fig. 2.*

ABOVE

DESIGN FOR AN INVALIDE'S EXERCISING CHAIR

1852

Fig. 1. elevation ⬩ *Fig. 2.* side view

*A light frame of wood, iron or other material, from the
sides of which are suspended by hooks (ee) or otherwise,
india rubber bands (ff), two on each side supporting the
seat (gg) of the Chair (hh). The weight of the sitter will
act on the elastic bands and depress the chair. The utility
consists in the facility with which an Invalid can obtain
exercise, with the least possible amount of exertion.*

OPPOSITE

**DR. TORBOCK'S APPARATUS FOR THE
TREATMENT OF FRACTURES OF THE LEG**

1846

(a) *is the crib or cradle in which the leg rests which is
suspended and swivels on the crane jib* (b). *This crane
jib is supported by the upright rod* (c) *and is capable
of being turned in any direction.*

OVERLEAF LEFT

DESIGN OF A TYPOGRAPH FOR THE BLIND

1852

Fig. 1. plan ⬩ *Fig. 2.* transverse sectional elevation
taken through the line (AB) on *Fig. 1.* ⬩ *Fig. 3.* section
elevation taken through the line (CD) on *Fig. 1.*

To the underside of the Sliding Frame (e) *is hinged
a Dial Plate* (g) *on the upper surface of which are
embossed letters, and figures, and stops, to enable blind
people to express their ideas on paper with great facility.*

OVERLEAF RIGHT

DESIGN FOR DOUBLE SPECTACLES

1846

Fig. 1. profile view ⬩ *Fig. 2.* similar view when the
additional lenses are in use ⬩ *Fig. 3.* plan view of *Fig. 2.*

*Extra pair of lenses so that the wearer may accommodate
the Instrument to the requirements of his eyes in viewing
either remote or proximate objects.*

Design of a Typograph for the Blind.

Provisionally registered for the Exhibition Hyde Park

FIG. 1.   FIG. 2.

FIG. 3.

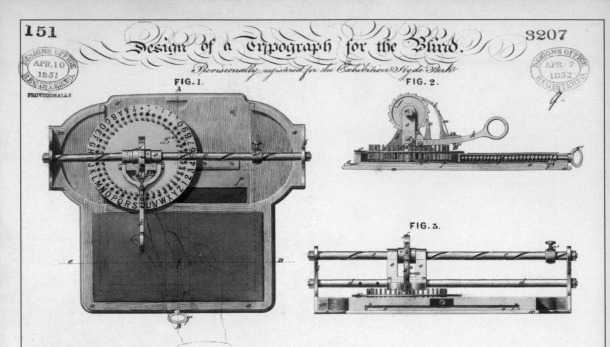

William Hughes, Governor of the Blind Asylum, Manchester, in the County of Lanc.r Proprietor

The purpose of utility to which the shape or configuration of the new parts of this Design have reference is to enable blind people to express their ideas on paper with great facility. Figure 1, is a plan of the Typograph. Figure 2 is a transverse sectional elevation of the same taken through the line A B on Figure 1, and Figure 3 is another sectional Elevation taken through the line C D, on Figure 1. The Drawings are made to a Geometrical Scale of six inches to one foot, a, represents the word frame to which the Standards b, are attached. These Standards b, support the screw c, and guide rail d; e, is a sliding frame supported by the Screw c, and guide rail d, and f is a ratchet wheel having a pin which passes through its boss and enters into the groove of the Screw c. To the underside of the Sliding Frame e is hinged a Dial Plate g, on the upper surface of which are embossed letters, and figures, and stops, as shewn in Figure 1. In the Dial Plate g, there is also a circle of countersunk round holes marked h, and another circle of holes for the upper ends of the types i, the lower ends of the types are guided by corresponding holes in the Lower Plate j. In setting the Type into their places the Letter B of the type, must be put in the hole facing the letter A of the Dial Plate, and all the other letters, figures and stops, are in the same relative positions. To the Sliding Frame e, is hinged the handle k, to which is jointed the click l, taking into the ratchet wheel f, and held in contact with it by the spring m. To the Sliding Frame e, is also hinged the retaining catch n, which is acted upon from below by a spring partly shewn in Figure 1. o, is a slide to which is hinged the frame p, which is furnished with a piece of transfer paper, under which the paper to receive the impression is placed, and q, is a screw with a wing head q¹, and ... Screw Nut q², which acts on the Slide o. In using the Typograph the operator puts his thumb into the opening at the end of the handle k, as shewn in figure 1, and brings the letter to be marked near to the said handle, on depressing which the underside of the handle presses on the upper end of the type and the lower end of the type by being brought in contact with the upper surface of the transfer paper, gives the requisite impression to the paper on the Slide o; and the guide pin k¹ by entering into one of the holes h, holds the dial plate firm during the operation. The handle k is raised off the type by the spring k², and the type is lifted up into its former position by a spiral spring wound around each of them as seen in figure 2. The operator then elevates the handle k sufficiently to move the ratchet wheel f, through a portion of a revolution equal to one tooth, this operation imparts also a lateral motion to the dial plate g, because the pin in the boss of the ratchet wheel f takes into the groove of the screw c which is held fast between the Standards b; the next letter that is required, is then brought near to the handle k which is again depressed and the operations are thus repeated until the Dial Plate arrives near the right hand end of the screw c, or until the Slide Frame e, comes against the stop c¹ which can be set in any convenient position. By drawing the retaining catch n, out of gear with the ratchet wheel f, and thrusting it back, the click l is also taken out of gear and the Sliding Frame e, is then at liberty to be moved back again to the left hand end of the screw c, the operator by then raising the handle k brings the catch n and click l again in gear and by turning the wing head q¹, the nut q² by acting on the Slide o, moves the paper on which the impressions are received into the proper position for commencing a new line.

The parts of this Design which are not new or original as regards the shape or configuration thereof are all the parts except the dial plate g; all the other parts are not new when taken separately but as here combined form part of a new Design.

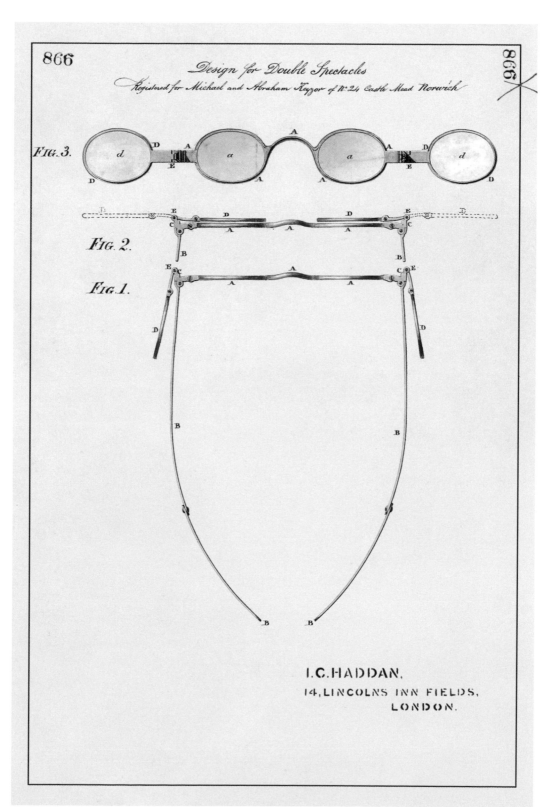

866   866

Design for Double Spectacles

Registered for Michael and Abraham Keyzor of N.º 24 Castle Mead Norwich

FIG. 3.

FIG. 2.

FIG. 1.

I. C. HADDAN,
14, LINCOLNS INN FIELDS,
LONDON.

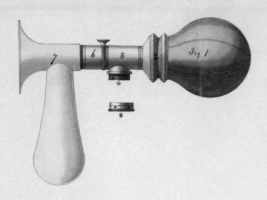

THE GUM ELASTIC BREAST RELIEVER
1849

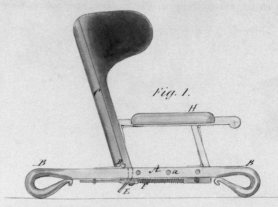

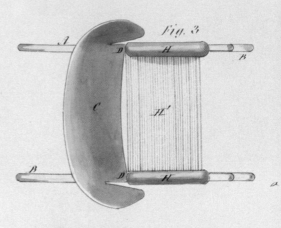

INVALID'S RECLINING BED COUCH
c. *1849*

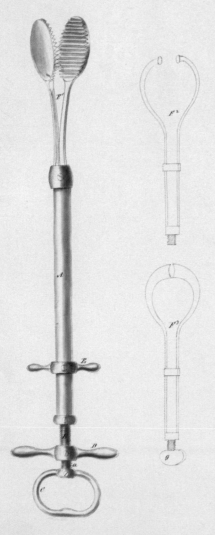

PARTURITION FORCEPS
1847

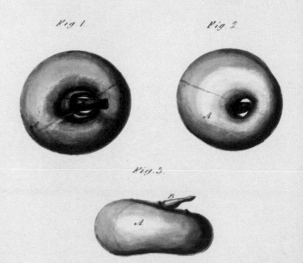

ELASTIC PESSARY (SURGICAL INSTRUMENT)
1849

DESIGN FOR THE CHEMICAL SANITARY BELT AND CHOLERA REPELLENT

c. *1848*

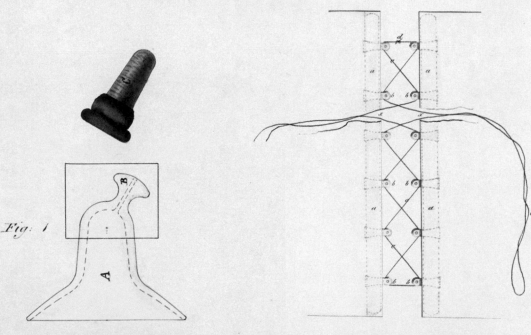

**NON-ORNAMENTAL DESIGN FOR
A NIPPLE PROTECTOR**

c. *1849*

**DESIGN FOR A FASTENING FOR BANDAGES
AND STAYS**

1845

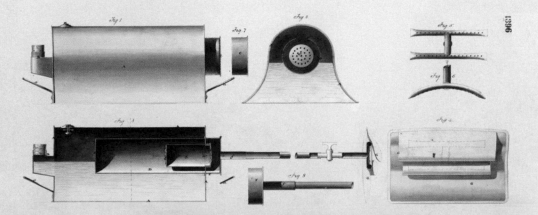

DESIGN FOR A FOOT-WARMER AND INFLUENZA VAPOUR BATH

c. *1848*

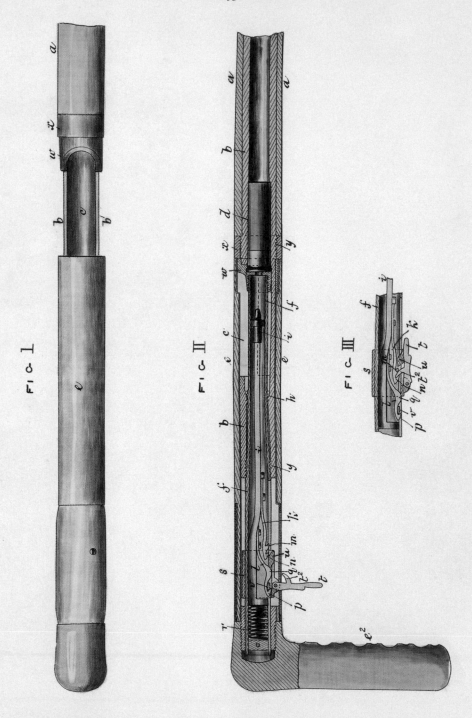

Simplicity and efficiency in closing cocking discharging and preventing accidental discharge of the gun and in extracting the empty cartridge cases.

SPORT & LEISURE

"TEN MINUTES' GALLOP
BEFORE BREAKFAST WILL
GIVE THE RIDER A WILTSHIRE
LABOURER'S APPETITE..."

• • •

Advertisement for Vigor's Horse-Action Saddle

The Sporting Times

1894

ike so many other aspects of life, leisure was completely transformed in the nineteenth century. A combination of industrialization, urban growth, improved transport links, new technology and the rise of the middle classes with their reforming zeal meant that many old traditional activities disappeared, others were organized and institutionalized, and completely new sports and entertainments were introduced. The sporting mania of the second half of the century created a market for new equipment and gadgets, which inventors and manufacturers were quick to exploit. Some of the designs registered, such as the tennis scoring system (see p. 174), seem practical, while others, such as the 'Apparatus for Gymnastic Performances', which allows for a scenic effect 'without combustibles of an explosive nature', less so.

In the first half of the century, as the middle classes grew and prospered, the question of how to fill their increasing leisure time in a morally acceptable way began to become a source of anxiety. There was also a growing concern that the disappearance of the traditional leisure activities of the working classes, eroded by the move towards industrialization, urban living, and suppression by the disapproving middle and upper classes, was creating social hardship and could leave a vacuum that might be filled by social unrest.

This situation in the middle of the century was completely transformed over the next thirty years. The 1847 Factory Act, which limited the working day to ten hours, the gradual introduction of half-days on Saturdays, the greater availability of cheap rail travel, and the increasing free time and prosperity enjoyed by the middle classes and a large section of the working classes led to a 'leisure revolution'.

Concerned that leisure activities should be respectable and productive, the reforming middle classes coined the term 'rational recreation', which came to be applied to any leisure activity deemed to be in some way improving. This Victorian spirit of self-improvement led to a drive for physical achievement and a concept of 'manliness', which encapsulated ideals of chivalry, courage, stoicism,

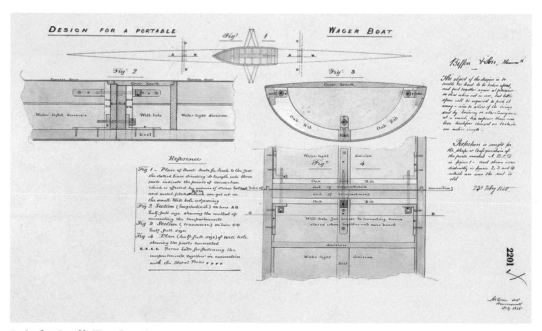

Design for a Portable Wager Boat, 1850

hardiness and endurance.[1] Sport was thought
to aid moral development in all classes, and there
was a widespread belief that a healthy body would
lead to an equally healthy mind. A historian of the
London School Board wrote: 'It is as true for the
children of mechanics and labourers, as for the
children of merchants and professional men, that
manly sports, played as they should be played,
tend to develop unselfish pluck, determination,
self-control and public spirit'.[2] Some regarded
physical fitness as the most important quality
in a man. A London lawyer and socialite writing
in 1861 commented that: 'the affected Dandy of
past years is unknown. If he exists, he is despised.
The standard or average English gentleman of
the present day must at least show vigour of body,
if he cannot display vigour of mind.'[3]

A kind of sporting mania took hold: a writer
in *Macmillan's Magazine* commented that: 'the
young men of that day seemed possessed by
a perfect mania for every species of athletic
contest'.[4] National bodies for the supervision
and coordination of the major sports were formed
in the 1860s and 1870s, and rules and regulations
for the conduct of sports and sporting fixtures
were put into place.

The most respectable sport throughout the
nineteenth century was cricket, which had an
impeccable background of support by members
of the aristocracy. From the 1850s to the 1870s
no other sport attracted so many players and
spectators. Exhibition cricket, with touring groups
such as the All-England Eleven and its rival the
United All-England Eleven, attracted huge crowds.
With the first test matches, cricket also began to
gain international popularity. W. G. Grace, the
greatest Victorian sporting hero, was a prime
attraction wherever he played.[5]

The University Boat Race between Oxford
and Cambridge Universities became an annual
event in 1856 and attracted enormous spectator

**"A MINGLED MASS OF PERFECTLY
LEGITIMATE PLEASURES EVER
THRUSTING THEMSELVES FORWARD
IN A VARIETY OF SHAPES…ALL
TOGETHER MAKING CONTINUALLY
INCREASING DEMANDS ON OUR
TIME, UPON OUR MONEY, AND
NOT LEAST, UPON OUR STRENGTH
AND POWERS OF ENDURANCE."**

THE TIMES, 20 JUNE 1876

interest. Hundreds of vessels crowded the River
Thames to watch, and the races were avidly
reported in the sporting press, alongside reports
on the individual rowers and their physical
condition and training regimes.

Athletics enjoyed a similar surge in popularity.
Although running competitions were common at
the beginning of the century, no attempt had been
made to standardize events, and professionals ran
with amateurs. As the century progressed, various
athletic clubs were formed and records of times
and distances began to be kept. Some impressive
records were set, sometimes in challenging
circumstances. In the English championships of
1868 Edward Colbeck ran the quarter mile in just
over fifty seconds, despite colliding with a sheep
midway. His record time for the event remained
unbroken for thirteen years.[6]

Because large numbers of professional and
intellectual men took part in activities such as
cricket, rowing, and athletics, these sports gained
respectability. Football, meanwhile, struggled to
overcome its association with the working classes.
It had been popular in various forms from the
middle ages, but throughout its history it had
tended to be condemned by the authorities. It had
been banned several times over the years, including
by Richard II, who believed it diverted young men

"VERY UNDERDONE MEAT, BREAD, AND GOOD SOUND BEER OR PORTER WAS CONSIDERED THE PROPER DIET; AND RUNNING AT TOP SPEED EARLY IN THE MORNING WAS ONE OF THE THINGS MUCH RELIED ON."

BISHOP WORDSWORTH OF ST ANDREWS, QUOTED IN *MODERN ENGLISH SPORTS*, 1885

from the study of archery.[7] Football as we know it today began with challenges between different pub teams, or groups from different streets. Other teams were formed by schools or churches, as a way of keeping local boys out of trouble. The original members of Aston Villa had links with the Bible class of a Wesleyan Chapel in Birmingham,[8] but the field the team played on belonged to a butcher, and the changing facilities were provided by a publican.[9]

The Football Association was formed in 1863, standardizing rules, and by the mid-1870s 'association football' was becoming the most popular national sport. The beginnings of professionalism came in the 1880s, when some clubs were expelled for paying players. The rise in popularity of football was driven by the general rise in living standards, which enabled working men to afford the price of travelling to matches, and gave them enough free time to watch or play in them. Footballers became heroes, and the allegiances of fans were exploited by the growing souvenir market, itself dependent on the working classes having spare cash.[10]

Gymnasiums, too, helped to promote the idea of 'manliness'. The first was built at Oxford University in 1859 by a Scot, Archibald MacLaren, who in 1860 implemented the training regime he developed there for the British Army. The gymnasium contained state-of-the-art equipment, including an area for fencing as well as jumping horses, horizontal bars, the trapezium, rope ladders, and wall-scaling.

There could not have been a greater contrast between these manly ideals and the expectations of women. Women were expected to maintain a ladylike decorum at all times, and their restrictive clothing prevented them from being anything other than minimally energetic. A distinction was made between sports, which were physically challenging, and games. Games allowed the less physically able – such as women and children – to take part, and were considered to be diversions, or 'amusements'.[11] Playing games in a genteel way was socially acceptable, and it reinforced an idealized image of family life.

Games parties and sports clubs provided cover for flirtation and courtship, and help to explain the popularity of mixed sports such as lawn tennis and croquet. Lawn tennis, invented by Major Walter Wingfield, who originally called it 'Sphairistikè,' was considered by a writer in the *Edinburgh Review* to be 'the most perfect of games', as one could watch as the ball was 'patted to and fro in lofty arcs by pretty young ladies, tripping gracefully to simple strokes which complaisant young gentlemen run about to recover from their random directions and make easy to return'.[12]

Croquet was first played in Ireland in 1852 and quickly became popular, with the first tournament being held in 1866. *The Gentlemen's Magazine* even ran a series of articles on the 'Science of Croquet', with illustrations showing how to adopt 'vicious stances'. Like tennis, it allowed young men and women to interact in a socially acceptable context. It became a huge craze, celebrated in music hall songs and lampooned in *Punch*.[13]

Having the right accoutrements was nearly as important as the competition itself, and pleasure was derived from buying the right equipment. Inventors were quick to try to exploit a potential market, coming up with pieces of equipment

A New and Useful Design for an Instrument to be attached to Lawn tennis Rackets for picking up balls from the ground, 1878

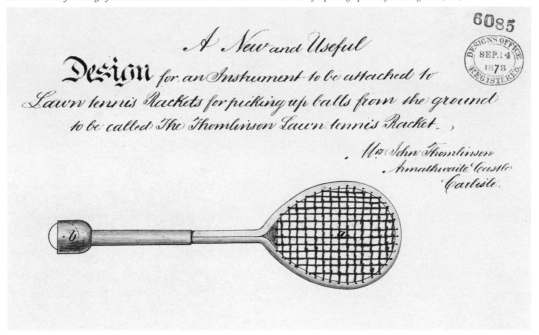

of mixed usefulness, such as the tennis racquet attachment for picking up balls, the "Umpire Croquet Register", and the "Croquet Clog" (to preserve lawns) (see pp. 171, 176 & 177).

Other sports became popular in the second half of the century, including golf – according to one writer 'there were districts in England where a person's moral character was considered of less importance than the precision and ease of his swing'. Ice-hockey, swimming, water handball and water polo became established sports, and in the 1870s workable roller skates were invented and 'rinkomania' took hold. By the end of the decade there were dozens of rinks in London alone. Prince's rink had 4,000 members, of whom 3,000 attended on a single day.[14] Around the same time cycling also became hugely popular across the social classes (see chapter IV). Railways excursions and overseas holidays also became increasingly popular. The *Saturday Review* remarked that 'The quietest sort of people are uncomfortable unless they, at least once a year,

tie themselves together in batches and go prowling over the tops of unexplored Alps.'[15]

Despite all this energetic activity, the respectable middle classes stressed the importance of recreation based around 'hearth and home'. Parlour games, musical evenings and craft activities were popular, and most middle-class homes would have had a piano. Cheap sheet music was published in abundance from the 1840s, and playing the piano was considered an essential accomplishment for young girls. There was a general flood of literature that kept the middle-class public well supplied with periodicals and novels. Private theatricals, quizzes and games, or older pastimes such as draughts or billiards were all popular family pastimes.[16]

Reviews in the increasing numbers of newspapers and magazines, as well as the spread of advertising, helped fuel the entertainment industry. *The Times* of 1 January 1862 carried dozens of advertisements for many and varied entertainments. Among the concerts, piano recitals, magicians and ventriloquists were thrilling spectacles, including 'VESUVIUS, Torre del Greco and the surrounding country fully delineated in BULFORD'S PANORAMA OF NAPLES' in London's Leicester Square. Children's entertainments included a Grand Juvenile Day at the Polytechnic, with 'Gratuitous Distribution of thousands of beautiful Ornaments, Toys, Pocket Knives, Cannons &c among the juvenile visitors'.

Many displays of special effects were given a scientific veneer for those who believed in 'rational recreation'. London's Polytechnic Institution was dedicated to the encouragement of invention and technology and the education of the working classes, but under this façade of 'rational recreation' entertainment seems to have been its true purpose.[17]

New technologies allowed ever more impressive theatrical special effects, and the 'sensation drama' became enormously popular, with productions including simulations of

"EVEN IDLENESS IS EAGER NOW – EAGER FOR AMUSEMENT: PRONE TO EXCURSION TRAINS, ART-MUSEUMS, PERIODICAL LITERATURE, AND EXCITING NOVELS..."

GEORGE ELIOT, *ADAM BEDE*, 1859

waterfalls, burning buildings, horse races and avalanches.[18] Magic lanterns, limelight, which produced intense illumination and made dissolving views possible, and in the early 1880s electricity, all added drama and realism to sets. Melodramas were popular throughout the Victorian period, with children and maidens being rescued from certain death a perennially popular theme.

Concert-going and music of many varieties, including classical performances, brass bands and music halls, were a feature of life for all the social classes. In 1833 Madame Tussaud had imported

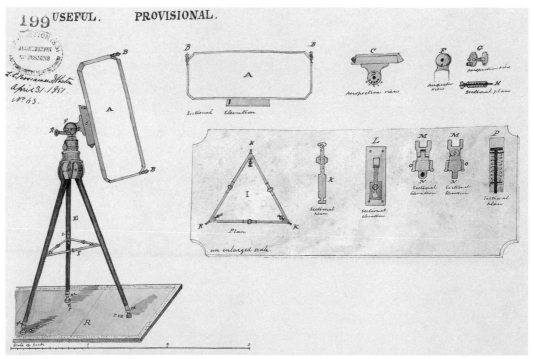

Design for a Useful Provisional Accordion Stand*, 1851

Design for a Self-Acting Music Turner (an apparatus for turning over the leaves of a music book)*, 1872

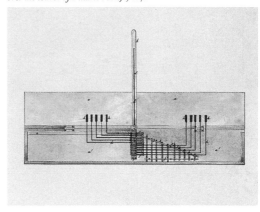

the French custom of promenade concerts, where audiences listened to music outdoors while walking and taking refreshments. The bandmaster Louis Jullien became known for his 'monster' concerts. At one of these an audience of 12,000 listened to extracts from Bellini's *Puritani* played on twenty cornets, twenty trumpets, twenty trombones, twenty ophicleides and twenty serpents.[19] As ever, inventors were quick to spot a trend, and a number of them registered designs for a variety of innovations for brass instruments (see pp. 182–83).

For the working classes, the music hall was the main form of musical entertainment. The first music hall was opened by a publican, Charles Morton, in Lambeth in 1852. Called the Canterbury Hall, it held 700 people, and audiences could enjoy food and drink as they watched the performers. The Alhambra, in Leicester Square, London, which opened in the 1860s, held an audience of 3,500; unlike earlier music halls it had seating facing the stage, as in a theatre. There were over thirty large music halls in London and at least 300 more purpose-built halls in the provinces.

Acts were many and varied (the beginning of 'variety'), including singers, comedians and acrobats.[20]

The Victorians left a legacy of enthusiasm for sports and of sporting organizations, many of which remain active to this day. Their many leisure interests and their thirst for novelty and excitement belie the stereotype of the insular, strait-laced Victorian and suggest that they took full advantage of the many new spectacles and experiences their new-found leisure allowed them to enjoy.

[1] J. A. Mangan and James Walvin, *Manliness and Morality: Middle-class Masculinity in Britain and America, 1800–1940*, New York: St Martin's Press, 1987, p. 1.

[2] H. B. Philpot, *London at School: The Story of the School Board*, 1904, quoted in Peter Bailey, *Leisure and Class in Victorian England*, London: Routledge & Kegan Paul, 1978, p. 128.

[3] S. M. Ellis (ed.), *A Mid-Victorian Pepys: Letters and Memoirs of Sir William Hardman*, 1923, quoted in Peter Bailey, *Leisure and Class in Victorian England*, London: Routledge & Kegan Paul, 1978, pp. 60–61.

[4] Bruce Haley, *The Healthy Body and Victorian Culture*, Cambridge, Massachusetts and London, England: Harvard University Press, 1978, p. 136.

[5] *Ibid.*, pp. 125–26.

[6] *Ibid.*, p. 130.

[7] *Ibid.*, p. 132.

[8] Peter Bailey, *Leisure and Class in Victorian England*, London: Routledge & Kegan Paul, 1978, p. 139.

[9] Judith Flanders, *Consuming Passions: Leisure and Pleasure in Victorian England*, London, New York, Toronto and Sydney: Harper Perennial, 2006, pp. 439–40.

[10] Sarah Levitt, *Victorians Unbuttoned*, London: George Allen & Unwin, 1986, p. 206.

[11] Haley, *op. cit.*, p. 125.

[12] *Ibid.*, p. 134.

[13] *Ibid.*, p. 135.

[14] *Ibid.*

[15] Bailey, *op. cit.*, p. 60.

[16] *Ibid.*, pp. 59–60.

[17] Flanders, *op. cit.*, pp. 271–72.

[18] Matthew Sweet, *Inventing the Victorians*, London: Faber and Faber, 2001, p. xi.

[19] Flanders, *op. cit.*, pp. 366–67.

[20] *Ibid.*, p. 375.

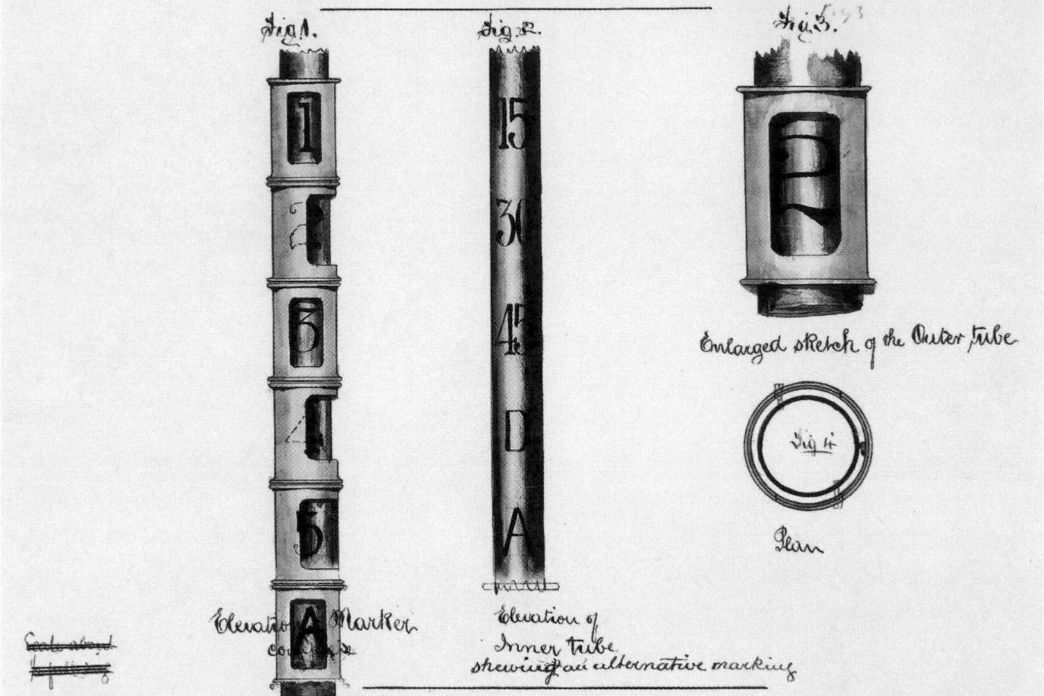

Apparatus for Scoring the Game of Lawn Tennis &c

6310

William Parham

Rothgate Works
Westmorelands
Bath

Fig 1.

Fig 2.

Fig 3.

Enlarged sketch of the Outer tube

Fig 4.

Plan

Elevation of Marker
complete

Elevation of
Inner tube
shewing an alternative marking

The purpose of Utility to which the Shape or Configuration of this design has reference is, that being slid or otherwise fixed in any Lawn Tennis or other poles, it affords a simple and convenient mode of marking the scores of the Game.

to by exposing the figures or letters marked on the tube to indicate such scores; the figures or letters being those that are necessary to mark the particular Game for which they are used.

Figure 1 — Represents the Scorer marking the Games in a set
Figure 2 — Represents the inner tube or body of the Scorer with the outer ones removed
Figure 3 & 4 — are enlarged details of Figure 1 & 2

The whole of this design is New so far as regards the Shape & Configuration thereof

Useful Design

A Receptacle for containing the ball (and arranged to the belt) employed in the game of Lawn Tennis

Isaac Evans, Birmingham

Proprietor

3276

DESIGNS OFFICE
FEB 21
1880
REGISTERED
PROVISIONALLY.

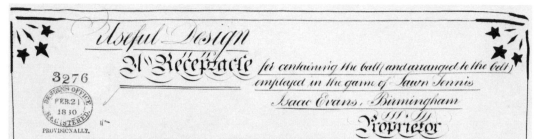

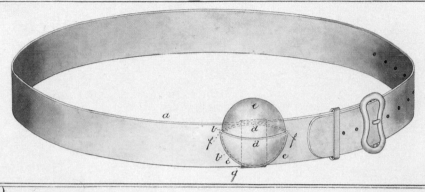

The purpose of utility arising from the *shape or configuration* of the new parts of this Design consists in connecting two segments of a circle thus forming a receptacle for the ball employed in the game of Lawn Tennis and other similar games the said receptacle is affixed to the belt by means of a loop or band but movable to any desired position of the wearer.

The Drawing is illustrative of the same

"*a*" is the belt, "*b*", *b*" are segments and the component parts of this Design being attached or connected at "*c c*", by applying pressure outwardly at "*d, d*" it will expand so as to receive the ball "*e*" (as illustrated) the points "*f, f*" compressing inwardly and holding the ball "*e*" in position, upon releasing the ball "*e*" the receptacle becomes compressed to the belt, to the back part of "*b*" is arranged the loop or band "*g*" which passes around the belt "*a*", but allows of the receptacle "*b*" being arranged in any required position.

Protection is sought for the *shape or configuration* of the parts marked "*b*" and "*g*" which are original or new the remainder is old.

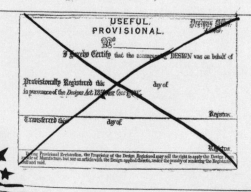

PREVIOUS LEFT

APPARATUS FOR SCORING THE GAME OF LAWN TENNIS &c.

1881

Fig. 1. the score marking the games in a set ◆ *Fig. 2.* the inner tube or body of the score with the outer ones removed ◆ *Figs. 3. & 4.* enlarged details

The purpose is that being slid or otherwise fixed in any Lawn Tennis or other poles, it affords a simple and convenient mode of marking the scores of the Game by exposing the figures or letters marked on the tube to indicate such scores.

PREVIOUS RIGHT

A RECEPTACLE FOR CONTAINING THE BALL (AND ARRANGED TO THE BELT) EMPLOYED IN THE GAME OF LAWN TENNIS*

1880

(a) is the belt, (b,b) are segments and the component parts being attached or connected at (c,c); by applying pressure outwardly at (d,d) it will expand so as to receive the ball (e) (as illustrated).

OPPOSITE

DESIGN FOR THE "UMPIRE" CROQUET REGISTER*

1870

The number of grooves around a player's mallet is twice that of the other mallets, used in a full game. The rings (c) are all placed either in the plain or coloured grooves (a,b), the player registering the balls he has 'croqueted' after each stroke by moving the India rubber rings from the plain to the coloured grooves or vice versa, to cover or uncover the grooves corresponding in colours to the balls he has 'croqueted'.

BELOW

DESIGN FOR A CROQUET CLOG

1872

Fig. 1. side view of the clog complete ◆ *Fig. 2. plan or top view of the same*

(aa) is the sole of the clog which is flat on its under surface, but is provided with pins on its upper surface to enter the sole of the boot or shoe of the player and thus prevent the clog from shifting about on the foot. The purpose is to prevent the heels of the boots of Croquet players from making holes in or injuring the lawn.

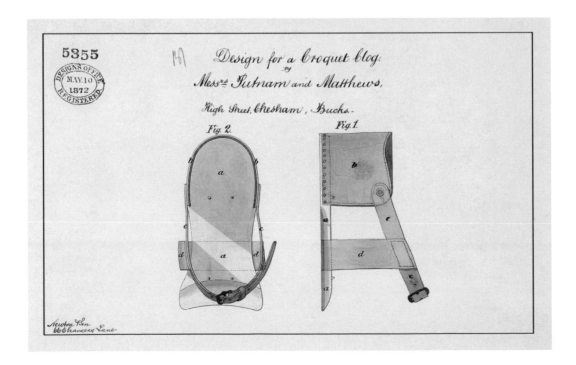

Design for the "Um- pire" Croquet Register.

Provisionally Registered for George Brown Councell of Thornbury, near Bristol, county of Gloster.

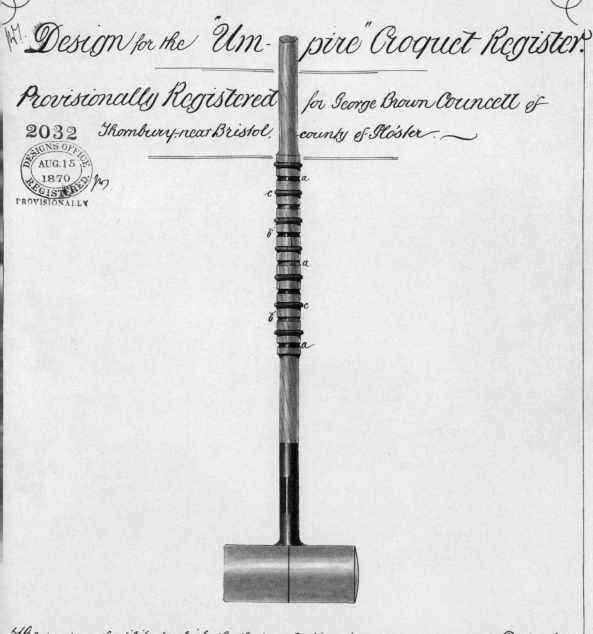

The purpose of utility to which the shape or Configuration of the new parts of this Design has reference is to enable a player to register the different balls which he may have "croqueted" during his stroke, to avoid mistakes when his turn comes again to play.

I provide a series of grooves around the handle of each player's mallet, at or about midlength. The number of grooves is twice that of the other mallets, used in a full game; and one half the number of said grooves (a) are each colored (or colored and numbered) to correspond with one of the other player's balls, every alternate groove (b) being uncolored, (c) are indiarubber rings which fit into and cover the colored grooves (a) there being one for each groove.

At the commencement of a game, the rings (c) are all placed, either in the plain or colored grooves, the player registering the balls he has "croqueted" after each stroke, by moving the indiarubber rings from the plain to the colored grooves or vice versa, to cover or uncover the grooves corresponding in colors to the balls he has "croqueted."

The parts of this design, which are new as regards the shape or configuration thereof, are those marked a, b, c.

1838

Design for an "Artificial Bird" Shooting Machine.

Registered for Mr Stephen Hartley
of 1 Alpha Place Manor St Chelsea

The annexed drawings represent a design for an artificial Bird shooting machine for the purpose of propelling an imitation bird on a wire to resemble such animals in their flight, Fig 1 represents a front view of this apparatus having the front of the cases removed in order to show the action of the machine. Fig 2 a side elevation with the side of case removed Fig 3 a plan with top of case removed, and Fig 4 a back view of the spindle b with the wheel removed. It consists of two wheels A & B mounted on spindles in cases C & D, the spindle a of B being merely to admit of its rotation and is pivoted in the back & front of the case D while the spindle b of the wheel A has a rotary motion communicated to it by a spring barrel E in which a spring is wound similar to the spring of a clock, the one end of the spring being

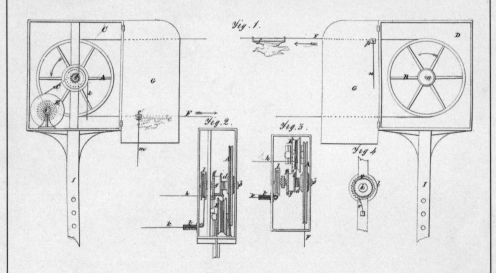

Fig.1. *Fig.2.* *Fig.3.* *Fig 4*

secured to a fixed spindle S & the other to the barrel E. The cord C from this barrel E is also wound on a barrel d on the spindle b & this when wound up to its full extent, will by the action of the spring cause the wheel A to rotate rapidly in the direction of the arrow thereby giving motion to the endless wire F which encircles the wheels A & B. On the wire F are suspended two small frames e & f carrying the imitation birds & to which the passage of the wire imparts a corresponding motion producing their passage from C to D & vice versa & during which they are to be fired at by the marksman, the birds being cut out in sheet iron & whitened in order to show when struck. The barrel d is of two different diameters as at g d so as to obtain a quick & slow movement to the bird, this is effected by pulling the wire h during the winding up of the cord C causing it to pass onto the larger barrel g producing the quick speed while if passed on to the smaller part a slow speed will result, serrations are made at it in order to cause the cord C when pulled as shown by dotted lines in Fig 3 to pass on to the larger diameter. The winding up is effected by the cord K wound on the barrel b fixed on spindle b this cord as well as the cords h m & n are conveyed to the firing stand where by pulling the cord K it will be unwound from the barrel b causing the cord C to be unwound from the barrel E on to the barrel d & when released the spring will return rapidly to its original position producing the action before described. A knot or other obstruction should be placed on cord K so as to stop the spring barrel from running quite down, this comes in contact with the spiral spring t through which the cord passes thereby breaking the concussion. & C are blinds from behind which the imitation birds start, in order to intercept the view of them till started, if it be desired that one only should start, the blinds G & are furnished with spring bolts O & p which by loosening either of their respective ends the bolt will shoot out & retain the bird, as soon also the wire sliding through its suspending frame, it being merely hung upon it while the other bird will be carried along with the wire & thus desire the marksman, as to where the bird is to proceed from. The toothed ratchet G is for the purpose of creating a noise with its spring N during the passage of the bird to resemble the sound of the wings produced by birds during flight. The support posts I I are arranged with a number of holes for the purpose of varying the height from the ground – Protection is desired for the whole design it being entirely new & never before used.

1838

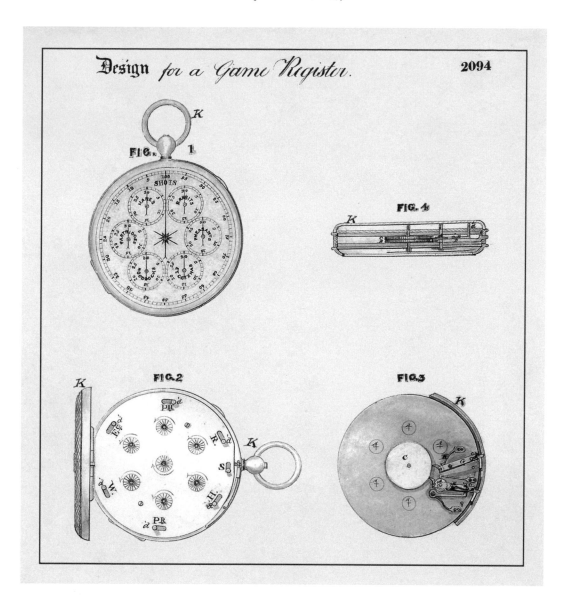

Design for a Game Register. 2094

FIG. 1

FIG. 4

FIG. 2

FIG. 3

OPPOSITE

DESIGN FOR AN "ARTIFICIAL BIRD" SHOOTING MACHINE

1849

Fig. 1. front view having the front of the cases removed
Fig. 2. side elevation • *Fig. 3.* plan with top of case
removed • *Fig. 4.* back view of the spindle (b)

*On the wire (F) are suspended two small frames (e & f)
carrying the imitation birds & to which the passage of
the wire imparts a corresponding motion producing their
passage from (C) to (D) & vice versa.*

ABOVE

DESIGN FOR A GAME REGISTER

1849

Fig. 1. external or face view • *Fig. 2.* back of the
instrument, the outer case being opened or removed
Fig. 3. plan of the works or apparatus as applied to
one game dial and the shot dial • *Fig. 4.* cross section

*A series of dials on the face of the instrument correspond
with the various descriptions of game intended to be
registered; there is a large dial or table on the outer circle
of the plate for indicating the total number of shots fired.*

Useful Design

"An Apparatus" for Gymnastic Performances

Alfred Short. Birmingham.

Proprietor

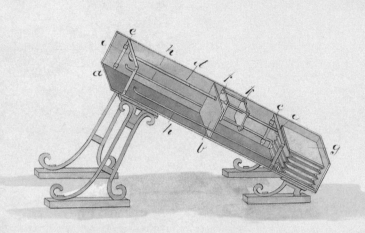

The Purpose of Utility arising from the Shape or Configuration of the new Parts of this design consists in Propelling the Performer to a required distance without injury to his Person

The Drawing is illustrative of the same; "A" is the receptacle or case (the one side and upper Portion of which is removed for a clearer explanation) into which the Performer is placed, with his or her feet resting against the Platform or Stand "b", "c.c." are two brackets answering the double Purpose of bracing the sides of the recep-table but chiefly for sustaining the guide rod "d", permanently affixed at the Parts marked "e.e." "f.f." are guide plates connected together by ruts and bolts and traverses the guide rod "d", freely in either desired direction carrying with it to and fro the Platform "b". "g" indicates a pair of bellows to which is connected the pipes "h. h." while at the aperture of the said Pipes is arranged a jet of gas (not thereon) so that when the bellows "g" are operated a Scenic effect is Produced without combustibles of an explosive nature

Protection is sought for the Shape or Configuration of those Parts coloured red and marked "c.c." "d". "f.f." "g". "h.h." which are — original or new the remainder is old.

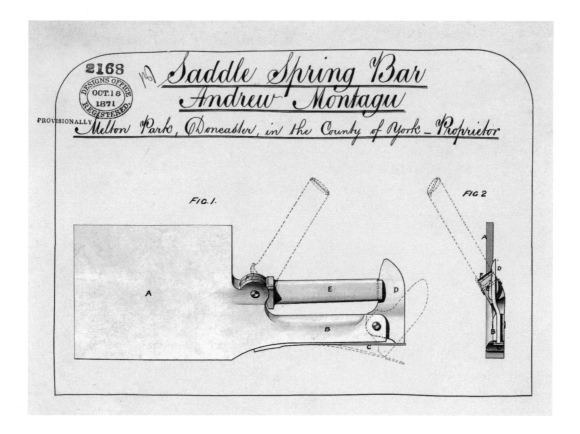

ABOVE

SADDLE SPRING BAR*

1871

Figs. 1. & 2. side and end view

Above the bar (B) there is another bar (E) from which the stirrup leather is suspended which has a hinge joint (F) formed at its forward or front end connecting it to the metal plate (A). The purpose is to instantly release a horseman when thrown with his foot entangled in one of the stirrups.

OPPOSITE

"AN APPARATUS" FOR GYMNASTIC PERFORMANCES*

1879

For propelling the performer to a required distance without injury to his person — (g) indicates a pair of bellows to which is connected the pipes (hh), while at the aperture of the said pipes is arranged a jet of gas so that when the bellows are operated a scenic effect is produced.

OVERLEAF LEFT ABOVE

DESIGN FOR A VALVE PERFECTING SPRING SLIDE FOR CORNETS &c.

1847

Fig. 1. front view • Fig. 2. section of the novel parts

The object is to give to the performer of Cornets or other valve instruments the power to sharpen or flatten any one or a given number of notes in the Scale with facility while playing on such instrument.

OVERLEAF LEFT BELOW

DESIGN FOR A SAX-HORN (A MUSICAL WIND INSTRUMENT)

1845

Fig. 1. side elevation • Fig. 2. plan view of some parts Fig. 3. partial sectional elevation • Fig. 4. detached view of a mouthpiece

The wind has a free passage through the instrument without the obstruction of sudden angles as in other wind instruments.

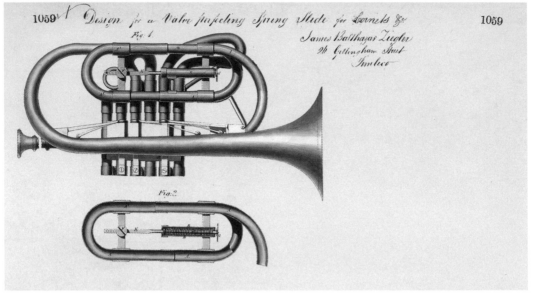

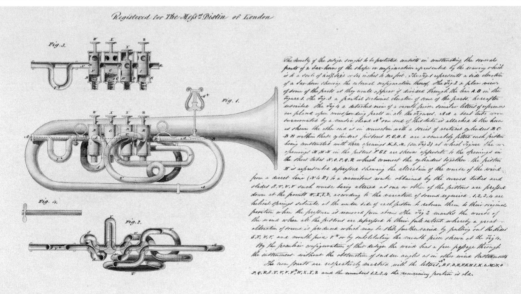

OPPOSITE

DESIGN FOR A SOLOCORNU

1855

Fig. 1. side view • Fig. 2. top view of the same

A reference to the diagram will shew the peculiar configuration of graduated bore which we propose to adopt. By the adoption of this form of tube we are enabled to ensure a rich, sonorous and brilliant quality of tone.

OVERLEAF

PLAN OF THE NEWLY INVENTED GEOMETRICAL KEY BOARD FOR THE PIANOFORTE

1845

In the Geometric Key Board the distance between all the short keys is exactly the same which must give a greater regularity in the Fingering and render the Instrument much more easy to learn and will enable many persons with a small hand to reach an octave which they are unable now to do.

Design for a Solocornu

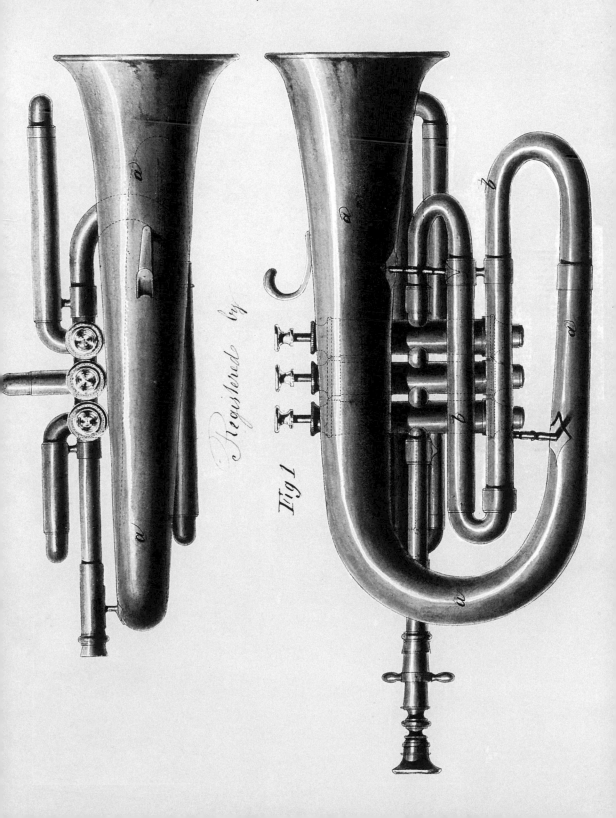

Registered by

Fig 1

448 —— *Explanation.* ——

The difference between the Geometric Key Board newly invented by Miguel Theodore De Folly and the old Key Board as commonly used is as may be seen by the Drawings from the regularity of distance between the Short Keys. In the old Key Board the distance between D (1) and F sharp (2) is not the same as between F (3) and G sharp (4) the same distance occurs between A sharp (5) and C sharp (6) which is not the same as between C sharp (7) and D sharp (8) consequently produces a great complication of

PLAN
OF THE
NEWLY INVENTED
GEOMETRICAL KEY
FOR THE
PIANOFORTE

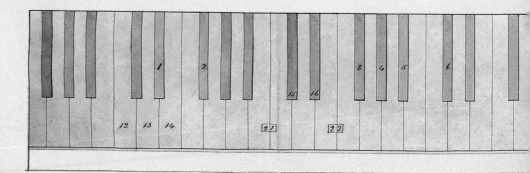

PROPOSED NEW ARRANGEMEN

SCALE OF

KEYBOARD AS USUALLY

...s and renders the Instrument most difficult to learn — In the Geometric Key Board the distance between all ...s is exactly the same See Drawing/which must give a greater regularity in the Fingerings and render the ...t much more easy to learn — It will be necessary to state that by the system upon which my Key Board (See Drawing) the notes C (9) D (10) and E (11) are played upon the short Keys whilst on the Old Key Board the same ...played upon the long Keys, 12, 13, and 14 / — The reverse occurs with C sharp (15) and D sharp (16) which on the

ARD ...Old Key Board are played on the short Keys, but on my New Key Board are played on the long ...Keys (19) and (20) — Another difference between the old and New Key Board is, that on the old one ...t of one octave say from A to A (12 Keys) two long Keys are twice joined together (21 and 22) whilst on the New ...the long and short Keys are always alternate — Another difference is that the old Key Board has in the ...n octave 7 long white Keys and 5 short Black ones but in my New Key Board there are in the extent of each

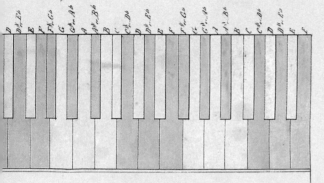

KEYBOARD

⎯⎯ INCHES

✳ Octave 3 short white Keys and 3 short Black ones as 3 long white Keys and 3 long Black ones which difference makes the octave shorter to the hand and will enable many persons with a small hand to reach an octave which they are unable now to do and any ordinary hand may be enabled to reach and play to the extent of tenths which cannot now be done —

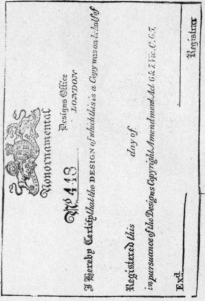

Nonornamental

Designs Office
LONDON

№ 448

I Hereby Certify that the DESIGN of which this is a Copy was on behalf of

Registered this   day of

in pursuance of the Designs Copyright Amendment Act 6 & 7 Vic. C. 65.

Registrar

Exd.

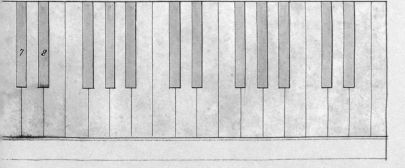

7   8

ANGED

Miguel Theodore De'Folly.
of 29 Harrington Street Hampstead Road
and 8 Lowther Arcade Strand — Musician.

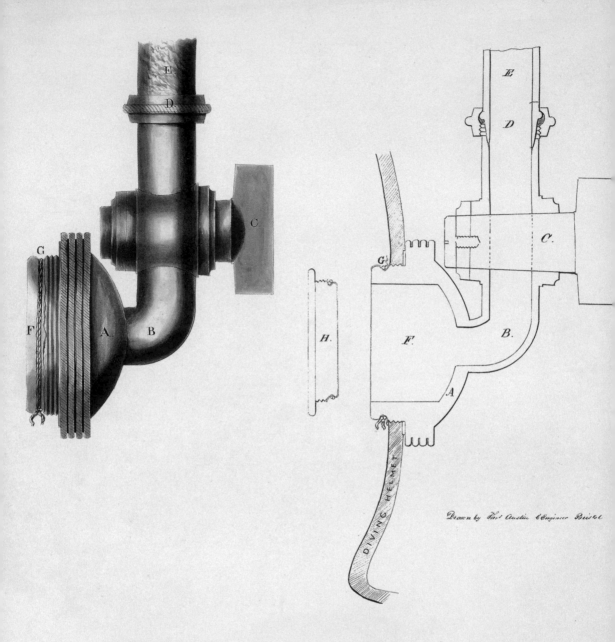

Drawn by Thos Austin C Engineer Bristol

SUBMARINE COMMUNICATOR

Designed by John Moore Hyde Optition & instrument maker of Bristol

This drawing represents the communicator as attached to the diving helmet opposite the ear of the diver: it consists of a chamber of metal (brass) marked a, a tube b, stop cock c, a union joint d, to which the flexible pipe e, is screwed: over the opening of the chamber at f a piece of membrane is streched and fastened round the groove g. (for instance) like a piece of bladder tied over the mouth of a bottle; or it may be screwed into the chamber by means of the cell H: the use of which membrane being to transmit the voice; the stop cock is used in the event of the membrane being injured to prevent the escape of the air from the helmet; This communicator is also applicable to the diving bell.

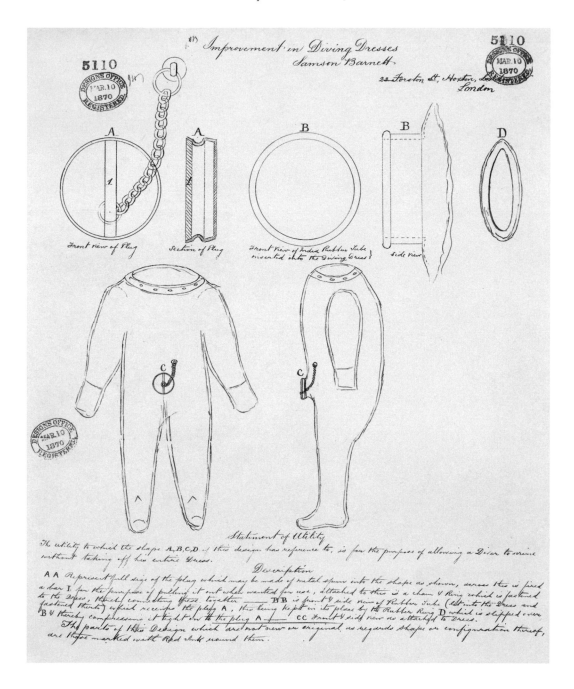

OPPOSITE

SUBMARINE COMMUNICATOR

1847

A chamber of metal, a tube, stop cock, a union joint,
to which the flexible sheathing pipe is screwed: over the
opening a piece of membrane is stretched and fastened;
the use of which membrane being to transmit the voice.

ABOVE

IMPROVEMENT IN DIVING DRESSES

1870

An India Rubber Tube inserted into the Diving Dress,
being kept in its place by the Rubber Ring. The utility
is for the purpose of allowing a Diver to urinate without
taking off his entire Dress.

**DESIGN FOR DALLMAN'S PATENT INVISIBLE SPRING
HUNTING EYE GLASS & SPECTACLES**

1842

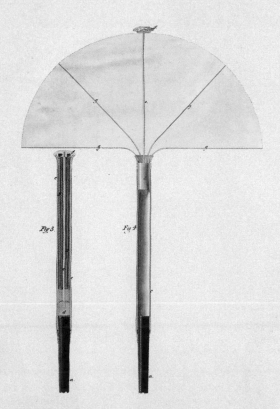

DESIGN FOR A FAN RIDING WHIP

1850

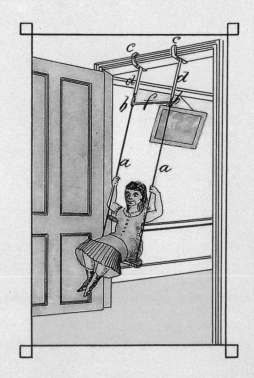

DESIGN FOR THE LONDON SWING*

1880

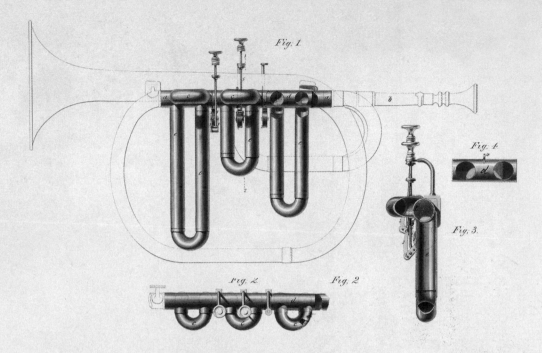

**DESIGN FOR ROLLING VALVE
BRASS INSTRUMENTS**

1848

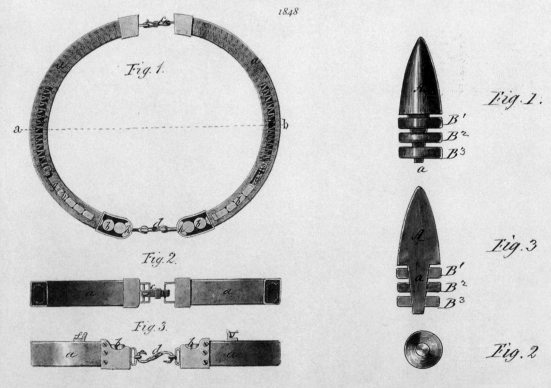

DESIGN FOR A CARTRIDGE BELT

1847

LIGHTWEIGHT RIFLE BALL

1852

DESIGN FOR A FIRE ESCAPE

1845

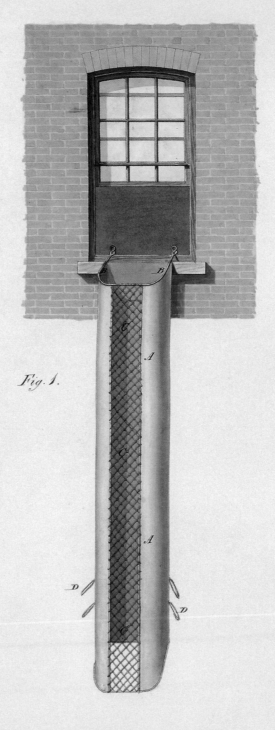

Fig. 1.

*An apparatus or machine by the assistance of which life may be saved
and represents the same as placed against the window of a house.*

SAFETY & SECURITY

"WARRANTED TO WITHSTAND THE GRIP OF THE MOST MUSCULAR RUFFIAN IN THE METROPOLIS"

◆ ◆ ◆

Advertisement for the Antigarrotte Collar,
by White, Choker & Co.

Punch

1856

ontemporary newspapers and journals reveal how the middle classes in the nineteenth century worried about their safety and security. This included a fear of crime, fire, drowning and of accidents in the home – which became more common as a result of new technologies. Many of the hazards they worried about were exacerbated by urban living, and many were scares created in part by the press as it competed for sales. Real or imagined, these problems presented inventors with opportunities to think up new and imaginative – although sometimes less than effective – solutions.

In the early nineteenth century England was policed lightly, mainly by the traditional system of the parish constable. There was widespread opposition to the idea of a paid police force which, it was feared, would be open to corruption and would threaten the liberties of the English people. By the early twentieth century, England had paid, uniformed police forces for every county and

borough.[1] This change in attitude was triggered in part by a series of panics around crime that occurred at intervals throughout the nineteenth century. The expanding middle classes in particular felt the need for greater protection from what they perceived as criminal elements in their midst.

Two 'garotting panics' occurred in 1856 and 1862. Fanned by constant press reports about attacks, fears were also exacerbated by 'ticket-of-leave men' – men who had returned from the colonies with a conditional pardon as the system of transporting criminals drew to an end. Their presence felt threatening, and was associated with a perceived increase in crime. 'Garotting' at that period meant the partial strangulation of a victim in order to incapacitate them and allow a robbery, although unsurprisingly it was not unknown for victims to be killed. Later in the century it came to mean what we would now call mugging. A letter writer to *The Times* in 1856 laments: 'There is not a town in the kingdom in which these [ticket-of-leave] men are known to be the inhabitants of which are not kept in a state of fear; if we go out after dark we are in dread of garotting, or if we remain at home we are not safe from housebreaking.'[2]

Gradually the fear died down, only to be triggered again in 1862 by the near-strangulation and robbery of Hugh Pilkington, MP for Blackburn, in July of that year. A celebrity victim ensured that the subject began to be reported again by the press, fuelling a further panic. The number of attacks was greatest in the north of England, especially in Manchester and Liverpool, although the press tended to focus on attacks in London – perhaps because that was where there seemed to be the greatest number of middle-class victims. The *Daily News* believed London to be: 'a battlefield of raging cabmen by day and a lair of assassins and footpads by night'.[3]

There was much discussion in the middle-class press about the need for self-protection, and

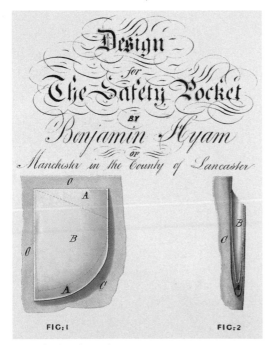

Design for the Safety Pocket, 1851

adversity fuelled invention. The fear of garotting and robbery led to a number of devices designed to protect the wearer and his property (women would not usually be walking around alone, especially after dark). These included the '"Antipickpocket" or Pocket Protector' and the 'Safety Pocket' (see pp. 212 and 192). One wonders how many lives were saved by the 'Anti-Garotting Cravat' (see p. 213).

Stories of intruders and worse still, murder by a stranger, created both terror and enjoyment. Fear and fascination were fuelled by torrid reporting of gruesome crimes in the press and in 'broadsheets' – cheap single-sheet publications which reported the latest crimes and scandals. There was frequently little or no concern for accuracy, and suspects were named and often effectively tried within their pages. People of all classes were transfixed by these stories of crimes, legal proceedings, convictions and executions. They could also view the crime scenes. Bodies were left *in situ* until an inquest, during which time visitors could take a day trip to see the reality for themselves. In 1842 Jane Jones, a London laundress, was murdered in a stable. Her body had been dismembered and she was disembowelled. Prior to the inquest, her body was on view to the public – *The Times* reported that 'very properly', the police were only allowing entry to 'the principal inhabitants of the neighbourhood'. Four days later, 'vehicles of every description, from the aristocratic carriage to the costermonger's cart' were permitted to enter, and the scene had become 'a disgusting exhibition'.[4]

A further panic surrounded murder by poisoning, especially the use of arsenic, which was contained in many household products. Again, fears were fuelled by extensive reporting of horrific cases in the press. In the 1860s *Punch* joked about a new publication to be called *The Sensation Times*. It would be devoted to 'Harrowing the Mind, Making the Flesh Creep, Causing the Hair to Stand on End…and generally Unfitting the

"THE FIREMEN WERE ON THE ROOFS OF HOUSES, HANDSOME AS GREEK HEROES, AND IT REALLY DID LOOK AS IF THEY WERE ENGAGED IN SLAYING AN ENORMOUS DRAGON."

GEORGE MEREDITH, *THE ADVENTURES OF HARRY RICHMOND,* 1871

Public for the Prosaic Avocations of Life…Murder, of course will have in these columns the foremost place…Arsenical Literature will find in these columns its best exponent, and all Poison Cases will be watched by a staff of special reporters who have been medically educated…'[5]

Once a trial – and if the press was lucky an execution – were over these stories were often translated almost immediately into other forms of entertainment, such as theatre productions, exhibitions, and 'sensation novels'. Madame Tussaud's would put on displays of the scenes

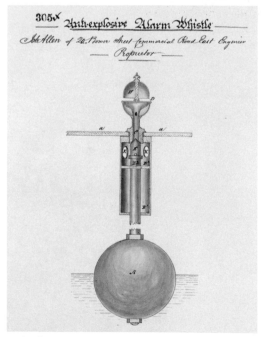

Design for an Anti-explosive Alarm Whistle, 1844

of crime, often buying household objects and even items of clothing that had belonged to the victims, and creating waxworks of those involved. Not surprisingly, these crimes, so widely publicized thanks to new technology (which allowed broadsheets and newspapers to be published more quickly and cheaply than ever before) created a market for items to make the home secure. This is reflected in the designs registered for copyright: there are alarms, padlocks, the 'Anti-explosive Alarm Whistle', and the rather Draconian-sounding 'Alarm Gun' (see pp. 193 and 203).

Another danger was death by drowning. The high number of drownings in Britain during this period is reflected in the registered designs, which include a number of different 'life preservers'. In the middle of the nineteenth century only about one in ten of those who made their living on the sea were able to swim[6] – this figure would have been much lower among the general population. In 1878 3,659 people drowned accidentally in England and Wales and 369 committed suicide by drowning. By the mid to late nineteenth century there was growing concern about these figures, which seemed to indicate a large-scale problem.[7] There appears to have been a certain embarrassment about the

wish to take safety precautions on the water. Often 'life preservers' were disguised as ordinary items of clothing, such as braces or waistcoats; perhaps it was considered 'unmanly' to be concerned about safety, or even to be unable to swim. However, this does not seem to have worried the wearer of the 'Apparatus for Saving Lives from Drowning' (see p. 199).

With the advent of railways and the consequent growth in the popularity of trips to the seaside (see chapters IV and VI), sea-bathing became increasingly popular. However, this did not usually entail swimming, but instead submersion or soaking in seawater, which was thought to have health benefits. Bathing machines – wheeled huts pulled by horses, which carried their occupants into the sea – not only protected the modesty of bathers by shielding them from view until they were in the water, but allowed them to immerse themselves in deep water without needing to swim out.[8]

As early as 1776, when the Royal Humane Society was established, attempts had been made to reduce the number of deaths by drowning. The Society was dedicated, among other things, to the resuscitation of the apparently drowned. However, the person with resuscitation skills would not necessarily be able to swim: instead they would be stationed near areas of water in case of accident, when the bodies of those apparently drowned would be brought to land by boat.[9]

It was not until the last quarter of the century that the importance of teaching children to swim, and of teaching life-saving techniques, began to be widely recognized. This was in large part thanks to William Henry, a champion swimmer with a particular interest in life-saving. He and another influential amateur swimmer, Archibald Sinclair, became the first joint secretaries of the Life Saving Society (now Royal Life Saving Society UK) in 1891. Its handbook stated the

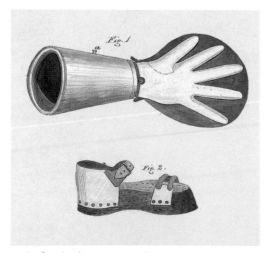

Design for swimming apparatuses, 1845

Design for Lee's Marine Life Preserver, 1844

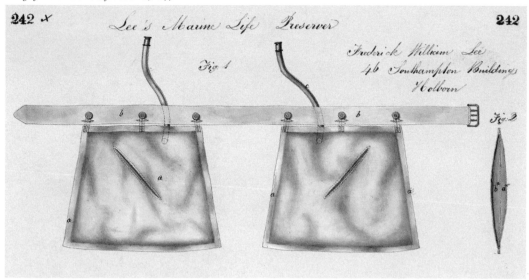

Society's ambitious goal: to teach every young person in the United Kingdom how to swim and how to save life. By the end of the nineteenth century the teaching of swimming and life-saving techniques had become widespread; 2,058 people across the country had passed at least one of the Society's proficiency tests by the end of 1898.[10]

Fires, firefighting equipment and firefighting techniques inspired a mixture of dread and fascination throughout the nineteenth century. The public were engaged with fires either as enthralled spectators of the real thing, as unfortunate victims, by reading the torrid accounts of fires in the press, or by attending the many simulations of fire dramas in plays, panoramas and dioramas.[11] When the Houses of Parliament burned down on 16 October 1834, a panorama of the fire was opened to the public a week later, and within two months of the fire the Cosmorama Rooms in Regent Street, London, showed a diorama of a 'Grand Tableaux, of the Interiors of the Lords & Commons, As They Appeared Previous to Their Destruction by Fire…And a Splendid Representation of the Conflagration with Dioramic & Mechanical Effect.'[12]

By the nineteenth century disastrous fires involving large numbers of buildings had greatly reduced. This was largely because of the use of brick and tiles in building rather than timber and thatch. However, the number of catastrophic fires in single buildings increased. The growth of cities, the increase in size of commercial buildings and places of entertainment, including factories, warehouses, tenements and theatres, meant that individual fires could cause greater loss of life and property. Fires in the home were also common, thanks to the use of gas and oil lamps and new technologies such as boilers for heating water.

Whereas public opinion about policemen was ambiguous (their motives and respectability were often considered suspect), the fireman became a heroic figure in the public imagination. Men of all social classes formed volunteer fire brigades – even the Prince of Wales, the future Edward VII, kept a fireman's uniform at Charing Cross Fire Station so that he could attend any major fires in London. By the end of the century the fireman had become something of a cult figure, celebrated throughout the arts, high and low. He was the epitome of idealized manhood so worshipped

Useful Design for a Family Fire Escape, 1855

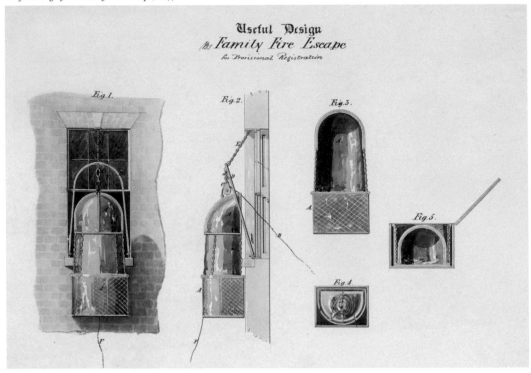

in the Victorian period. By contrast, when a group of women at Girton College, Cambridge, formed a volunteer fire brigade, soon followed by other college women, their efforts were greeted by hostility in the press. This was largely on the grounds of immodesty. The *New York Times* pronounced: 'That the firegirls should actually ascend the ladders in full gaze of the public, and while the fierce light of fire plays about their ankles, is of course, unthinkable.'[13]

The new household technologies that were becoming increasingly popular in middle-class homes were a common cause of house fires. Kitchen ranges, when they were first introduced in the early part of the century, could sometimes explode, as could geysers, or small boilers, installed in bathrooms to heat the water just before it was used.[14] Oil and gas lamps, stoves, and boilers were all fire hazards, and hearth and chimney fires were common. The fireplace was a symbol

of Victorian domestic life – of 'hearth and home' – and much of family life would revolve around it. Unfortunately, it could also be a cause of household accidents.

In the period when crinolines were fashionable dress – at the height of their popularity they could be six feet in diameter – there were many reports in the newspapers of horrific deaths caused by women's dresses catching fire as they moved too close to hearths or stoves. The crinoline would cause the fire to engulf the woman in flames, and other women, also wearing crinolines, would be unable to come to the rescue. A report in *The Times* of an inquest in 1862 records how Anna Maria Grant was killed after her dress caught fire. She tried to cut off her clothes before raising the alarm, but her friends when they arrived were unable to help her. In summarizing the evidence the coroner observed that 'he did not like to be making crinolines a constant theme at inquests, but there could be no doubt…that fatal accidents arising from a similar cause were a frequent occurrence….He hoped the large number of dreadful deaths of which it was the cause would induce the ladies to give it up.'[15]

These fire risks help to explain the large number of inventions, which would mainly have been aimed at middle-class consumers, designed to enable the owner to escape from a burning building. These range from the discreet ('portable apparatus with self-acting friction band, spring, or grip, for escape from elevated places in cases of fire'), to the hair-raising ('Design for a Fire-Escape') (see pp. 198, 200–201).

A massive fire in London's Tooley Street in 1861 led to new legislation governing the fire services and the adoption of strict commercial building regulations. The fire, at Cottons Wharf, where many warehouses were located, was thought to be the greatest since the Great Fire of London in 1666. Smoke was discovered at a warehouse storing hemp and jute, and the fire spread quickly to surrounding buildings. The blaze lasted for fourteen days, and its victims included James Braidwood, the Superintendent of the London Fire Engine Establishment. This organization had been established in 1833 by a group of ten insurance companies. People from all over London came to view the fire. With more than 30,000 spectators, sellers of drinks and cheap refreshments did a roaring trade, and public houses stayed open.[16]

In 1862, the insurance companies wrote to the Home Secretary stating that they could no longer be responsible for the fire safety of London. The Metropolitan Fire Brigade Act was passed in 1865 establishing the Metropolitan Fire Brigade as a public service. Across the United Kingdom hundreds of professional and volunteer fire brigades continued to operate separately until 1938, when legislation centralized control of fire services in Great Britain and required local authorities to provide an effective fire service.

Industrialization, urban living and a greater range of activities both in leisure time and at work brought with them dangers and challenges. It is sometimes hard to tell from this distance which were real and which were imagined, but nineteenth-century inventors, both the spectacularly successful and the spectacularly hopeful, were quick to come up with ways to help make life feel safer.

[1] David Taylor, *The New Police in Nineteenth-Century England*, Manchester: Manchester University Press, 1997, p. 1.

[2] *The Times*, 30 October 1856, p. 5.

[3] Quoted in R. Sindall, 'The London garotting panics of 1856 and 1862', *Social History* 12(3), p. 355.

[4] Judith Flanders, *The Invention of Murder*, London: HarperPress, 2011, pp. 141–43.

[5] Flanders, *ibid.*, p. 247.

[6] Matthew Sweet, *Inventing the Victorians*, London: Faber and Faber, 2001, p. 119.

[7] Christopher Love (ed.), *A Social History of Swimming in England, 1800–1918: Splashing in the Serpentine*, London: Routledge, 2007, p. 103.

[8] Sweet, *op. cit.*, p. 119.

[9] Love, *op. cit.*, p. 100.

[10] Love, *op. cit.*, p. 107.

[11] Robyn Cooper, 'The fireman: Immaculate manhood', *The Journal of Popular Culture*, 28(4), p. 139.

[12] Judith Flanders, *Consuming Passions: Leisure and Pleasure in Victorian England*, London, New York, Toronto and Sydney: Harper Perennial, 2006, pp. 267–68.

[13] Cooper, *op. cit.*, p. 149.

[14] Judith Flanders, *Inside the Victorian Home*, London and New York: W. W. Norton & Company, 2003, p. 326.

[15] *The Times*, 31 December 1862, p. 4.

[16] http://www.london-fire.gov.uk/ AnniversaryTooleyStreetFire.asp. (last accessed 27/05/2014).

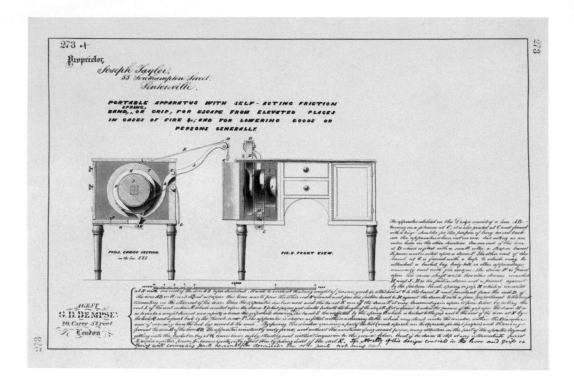

ABOVE

PORTABLE APPARATUS WITH SELF-ACTING FRICTION BAND, SPRING, OR GRIP, FOR ESCAPE FROM ELEVATED PLACES IN CASES OF FIRE &c; AND FOR LOWERING GOODS OR PERSONS GENERALLY

1844

Fig. 1. cross-section ◆ *Fig. 2.* front view

The apparatus consists of a lever (AB) turning on a fulcrum at (C) over one end of this lever at (D) which is fitted with a small roller, a strap or band (E) passes and is coiled upon a drum (F). The other end of the band at (G) is formed with a loop to which may be attached a basket, bag, body-belt or other appendage commonly used with fire-escape. By opening the window and throwing forward the arm (A) of the lever (AB), the apparatus is instantly ready for use. The operator getting the basket or bag at (G), lowers himself safely, readily and without concussion to the ground below.

OPPOSITE

APPARATUS FOR SAVING LIVES FROM DROWNING

1850

Fig. 1. a man attired with the apparatus complete, (a) is a float formed of the Globular shape, concave on the under side shewn in *Figs. 2. & 3.* ◆ *Fig. 4.* consists of two floatable converse oblong buoys ◆ *Fig. 5.* plaited rope and buoys

The purpose of utility is that it is more easily fitted to the Body of a Man, and enables him to support himself and others in the Water, with greater facility than by the usual formed floats.

OVERLEAF

DESIGN FOR A FIRE-ESCAPE

1843

Fig. 1. apparatus expanded or ready for use ◆ *Fig. 2.* the compact and portable form of the apparatus when closed

(a,a) the Framework to which is attached the sail-cloth or other suitable material (b,b) for persons to jump on, the springs (c,c) being for the purpose of breaking the shock.

Apparatus for Saving Lives from Drowning

2603

DESIGNS OFFICE
DEC. 28
1850
REGISTERED

The Invention of John Keyse, Proprietor thereof, residing at No. 10 Cross Street, Newington Butts, Surrey.

72

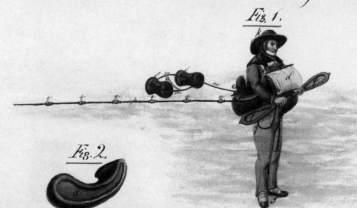

Fig. 1.

Fig. 2.

Fig. 3.

Fig. 1. Represents a Man attired with the Apparatus Complete. a. is a float formed of a Globular shape, concave in the under side shewn in Fig. 2. b.b. shape to support apparatus. a. &&. ropes to apparatus to support persons. d. sail with yards. e. belt to support. d, and f. by means of a line passing inside a. f. hand paddle, with blades dished on both sides. g. line to secure hand paddle to e. h. ends of line for securing a. f. clogs dished on the under side shewn at Fig 3. k. a shield, cap and cape secured by straps under the chin.

Fig. 4.

Fig. 4. letter c. consists of two floatable convex oblong buoys, formed of the shape shewn, secured by ropes n. see Fig. 1. n. rope to apparatus for supporting persons. O. seat belt.

Fig. 5.

Fig. 5. h. plaited rope and buoys. q. secured and also secured to Fig. 1.

The parts of this Design which are not new, are coloured light Brown.

The purpose of Utility is that it is more easily fitted to the Body of a Man, and enables him to support himself and others in the Water with greater facility than by the usual formed floats.

The whole of the above parts are necessary to constitute a Single design.

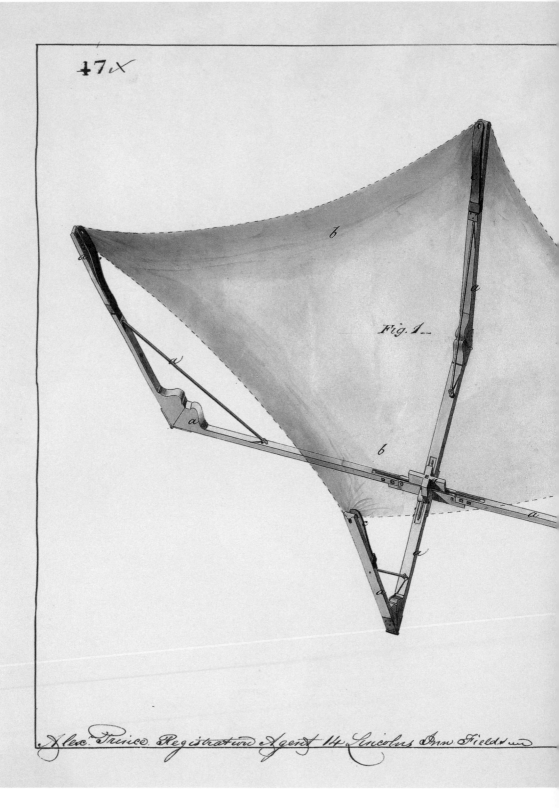

47 X

Fig. 1.

DESIGN for a FIRE-ESCAPE

Registered for Joseph Taylor.
of 55 Southampton Street
Pentonville

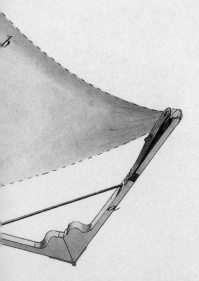

Fig. 2.

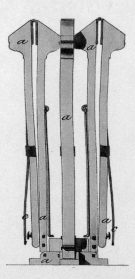

In the annexed Drawing Fig.1 represents the apparatus expanded
or ready for use — a.a the framework to which is attached the sail-cloth a other
suitable material b.b for persons to jump on. the springs c.c being for the
purpose of breaking the shock caused thereby. Fig. 2. shews the compact and
portable form of the apparatus when closed up (the sail-cloth being removed)
The design sought to be protected is represented by the entire Drawing

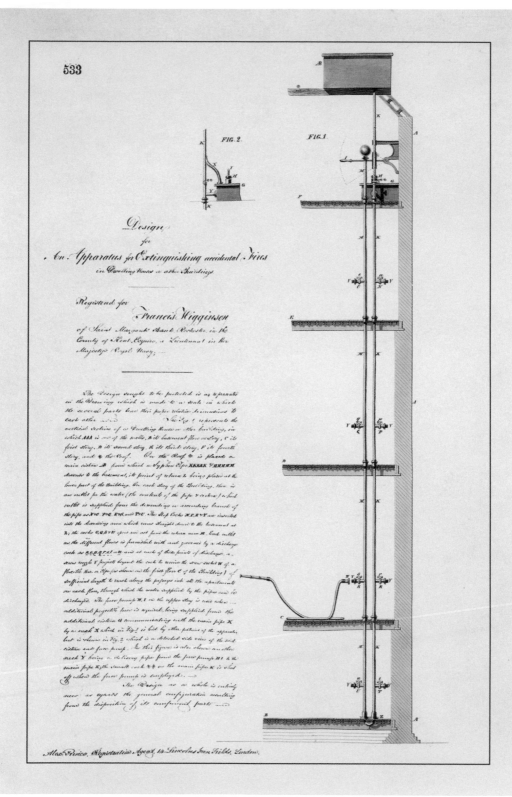

OPPOSITE

AN APPARATUS FOR EXTINGUISHING ACCIDENTAL FIRES IN DWELLING HOUSES OR OTHER BUILDINGS

1845

Fig. 1. the vertical sections of a Dwelling House or other building, in which (A) is one of the walls, (B) its basement floor or story, (C) its first story and (*) the Roof • *Fig. 2.* close-up view

On the Roof is placed a main cistern (AB) from which a Syphon Pipe (K) & (M) descends to the basement. On each story of the Building, there is an outlet for the water by a flexible Hose or Pipe (as shewn in the first floor (C) of the Building) of sufficient length to reach along the passages into all the apartments of each floor, through which the water supplied by the pipes can be discharged.

BELOW

IMPROVED ALARM GUN

1850

Fig. 1. alarm gun with one end left open • *Fig. 2.* sketch exhibiting the manner of its application

(AA) *is the body of the gun which consists of a rectangular block of solid metal in which there are bored six holes or barrels* (BB) *intended to be charged with gun-powder and the channel* (C) *with a slow burning composition or fuse by which the powder is to be fired. When the string is pressed, it draws the small weight* (O) *up to the eye-pin and then the large one* (M) *off its pin by which its fall withdraws the prop* (E), *lets the trigger* (D) *free and fires the gun.*

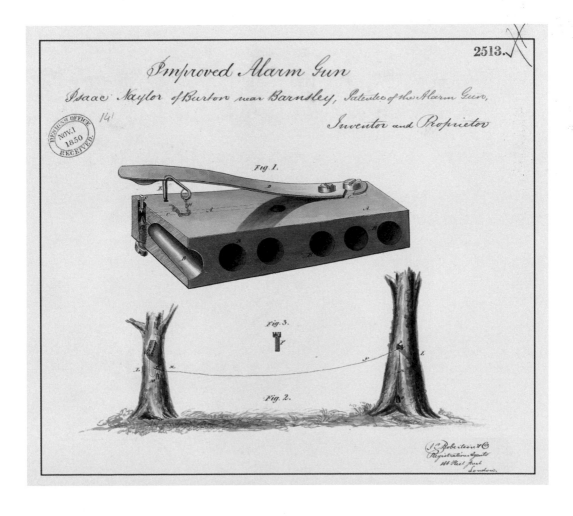

2649.

JAN.27
1851

124

Design for a Stink Trap.

FIG. 1.

FIG. 2.

ABOVE

DESIGN FOR A STINK TRAP

1851

Fig. 1. transverse section • *Fig. 2.* longitudinal section

(aa) *represents the outside casing of the Stink Trap,*
furnished with the ribs (b) *and* (c) *forming the Syphon*
(d) *is an inclined partition reaching the top of the grate*
(e), *which latter is attached to the Stink Trap by a*
chain (f). *When it is requisite to remove the impurities*
collected in the Stink Trap the grate (e) *is raised and*
placed over the Syphon, the operator is then enabled,
by means of a suitable implement, to scoop the impurities
up the inclined partition (d), *to the level of the road.*

OPPOSITE ABOVE

DESIGN FOR AN IMPROVED VERMIN TRAP

1863

Fig. 1. vertical section • *Fig. 2.* top plan view (with
the cover removed) • *Fig. 3.* perspective elevation

(A) *is an opening for admitting the Vermin.* (B) *is a*
T shaped platform turning on a fulcrum at (b). (C) *is*
a horizontal partition with two openings (c,c) *covered by*
hinged retaining gratings, (d,d). *The receptacles* (e,e)
and (f,f) *are for holding inaccessible baits.*

OPPOSITE BELLOW

DESIGN FOR A PERPETUAL MOUSE-TRAP

1866

(A) *is one of the two entrances for mice.* (BB) *is a*
tilting gang-way or platform inducing the mice through
the wire drop grate (C) *to the receiving chamber* (D).
Within the glass covered receptacles (E,G) *are placed*
baits which are inaccessible to the mice. The Purpose is
the continuous catching of mice, without resetting traps.

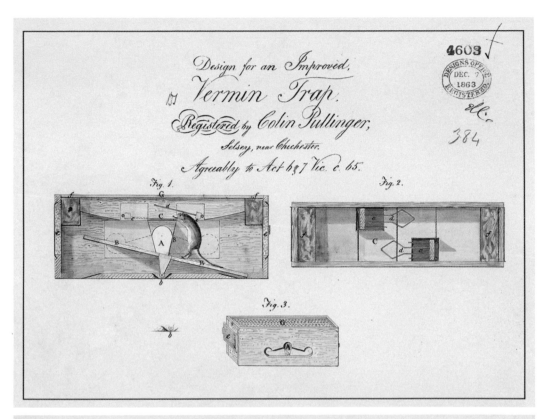

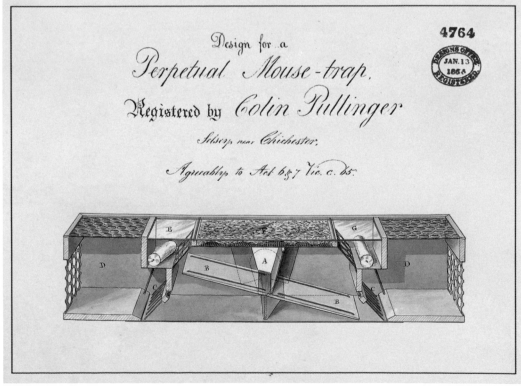

BELOW

A TELL-TALE KEYLESS PADLOCK

1878

Fig. 1. padlock with cover closed • *Fig. 2.* padlock with cover removed • *Fig. 3.* back part of the padlock with spring chamber • *Fig. 4.* transverse section

The parts (A) and (B) are spring jointed. In part (B) there is a slot through and into which a card or paper or any thin substance can be placed covering and concealing the spring. To actuate the spring to release (A) from (B) the card or other interposing medium must be broken shewing that the instrument has been tampered with. The purpose is by avoidance of use of keys to secure enclosures of goods from observation or theft, except with obvious and certain discovery.

OPPOSITE

DESIGN FOR A PICK PREVENTION KEY

1852

Fig. 1. an elevation • *Fig. 2.* side view • *Fig. 3.* side view, shewing the action of the 'pick preventives' after the handle of the key has been removed • *Fig. 4.* end view with the preventives closed • *Fig. 5.* end view with the preventives open

An effective way of preventing the introduction of picking apparatus is by filling the aperture at which the instruments must necessarily be introduced, and this is effected by the Design which fills up the principal aperture, and also provides effective spring catches to prevent removal of the impediments.

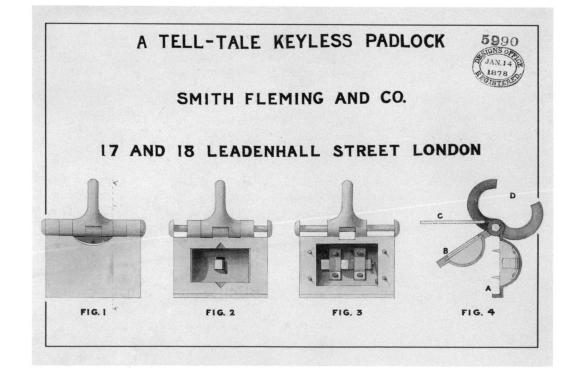

Nº 440

DESIGNS OFFICE
JULY. 1
1852
REGISTERED
PROVISIONALLY

DESIGN
for
a Pick prevention Key

Provisionally Registered for Joseph Schloss 18 Friday Street Cheapside London

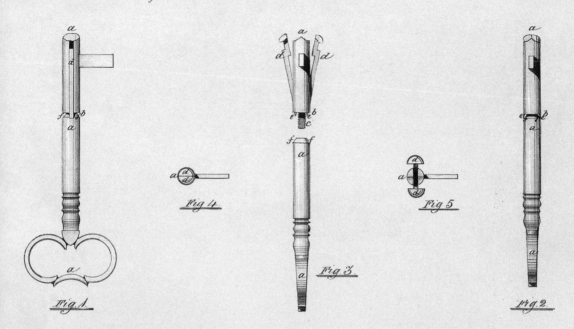

Fig 4

Fig 3

Fig 5

Fig 1.

Fig 2.

Description

The Drawing represents five views of the Design drawn to a Geometrical scale. Figure 1 being an elevation. Figure 2 a side view. Figure 3 also a side view, shewing the action of the "pick preventives" after the handle of the key has been removed. Figure 4 an end view with the preventives closed, and Figure 5 an end view with the preventives open, in all of which similar letters denote similar parts a. a. a, the key divided into two portions at b, the screw c admitting of the two being screwed up into the position shewn in Figures 1 and 2. The lock end is furnished with two longitudinal levers d. d. which are kept apart as shewn in Figure 3, by means of small springs, when the handle is taken off. The extremities e. e. of these levers are formed into small points, and are acted upon by the obliquity of the wedge end section of the end f. f. of the handle which terminates in the frustrum of a cone of about 45 degrees. When the handle is screwed on the sides of the frustrum f. f. pressing obliquely against the inner sides of the parts e. e. gradually closes them, as shewn in Figures 2 and 4. An effective way of preventing the introduction of picking apparatus, is by filling the aperture at which the instruments must necessarily be introduced, and this is effected by the Design which fills up the principal aperture, and also provides effective spring catches to prevent the removal of the impediments.

The Utility of the shape and configuration of this Design consists in the security afforded against the picking of the simplest Lock.

Claim is made for the shape and configuration of the parts marked b, c, d, e, f. The remainder is Old.

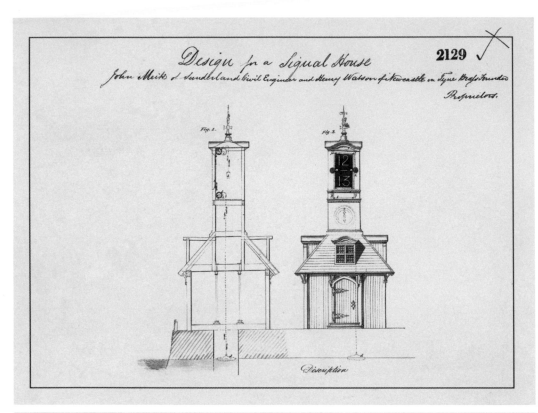

Design for a Signal House

John Meik of Sunderland Civil Engineer and Henry Watson of Newcastle in Tyne Brass Founder

Proprietors.

2129

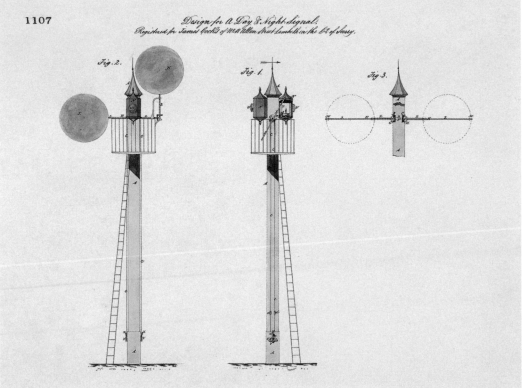

1107

Design for A Day & Night Signal:

Registered for James Cook of Wm Allen Street Lambeth in the C^{ty} of Surry.

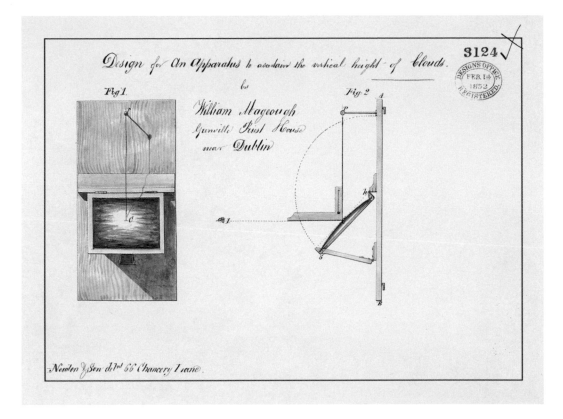

OPPOSITE ABOVE

DESIGN FOR A SIGNAL HOUSE

1849

Fig. 1. section • *Fig. 2.* elevation of the same

When the float (d) *rises with the tide the balance weight*
(h) *moves the whole apparatus in the direction of the*
arrows coloured blue, and when the float falls with the
ebb of the tide the movements are indicated by the arrows
coloured red. The utility is more useful figures for tide
gauges or indicators for ships entering or leaving harbour.

OPPOSITE BELOW

DESIGN FOR A DAY AND NIGHT SIGNAL

1847

Fig. 1. side elevation • *Fig. 2.* front elevation
Fig. 3. transverse and vertical section of certain parts

(T) *marks a reflector fixed to the plate* (Q) *in this*
reflector there are fixed three colored glasses, one or
other of which may be brought opposite to the bull's eye.

ABOVE

DESIGN FOR AN APPARATUS TO ASCERTAIN THE VERTICAL HEIGHT OF CLOUDS

1852

Fig. 1. front elevation • *Fig. 2.* transverse vertical
section

(AB) *is a thick board provided with means of being*
fastened in a truly vertical position to a wall or post:
(C) *is a convex mirror of black glass framed and*
attached to the board (AB) *by means of a hinge at* (h).
(P) *is a pin which is perpendicular to the surface of the*
board. In the head of the pin a hole is made in a direction
parallel to the board and consequently perpendicular to
the horizon. This Design is for an apparatus to be used
in making meteorological observations, and whereby
the vertical distance of clouds from the earth may be
ascertained with tolerable accuracy.

DESIGN FOR A LIFE RAFT

Registered for Walter Raymond

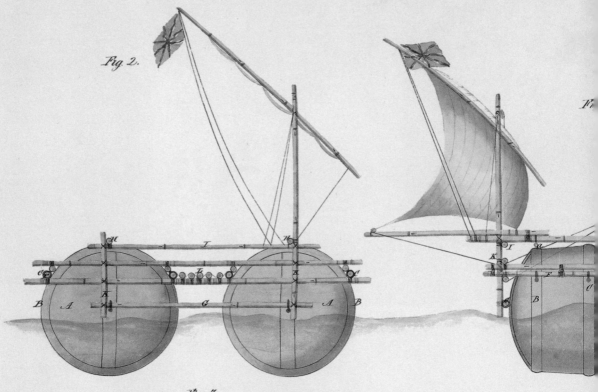

Fig. 2.

Fig. 3.

The drawing exhibits several views of the
appear when in use. Fig. 2 an end view the
described and referred to. — Similar letter
respectively. — AA mark two vessels of ga
mentioned. — DD mark openings for filling
CC serve also to lash the said vessels to the
of admitting atmospheric air therein u
for the purposes of this design — the ship's
and to reeve bamboos FF through the ring
bamboos are then securely lashed together
bamboos HH are then passed through the rin
pieces KK which serve as masts for attaching
other available material intermatted as shown
thus designed and constructed, may be steered
  The Utility of this design envi
forming the raft may be lashed together
   The Claim is for

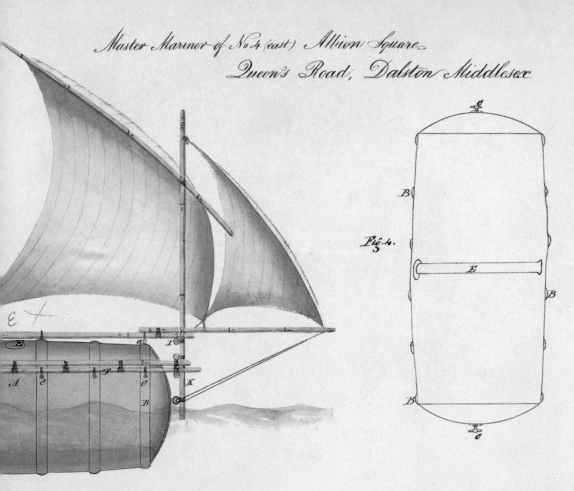

Master Mariner of No 4 (east) Albion Square
Queen's Road, Dalston Middlesex

Fig. 4

Description.

...wn to a geometrical scale of half an inch to a foot. — Fig. 1 exhibits a side elevation of the design as it would

...3. a top plan view without the rigging. — Fig. 4 a transverse section of one of the parts hereafter particularly ...

...ce are employed to denote corresponding parts in so far as such parts appear or can be seen at each of the 4 figures

...ed, are constructed with hollow bands BB to which are attached swivels and rings CC for the purpose hereafter...

...vessels with fresh water for the ship's use when such said vessels are not required for the purposes of a raft; the rings

... It will be observed by referring to Fig. 4 that each of the vessels AA are furnished with a pipe E for the purpose

...contents may be readily and speedily discharged therefrom — And supposing said vessels to be required

...ing discharged the contents thereof, and stopped the openings D and E proceed to turn the vessels AA overboard

...d at the sides of the vessels AA and subsequently pass bamboos CC through the rings at the ends of said vessels, the

...the vessels at the required distance asunder or the raft may be constructed on deck according to circumstances:

...ate at the top of the vessels AA and to the pieces IIII transverse pieces II are securely lashed as also the vertically placed

...and rigging to the bamboos I form the platform or deck of the raft and are designed to be covered with sail cloth or

...o protect such part from the force of air & water from rushing upwards; the parts 1.1 of the vessels AA serve as seats:— the raf

...e astern of the raft.

...ndering available the principal parts thereof for the ship's use and secondly in the facility with which the part

...l shape or configuration of the design as exhibited and described which is entirely New.

V 2458.

PREVIOUS PAGE

DESIGN FOR A LIFE RAFT

1850

Fig. 1. side elevation • *Fig. 2.* end view • *Fig. 3.* top
plan view without rigging • *Fig. 4.* transverse section

(AA) *mark two vessels of galvanized sheet iron constructed
with hollow bands* (BB) *to which are attached swivels
and rings* (CC) *through which to reeve bamboos* (FF)
when the design is needed as a life raft. The vessels (AA)
are furnished with a pipe (E) *to admit atmospheric air.*

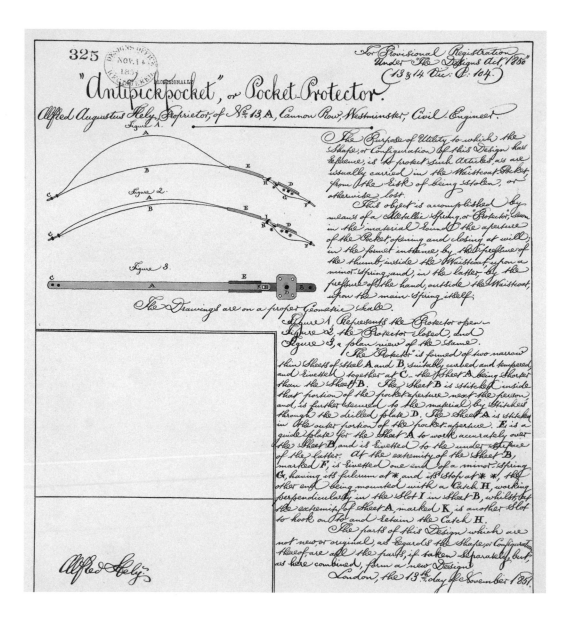

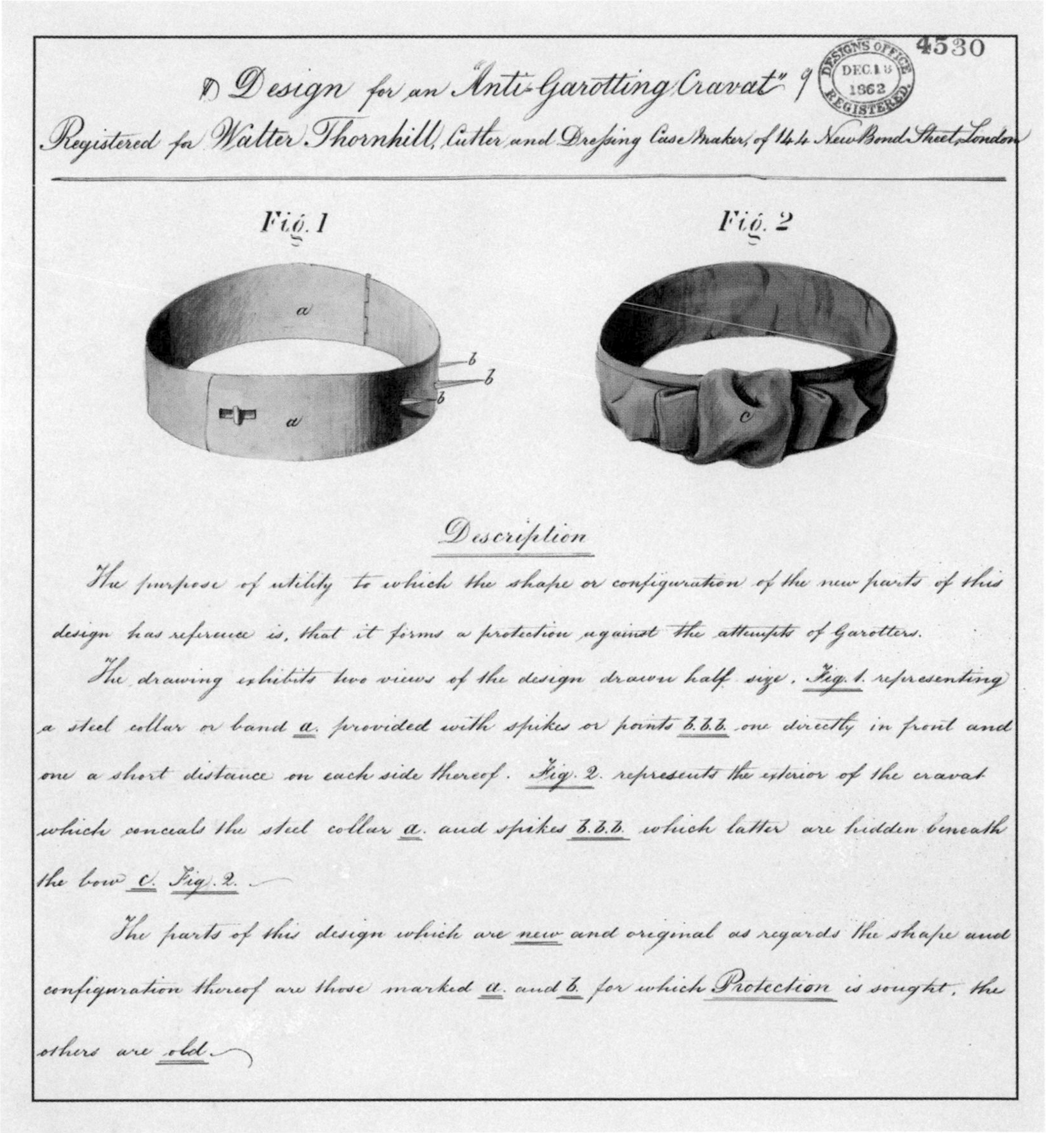

Design for an "Anti-Garotting Cravat"
Registered for Walter Thornhill, Cutter and Dressing Case Maker, of 144 New Bond Street, London

4530

Fig. 1

Fig. 2

Description

The purpose of utility to which the shape or configuration of the new parts of this design has reference is, that it forms a protection against the attempts of Garotters.

The drawing exhibits two views of the design drawn half size. *Fig. 1* representing a steel collar or band *a*, provided with spikes or points *b.b.b.* one directly in front and one a short distance on each side thereof. *Fig. 2*. represents the exterior of the cravat which conceals the steel collar *a*. and spikes *b.b.b.* which latter are hidden beneath the bow *c*. *Fig. 2*.

The parts of this design which are *new* and original as regards the shape and configuration thereof are those marked *a*. and *b*. for which *Protection* is sought, the others are *old*.

OPPOSITE

"ANTIPICKPOCKET", OR POCKET PROTECTOR*

1851

Fig. 1. the Protector open ⬧ *Fig. 2*. the Protector closed
Fig. 3. plan view of the same

The 'Protector' is formed of two narrow thin sheets of steel (A) and (B), suitably curved and tempered, and rivetted together at (C). The purpose is to protect such articles, as are usually carried in the Waistcoat Pocket, from the risk of being stolen, or otherwise lost.

ABOVE

DESIGN FOR AN "ANTI-GAROTTING CRAVAT"

1862

Fig. 1. a steel collar or band (a) provided with spikes or points (bbb) one directly in front and one a short distance on each side thereof ⬧ *Fig. 2*. the exterior of the cravat which conceals the steel collar (a) and spikes (bbb) which latter are hidden beneath the bow (c)

The purpose is, that it forms a protection against the attempts of Garotters.

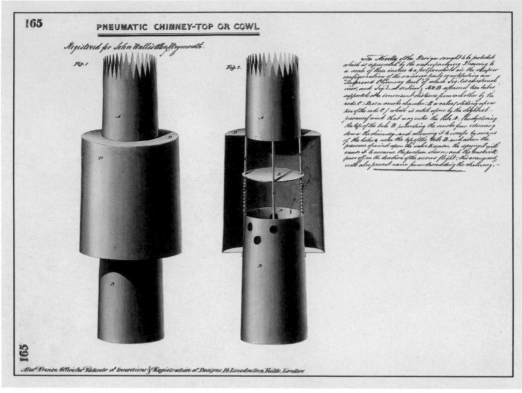

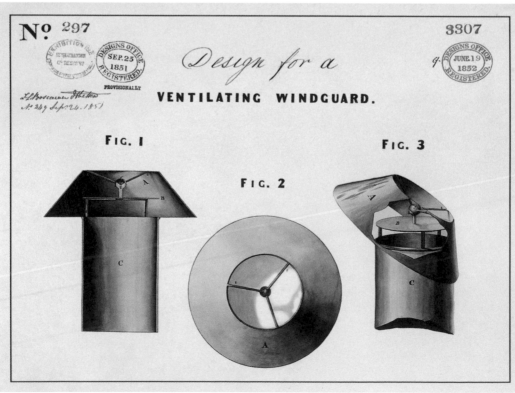

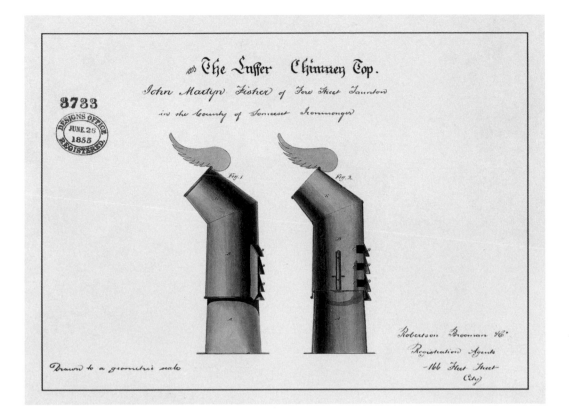

3733

OPPOSITE ABOVE

PNEUMATIC CHIMNEY-TOP OR COWL

1844

Fig. 1. external view ✦ *Fig. 2.* section

Tubes (A, B) are supported at a convenient distance from each other by rods (C); (E) a valve sliding upon the rods which is acted upon by the slightest pressure of wind that may enter the tube (A) thereby closing the top of the tube (B) preventing smoke from returning down the chimney.

OPPOSITE BELOW

DESIGN FOR A VENTILATING WINDGUARD

1852

Fig. 1. vertical section ✦ *Fig. 2.* plan of the cap ✦ *Fig. 3.* elevation of the windguard, as fixed to a chimney pot

The wind rushes through the top of the cap and is dispersed by the plate (B) through the wide opening at the bottom, thereby producing a tendency to exhaust the air in the chimney.

ABOVE

THE SAFFER CHIMNEY TOP

1855

Fig. 1. side elevation ✦ *Fig. 2.* section of this improved chimney top

(AA) is the fixed portion of the chimney top and (B) the moveable portion which is free to turn round upon the central pin (a) in whatever direction the wind is blowing. (CCC) is a series of openings covered by the louvres (DDD) the angle of each of which is such that the wind impinging upon them is deflected upwards and makes its exit from the mouth (E). The purpose is the effectual curing of smoky chimnies by increasing the upward current as hereinbefore explained.

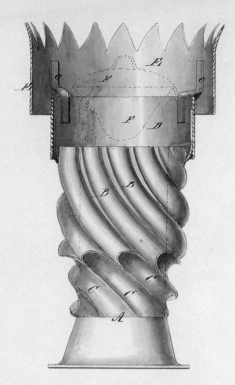

A DEFIANCE WINDGUARD AND TRUE VENTILATOR
1849

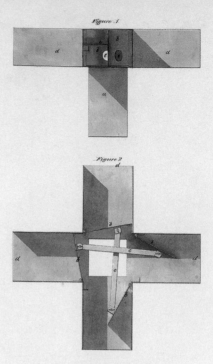

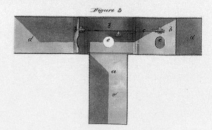

**NON-ORNAMENTAL DESIGN FOR
A SMOKE PREVENTATIVE**
1852

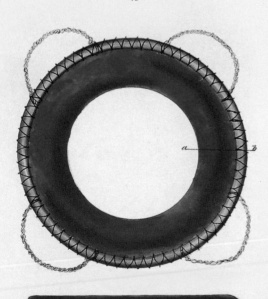

THE YARBOROUGH LIFE BUOY
1845

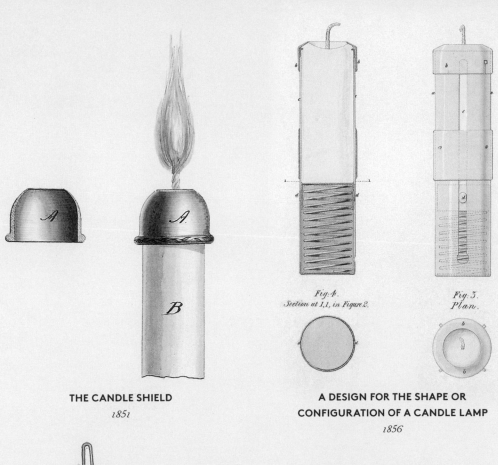

THE CANDLE SHIELD

1851

**A DESIGN FOR THE SHAPE OR
CONFIGURATION OF A CANDLE LAMP**

1856

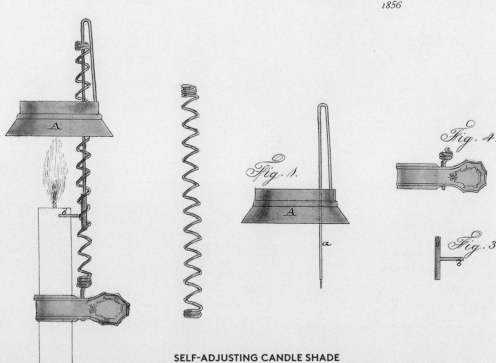

SELF-ADJUSTING CANDLE SHADE

1852

PICTURE CREDITS <small>(pages 1–152)</small>

1 BT 45/5/950 *Ventilating Window Pane*, Robert Bowie, Surgeon, Fowkes's Buildings, Tower Street, London, 05/02/1847

2 BT 45/18/3514 *Spring-Loaded Bible Case*, Thomas Brindley, 2 Leonards Square, Finsbury, 24/09/1853

4–5 BT 45/9/1708 *Placard Holder*, William Henry Neuber, 76 Long Acre, London, 19/12/1848

6–7 BT 45/4/744 *Fire Escape*, James Walby, 59 Greek Street, Soho 16/06/1846

8 BT 45/28 front cover, 5/09/1874–14/02/1878

10 BT 45/14 spine, 27/12/1850–29/04/1851

11t BT 45/16/3008, *The Oblique Pen Holder* (detail), Frederick Samuel Bremner, Gentleman, Camden Town, 06/11/1851

11b BT 47/10/3817, *Field Sketching Protractor* (detail), Major Edward Gunter, Winchelsea House, Folkestone Road, Dover, 14/11/1883

12 BT 47/7/2057, *Spiral Grooved Candle*, Mathew Lawson, Cookeridge Street, Leeds, County of York, 11/11/1870

14 BT 45/26/5196, *Clip for Attaching Grapes to Epergnes*, William Brearley, 12 Carver Street, Sheffield, 18/11/1870

15 120 BT 45/9/1693, *Pedo-Manu-Motive*, James Hayes, Elton, Huntingdonshire, 05/12/1848

16 BT 45/13/2442, *'Cantab' Braces*, Joseph Welch & John Margetson, 17 Cheapside, 08/09/1850

18 BT 45/8/1425 *Somapantic Bath*, Samuel Gilbert Junior, Ironmonger Street, Stamford, 22/04/1848

20 BT 45/4/634 *Knife & Fork Cleaner*, George Farrow, Park Lodge, Peckham, Surrey, 23/01/1846

21 BT 45/18/3436, *20-Option Extending Table*, De Jean Louis Benoit Vandenbosch, Montagne aux herbes potagères à Bruxelles, 30/03/1853

22 BT 45/24/4739, *Sectioned Bar of Soap*, Whitaker & Grossmith, 120 Fore Street, London, 05/09/1865

23 BT 45/11/2032, *Self-Acting WC*, Charles Chapman Clark, Reading, Berks, 18/09/1849

24 BT 45/1/32, *Omnidirective Shower Bath*, Charles Lewis and Company, Bath Manufacturers, Stangate Street, Lambeth, 12/10/1843

25 BT 45/1/125, *Horticultural Water Circulator*, Benjamin Fowler, Dorset Street, Salisbury Square, London, 20/02/1844

26 BT 45/4/789, *Jack for Putting on & Pulling off Boots*, Edward Fox, 15 Penrhyn Street, Liverpool & James Brown Carson, Drury Lane, Liverpool, 13/08/1846

27 BT 45/23/4553, *Boot Warmer*, Henry Doulton & Co., 63 High Street, Lambeth, 27/04/1863

28 BT 45/6 1046, *Heatable Spatula*, Samuel Backler, 4 Cambridge Terrace, Islington, 28/04/1847

29 BT 45/13/2504, *Knife & Fork Cleaner*, Thomas Parker, Kensington, Middlesex, 29/10/1850

30 BT 45/7/1305, *Counterbalance Candle Holder*, James Mellin, Levengrave near Rochdale, 30/12/1847

31 BT 45/6/1032, *Illuminated Night Clock*, James Parkes & Son, 5 St Mary's Row, Birmingham, 08/04/1847

32 BT 45/5/889, *Improved Bread Knife*, William Batty Mapplebeck, Ironmonger, Bull Ring, Birmingham, 05/12/1846

33 BT 47/9/3395, *Combined Knife & Fork*, Messrs Arnold & Son, Surgical Instrument Makers, West Smithfield, London, 01/02/1881

34 BT 45/11/2041, *Gravy Dish*, John Gray, Edinburgh, 01/10/1849

35 BT 45/17/3369, *Oyster Opener*, Adolph Aubert, Nantes, France, 11/09/1852

36 BT 45/25/4813, *Curved Roller Blind*, Rudolph Lindenzweig & William Jolly, Islington, 20/09/1866

37 BT 45/4/733–34, *Apparatus for Raising & Lowering Chandeliers*, John & Charles Ratcliff, 140 Suffolk Street, Birmingham, 02/06/1846

38 BT 45/2/335, *Portable Bed Warmer*, Messrs Ratcliff, Birmingham, 18/12/1844

39 BT 45/12/2219, *Bed Supporter*, Joseph Gardner, Agent to the Midland Railway Company, 39 Cross Street, Hill Street, Birmingham, 07/03/1850

40 BT 45/7/1295, *Baby Jumper*, Henry Sylvester Rogers, Salisbury Street, Strand, 16/12/1847

41 BT 45/13/2545, *Fixed Position Rocking Horse*, John Allen, Clarence Place, Hackney Road, 21/11/1850

42 BT 47/5/1261, *Portable Bath*, Thomas Simmons, Ann Street, Birmingham, 22/08/1861

43 BT 45/17/3392, *Improved Cistern for WCs*, Thomas Crump, Plumber, Derby, 24/11/1852

44 BT 45/10/1863, *Hydro Vapour Bath*, John Goodman M.R.C.S., Manchester, 26/04/1849

45 BT 45/3/457, *Portable Shower Bath*, William Day, 353 Strand, London, 24/05/1845

46t BT 45/3/454, *Improved Irrigator*, Bentley & Bailey, Bedford, 20/05/1845

46b BT 45/11/2189, *Sawing Instrument*, Anthony Mayer, Civil Engineer, Savage Gardens, Tower Hill, 18/02/1850

47 BT 45/14/2676, *Apparatus for Destroying Insects*, William & John Sangster, Cheapside, 08/02/1851

48–49 BT 45/12/2239, *Peach Protector*, Christopher Halliman, Gardener, Kensington 22/03/1850

50 BT 45/2/387, *Fruit Gatherer*, Thomas Dray, Chiswell Street, Finsbury, 05/03/1845

51 BT 45/20/3992, *Flower & Fruit Gatherer*, Jonathan White Haythorn, Net Manufacturer, Nottingham, Hexagon Gardens, 25/05/1857

52tl BT 45/4/785, *Design for Bottom of a Kettle Or Saucepan*, Samuel John Deeble, Potton in the County of Bedford, 08/08/1846

52tr BT 45/21/4063, *Swing Kettle Stand*, Thomas Pettiver, Trinity Street, Islington, 01/03/1858

52b BT 47/3/78, *Winder Expanding Dining Table*, Thomas Geake, Sherborne, Dorset, 28/02/1851

53tl BT 47/1/561, *Split Bottle*, James Edward Boyd, Hither Green, Lewisham, Kent, 26/03/1861

53tr BT 45/9/1791, *Pump Action Shower*, Robert Wilson & William Wilson, 95 Wardour Street, Soho, London, 24/02/1849

53c BT 45/22/4300, *Improved Pickle Fork*, Sherwood & Barrett, 52 Great Hampton Street, Birmingham, 09/11/1860

53b BT 47/3/457, *Noiseless Cornice Pole & Ring*, Martin Billing, Brass Founder & Cornice Role Maker, 142 High Holborn, London, 19/08/1852

54 BT 45/16/3072, *The Hand Hard Labor Machine*, George Nelson Haden, Engineer, Trowbridge, Wiltshire, 01/01/1852

56 BT 45/1/159, *Ventilator for Buildings*, William Hill, 12 Tottenham Court, New Road, 30/03/1844

57 BT 45/18/3431, *Sausage Machine*, W. Brooks, Aldgate, London, 11/03/1853

58 BT 45/5/802, *Portable Kiln*, Jasper Wheeler Rogers C.E., 1 Nottingham Street, Dublin, 22/08/1846

59 BT 45/5/860, *Optical Pencil*, John Moore, Pencil Manufacturer, Birmingham, 29/10/1846

60 BT 45/4/607, *Distance Measurer for Maps & Charts*, Brookes Hugh Bullock, Gentleman, No. 2 Chester Street, Grosvenor Place, c. 1845

62–63 BT 45/1/183, *Standing & Sitting Machine*, William Warne, Lark-Hall Lane, Clapham, 14/05/1844

64 BT 47/5/1152, *Portable Scaffold*, Thomas Tunbridge, Spring Gardens, Spittle Gate, Grantham, 11/06/1860

65t BT 45/12/2317, *Portable Smelting Apparatus*, John Marvin, London Gas Works, Vauxhall, 31/05/1850

65b BT 45/1/184, *Portable Forge*, Benjamin Hick & Son, Bolton, Lancashire, 11/05/1844

66 BT 45/18/3464, *Clover Head Seed Extractor*, W. Batley, Engineer, Bridge Street Works, Northampton & John Rivet of Brington, Huntingdonshire, 23/05/1853

67 BT 45/16/3163, *Machine to Fold Paper Bags*, Peter Pearson, Manchester, 05/03/1852

68 BT 45/1/54, *Mechanical Poultry Feeder*, Alexander Bollenot, Cook, Adam Street East, 31/10/1843

69 BT 45/3/435, *Improved Clod Crusher*, W. Grounsell, Louth, Lincolnshire, 23/04/1845

70 BT 47/9/3399, *Combined Lamp & Oil Can*, John Murrell Timmis, Birmingham, 11/02/1881

71 BT 45/16/3023, *Wheel Supporter*, Stephen Mendham Feary, Farmer, Willingham near Cambridge, 21/11/1851

72 BT 45/19/3755, *Portable Fireproof Building*, Samuel Hemming, Cliff House Works, Bow, 11/09/1855

73 BT 45/28/5973, *Portable Sheep House*, James Buchanan, Campden, Gloucestershire, 14/11/1877

74 BT 47/3/103, *Calling Machine*, Walter Smith, 6 Wyatt Street, Maidstone, Kent, 13/03/1851

75 BT 45/16/3046, *Telekouphonon*, Francis Whishaw, 9 John Street, Adelphi, London, 25/12/1851

76 BT 47/3/369, *Advertising Vehicle*, James G. Wilson C.E., Lindsey House, Chelsea, 26/02/1852

77 BT 47/3/373, *Rotary Advertising Vehicle*, James G. Wilson, Lindsey House, Chelsea, 11/03/1852

78 BT 47/3/344, *Elliptical Compasses*, Moritz Pillischer, Optician, 398 Oxford Street, London, 23/12/1851

79 BT 45/16/3008, *The Oblique Penholder*, Frederick Samuel Bremner, Gentleman, Camden Town, London, 06/11/1851

80 BT 47/4/562, *File for Papers & Bills*, Stephen Norris, New Peter Street, Horseferry Road, Middlesex, 23/02/1854

81 BT 45/11/2175, *Universal Reservoir Ink Stand*, J. & E. Ratcliff, Manufacturers, 58 St Paul's Square, Birmingham, 09/11/1850

82 BT 47/7/2476, *All-Seeing School Room*, Walter Rumble, School Stationer, Snodland, Kent & George Friend, County Architect, Maidstone, Kent, 14/08/1872

83 BT 45/13/2402, *Folding Trencher Cap*, Joseph Welch & John Margetson, 17 Cheapside, 08/08/1850

84t BT 42/5/890, *Turnip Cutting Machine*, James Richmond, Salford, 22/10/1841

84br BT 45/21/4142, *Shape & Configuration of a Block of Black Lead*, George Augustus Breillat Chick, Milk Street, Leek Lane and Callow Hill Street, Bristol, 20/12/1858

84bl BT 45/18/3460, *Vertical Firebox Boiler*, J. Mackay, Engineer, Drogheda, 18/05/1853

85tl BT 45/5/833, *Castrating Knife*, Alfred Barnshaw, Sheep Shear Maker, No. 5 Hall Carr place, near Sheffield, 24/09/1846

85tr BT 45/26/5106, *Glue Pot & Stand*, George Burton, 232 St John's Street, Clerkenwell, London, 24/02/1870

85b BT 45/9/1621, *Portable Blacksmith's Hearth*, Alexander Chaplin, Engineer, Barnes Street, Limehouse, 17/10/1848

86 BT 45/10/1823, *Ventilating Hat*, John Fuller & Co., 95 & 96 Long Lane, Southwark, London, 26/03/1849

88 BT 45/11/2036, *Spring Muffler*, Foster Porter & Co., 124 Wood Street, Cheapside, 19/09/1849

89 BT 45/14/2699, *Unique Braces*, Joseph Welch & John Margetson, 17 Cheapside, 19/02/1851

90 BT 45/15/2853, *Hat Cigar Holder*, Godfrey & Nathaniel Levi, 26 London Road, Liverpool, 20/06/1851

91 BT 45/25/4834, *Moustache Protector*, Alfred Arculus, Birmingham, 22/01/1867

92 BT 45/11/2020, *Tailor's Measure*, Henry Holden, 29 Liverpool Street, Kings Cross, 30/08/1849

94 BT 45/6/1157, *Hat Suspender*, James Clark, 3 Wellington Street, Blackfriars Road, London, 04/08/1847

95t BT 45/1/107, *Elastic Opera Hat*, James Bickerton Junior, 36 Stamford Street, Blackfriars, 15/01/1844

95b BT 47/8 2960, *Duplex Hat*, Herbert Lintott, 2 Souvenir Villas, Tavistock Road, Croydon, & Charles Evelyn Smith, 4 Welford Terrace, Brook Road, Upper Clapton, 06/02/1878

96 BT 45/1/71, *Instrument for Measuring Heads*, Victor Jay, 11 Southwark Square, 23/11/1843

97 BT 45/1/172, *Portable Apparatus for Shaping Hats*, Henry Wier Collinson, 14 Stamford Street, Blackfriars, 29/04/1844

98 BT 47/5/1345, *Volunteer Reversible Trowsers*, Michael Mendelssohn, Tailor, 58 Millbank Street, Parliament Street, London, 28/04/1862

99 BT 45/19/3746, *The Trouser Alliance*, Samuel Benjamin Woolf, 45 Old Bond Street, 16/08/1855

100–101 BT 45/22/4316, *Design for Pantaloons*, Henry Cutler, 6 Conduit Street, Regent Street, London, 14/12/1860

102 BT 45/29/6222, *Combined Brace & Purse*, Henry Whitehead, 11 Hamsell Street, Leicester Square, London, 29/10/1879

103 BT 47/5/1257, *Combined Glove & Purse*, Henry Sumner, Architect, Liverpool, 09/08/1861

104 BT 45/3/501, *Spring Sole for Boots*, Henry Salter, 29 Charing Cross, London, 19/07/1845

105 BT 47/6/1892, *Amphitrepolax Boot*, Charles Isaac Swift, 99 High Street, Camden Town, 04/12/1868

106t BT 47/7/2187, *Pen & Pencil Calendar & Tape Measure*, John Wade Avery, 11 Surrey Grove, Surrey Square, London, 11/12/1871

106b BT 45/17/3336, *Revolving Pen, Pencil & Toothpick Holder*, Thomas Allison Readwin, 2 Winchester Buildings, London, 17/07/1852

107 BT 45/14/2638, *Cigar-Holding Pencil Case Knife*, Unwin & Rodgers, Sheffield, 22/01/1851

108 BT 47/7/2262, *Lobster Cigar Tube*, Theodor Lostorfer, 5 Arundel Street, Coventry Street, London, 07/11/1872

109t BT 45/28/5663, *Smoking Pipe*, J.P. Mazet & Co., 39 Monkwell Street, London, 02/04/1875

109bl BT 47/3/377, *Pipe Cane*, Edward Warren, 3 Blomfield Terrace, Hyde Park, 20/03/1852

109br BT 47/3/378, *Cigar Cane*, Edward Warren, 3 Blomfield Terrace, Hyde Park, 20/03/1852

110 BT 45/21/4122, *New Uniform Front*, Thomas Richard Barlow, 143 Tooley Street, Southwark, 09/10/1858

111 BT 45/30/6400, *Corset With Expansible Busts*, F. Parsons, Sunnybank, Chipping Norton, 11/04/1881

112 BT 45/3/424, *Triple Hairbrush*, Ross & Sons, 119 Bishopsgate Street, 08/04/1845

113 BT 45/24/4659, *Portable Hair Brushing Machine*, James Beckett, Lambs Building, Stephens Green, West Dublin & Nathaniel Lewis Griffin, 17 Suffolk Street, Dublin, 27/09/1864

114t BT 45/4/616, *Instrument for Holding Up Ladies Dresses*, Berens Blumberg & Co., 33 St Paul's Church Yard, London, 01/01/1846

114cr BT 45/10 1897, *The Mimosa Or Flower Cornet*, William Blackmore Pine, Strand, London, 25/05/1849

114cl BT 45/3/434, *Improved Economic Button for Ladieswear*, Thomas Hope, Newhall Street, Birmingham, 18/06/1852

114b BT 45/28/5617, *Portable Carrier for Multiple Umbrellas*, Moss Davids, Hat Manufacturers, 237 High Holborn, London, 15/10/1874

115t BT 45/16/3186, *Vulcan Porte Cigars*, Widow Henrietta Schloss & Simon Schloss, Paris, 19/03/1852

115br BT 45/22/4293, *Porte Monnaie*, Thomas Drayton, Pocket Book Manufacturer, 1 Holford Square, Pentonville, London, 27/09/1860

115bl BT 45/26/5061, *Hat Brush*, James Higgins, 5 Harrington Gardens, Maida Hill, 13/10/1869

116 BT 45/23/4421, *Travelling Case*, Messrs Mechi & Bazin, 112 Regent Street & 4 Leadenhall Street, London, 07/11/1861

118 BT 45/13/2477, *Plantoform*, Louis Dutreith, Veterinary Surgeon, 4 Wellington Street, Strand, London, 10/10/1850

119 BT 45/18/3417, *Railway Bolster*, William Eassie, Contractor, Gloucester, 01/02/1853

120 BT 45/6/1047, *Elastic Wheel for Carriages*, Felix Abate, Neapolitan Civil Engineer and Architect, London, 28/04/1847

121 BT 45/3/477, *Marine Steam Propeller*, John Manchee, Palatine Pace, Stoke Newington Road, 18/06/1845

123 BT 45/18/3401, *Portable Tent*, H. Harrison, Hoxton, London, 21/12/1852

124 BT 45/22/4321, *Pillow Cap for Travellers*, Walter Jessop, 4 Royal Crescent, Cheltenham, 22/12/1860

125 BT 45/20/3883, *Railway Rug*, Henry John Nicoll & Donald Nicoll, 114, 116 and 120 Regent Street and Cornhill, London, 06/10/1856

126tl BT 45/7/3348, *Combined Walking Stick & Railway Carriage Door Key*, William Agnew Pope, 42 Cannon Street, London, 11/10/1880

126tr BT 45/7/3360, *Combined Umbrella Handle & Railway Carriage Door Key*, William Agnew Pope, 42 Cannon Street, London, 23/10/1880

126b BT 45/15/2895, *Improved Travelling Label*, Cox & Wilson, Oxford Works, Oldbury, 31/07/1851

127 BT 45/20/3810, *Travelling Bottle & Glass*, P & F Schäfer, 12 Brewer Street, Golden Square, 15/02/1856

128–29 BT 45/6/1101, *Carriage Telegraph*, Frederick Richard Louis Koepp, 14 Chadwell Street, County of Middlesex, 17/06/1847

130 BT 45/18/3440, *Gold Digger's Dwelling*, Job Skudder, Lower Road, Deptford, 31/03/1853

131 BT 45/17/3328, *Gold Washing Cradle*, John Symonds, Manufacturer, Circus Minories, 09/07/1852

132 BT 45/5/957, *Folding Stool*, Alexander Pilbeam, 18 Adam Street, Adelphi, 09/02/1858

133 BT 45/3/478, *Portable Cooking Apparatus*, Henry Madden, 14 George Street, Adelphi, London, 19/06/1845

134 BT 45/30/6648, *Pack Saddle Boxes & Bedstead*, Bowring Arundel & Co., Outfitters, 11 & 12 Fenchurch Street, London, 20/03/1883

135 BT 45/29/6031, *Campaigning Waterproof Sheet & Valise*, Thomas White, Aldershot, 26/04/1878

136–37 BT 47/4/669, *Aerial Machine for the Artic*, Arthur Kinsella, Kilkenny, Ireland, 30/05/1855

138 BT 45/1/198, *Lunette Parasol*, William Sangster, Regent Street, Westminster, 11/06/1844

139 BT 45/11/2039, *Hearse*, Charles Edward Butler, 31 Farringdon Street, 22/09/1849

140t BT 45/29/6105, *Luncheon Casket*, Edward Burkhill Laycock, New Church Street, Sheffield, 8/11/1878

140cr BT 47/10/3813, *Field Sketching Holdall*, Major Edward Gunter, Winchelsea House, Folkestone Road, Dover, 14/11/1883

140br BT 45/18/3521, *Bennett's Locomotive Regulator*, J. Bennett, 25 Cheapside, London, 24/10/1853

140bl BT 47/10/3817, *Field Sketching Protractor*, Major Edward Gunter, Winchelsea House, Folkestone Road, Dover, 14/11/1883

141tl BT 45/18/3539, *Steam Engine Link Motion*, E. Reynolds, Derbyshire, 08/12/1853

141tr BT 45/18/3454, *Locomotive Clack Box*, J. Budge, Middx, London, 25/04/1853

141b BT 45/18/3452, *'The Imigrant's Companion'*, T. Youngs, Poplar, Middlesex, 19/04/1853

142 BT 45/2/328, *Design for a Truss*, Frederick Farmer, Brighton, 04/12/1844

144 BT 45/2/205, *Surgical Syringe*, Frederick Fovaux Weiss, Surgical Instrument Maker, Strand, London, 27/06/1844

145 BT 45/5 931, *Medical Galvanic Machine*, Gabriel Davis, Optician, Leeds, 25/01/1846

146 BT 45/5/988, *Portable Ether Inhaler*, M. Salt & Son, Surgical Instrument Makers, 21 Bull Ring, Birmingham, 05/03/1847

147 BT 45/30/6563, *Cholera Belt*, Dodd & Monk, Albert Mill, Canal Street, Congleton, Cheshire, 27/07/1882

148 BT 45/20/3946, *Fumigating Apparatus to Cure Syphillis*, Whicker & Blaise late Savigny & Co., 67 St James's Street, London, 21/02/1857

149 BT 45/2/261, *Drug Grinder*, J. Whitmee, Steel Mill Manufacturer, 70 St John Street Clerkenwell, 27/09/1844

150t BT 45/8/1533, *Artificial Leeches*, D.G. Wertheimber & Francois Perroncel, South Street, Finsbury, London, 09/08/1848

150b BT 45/8/1571, *Mechanical Leeches*, D.G. Wertheimber & Francois Perroncel, South Street, Finsbury, London, 05/09/1848

151 BT 45/9/1602, *Mechanical Artificial Leeches*, Prosper Alexandre Lambert, Civil Engineer, 10 Bedford Street, Covent Garden & 6 Passage de l'Entrepot des Marais, Paris, 04/10/1848

152 BT 45/3/484, *Scarificator*, Fred Fovaux Weiss, Strand, London, 03/07/1845

PICTURE CREDITS (pages 153–224)

153 BT 45/6/1055, *Pneumatic Inhaler*, William John Bowden, Surgeon, Ware, Herts, 05/05/1847

154–55 BT 45/11/2153, *Enema Fountain Syringe*, Joseph Gray & Henry Lawson, 37 Eldon Street, Sheffield, 19/01/1850

156 BT 45/6/1073, *Prolapse Support*, Joseph Schofield, Bradford, Yorks, 19/05/1847

157t BT 45/6/1143, *Inflatable Pessary for Prolapsed Vagina/Anus*, Keith Imray M.D., Devonshire Street, Portland Place, London, 21/07/1847

157b BT 45/4/758, *Truss*, Thomas Pool, Accrington, Lancaster, 04/07/1846

158 BT 45/7/1288, *Metallic Masticating Plates for Artificial Teeth*, Frederick Pedley, 32 Savile Row, Burlington Gardens, 10/12/1847

159 BT 47/3/82, *Masticating Knife & Fork for the Toothless*, Duffield, Offord, Market Row, Great Yarmouth, Norfolk, 03/03/1851

160 BT 45/4/654, *Dr Torbock's Apparatus for Fracture of the Leg*, Joseph Wood, Surgical Instrument Manufacturer, York, 24/02/1846

161 BT 47/3/371, *Invalid's Exercising Chair*, Robert Kerry, Lansdowne Road, Stockwell, Surrey, 01/03/1852

162 BT 45/17/3207, *Typograph for the Blind*, William Hughes, Governor of the Blind Asylum, Manchester, County of Lancaster, 07/04/1852

163 BT 45/5/866, *Double Spectacles*, Michael & Abraham Keyzor, 24 Castle Mead, Norwich, 11/11/1846

164tl BT 45/10/1845, *Breast Reliever*, Alexander Robertson, Surgical Instrument Maker, 22 Bachelor's Walk, Dublin, 14/04/1849

164tr BT 45/11/2076, *Invalid's Reclining Bed Couch*, Messrs Weiss and Son, Surgical Instrument Maker, 62 Strand, London, 03/11/1849

164br BT 45/10/1878, *Elastic Pessary*, Maurice Pierre Philip Bourjeaurd, Surgeon, Davies Street, Berkeley Square, London, 05/05/1849

164l BT 45/6/1049, *Parturition Forceps*, John Nelson, Highfield, Sheffield, 01/05/1847

165t BT 45/9/1610, *Sanitary Belt & Cholera Repellent*, Thomas Drew, Chemist, Plymouth, 09/10/1848

165cl BT 45/11/2002, *Nipple Protector*, Francis Taylor, Surgeon, Romsey, Hampshire, 21/08/1849

165cr BT 45/3/587, *Bandage Fastening*, Thomas Benbow, Camden Street, Birmingham, 19/11/1845

165b BT 45/7/1396, *Foot Warmer & Influenza Vapour Bath*, Richard Moss, Bartholemew Square, Old Street, London, 22/03/1848

166 BT 45/29/6252, *Walking Stick Gun*, John Clarke Barnes, Birmingham 27/12/1879

168 BT 45/12/2201, *Portable, Collapsible Boat*, Biffen & Son, Hammersmith, 25/02/1850

171 BT 45/29/6085, *Tennis Racket Attachment for Picking Up Balls*, Mrs John Thomlinson, Armathwaite Castle, Carlisle, 14/09/1878

172 BT 47/3/199, *Accordion Stand*, Edwin Faulkner, 11 York's Street, St James's Square, 31/04/1851

173 BT 47/7/2206, *Music Page Turner*, Richard Robinson, 8 Graham Terrace, Dalston, 23/02/1872

174 BT 45/30/6540, *Tennis Scoring System*, William Parham, Northgate Works, Westmoreland, 13/05/1881

175 BT 47/9/3276, *Belt Ball Holder for Tennis*, Isaac Evans, Birmingham, 21/02/1880

176 BT 45/27/5355, *Croquet Clog*, Putnam & Matthews, High Street, Chesham, Bucks, 10/05/1872

177 BT 47/7/2032, *Croquet Register*, George Brown Councell, Thornbury near Bristol, 15/08/1870

178 BT 45/10/1838, *Artificial Bird Shooting Machine*, Stephen Hartley, 1 Alpha Place, Manor Street, Chelsea, 07/04/1849

179 BT 45/11/2094, *Game Register*, Thomas Melling, Engineer, Rainhill Iron Works near Liverpool in the County of Lancaster, 23/11/1849

180 BT 47/9/3118, *Apparatus for Gymnastic Performance*, Alfred Short, Birmingham, 25/01/1879

181 BT 47/7/2168, *Saddle Spring Bar*, Andrew Montagu, Melton Park, Doncaster, County of York, 18/10/1871

182t BT 45/6/1059, *Valve-Perfecting Spring Slide for Brass Instruments*, James Balthazar Ziegler, 26 Gillingham Street, Pimlico, 07/05/1847

182b BT 45/2/345, *Sax-Horn*, The Messrs Distin, London, 10/01/1845

183 BT 45/19/3786, *Solocornu*, Key & Co., Charing Cross, London, 22/11/1855

184–85 BT 45/3/448, *Geometrical Keyboard for a Piano*, Miguel Theodore de Folly, 29 Hassington Street, Hampstead Road & 8 Lowther Arcade, Strand, 13/05/1845

186 BT 45/7/1208, *Submarine Communicator*, John Moore Hyde, Optician & Instrument Maker, Bristol, 27/09/1847

187 BT 45/26/5110, *Improved Diving Suit*, Samson Barnett, 23 Forston Street, Hoxton, 10/03/1870

188t BT42/5/1420, *Hunting Spectacles*, Thomas Dallman, 12 Tottenham Court Road, London, 29/08/1842

188br BT 47/9/3317, *The 'London Swing'*, Messrs Loeb & Co., 49 & 50 Aldermanbury, London, 13/07/1880

188bl BT 45/11/2152, *Fan & Riding Whip*, George Jacobs, Cockspur Street, Charing Cross, 16/01/1850

189t BT 45/8/1574, *Rolling Valve Brass Instrument*, John Calcott, 9 Roehampton Street, Vauxhall Bridge Road, 07/09/1848

189br, 45/16/3147, *Rifle Ball*, Charles William Lancaster, Gun Maker, 151 New Bond Street, 26/02/1852

189bl BT 45/5/928, *Cartridge Belt*, Parker Field & Sons, 233 High Holborn, 22/01/1847

190 BT 45/3/520, *Fire Escape*, F. Butler, 41 Sussex Street, London University, 15/08/1845

192 BT 45/15/2852, *Safety Pocket*, Benjamin Hyam, Manchester in the County of Lancaster, 20/06/1851

193 BT 45/2/305, *Anti-explosive Alarm Whistle*, Job Allen, 20 Bower Street, Commercial Road East, London, 01/11/1844

194 BT 45/3/545, *Swimming Apparatus*, John Keyse, 27 Crosby Row, Walworth Road, 02/10/1845

195 BT 45/2/242, *Life Preserver*, Frederick William Lee, 46 Southampton Buildings, Holborn, 09/08/1844

196 BT 45/19/3726, *Family Fire Escape*, Charles Tilston Bright, Engineer, Exchange Buildings, Liverpool, 06/06/1855

198 BT 45/2/273, *Portable Fire Escape*, Joseph Taylor, 55 Southampton Street, Pentonville, 19/09/1844

199 BT 45/14/2603, *Apparatus for Saving Lives From Drowning*, John Keyse, 10 Cross Street, Newington Butts, Surrey, 28/10/1850

200–201 BT 45/1/47, *Fire Escape*, Joseph Taylor, 55 Southampton Street, Pentonville, 25/10/1843

202 BT 45/3/533, *Apparatus to Extinguish Fires in Dwelling Houses*, Francis Higginson, St Margarets Bank, Rochester, County of Kent, 03/09/1845

203 BT 45/13/2513, *Alarm Gun*, Isaac Naylor, Burton near Barnsley, Yorkshire, 01/11/1850

204 BT 45/14/2649, *Stink Trap*, Peter Rothwell Jackson, Engineer, Salford Rolling Mills near Manchester 27/01/1851

205t BT 45/24/4603, *Vermin Trap*, Colin Pullinger, Selsey near Chichester, 07/12/1863

205b 45/24/4764, *Perpetual Mouse-trap*, Colin Pullinger, Selsey near Chichester, 13/01/1866

206 BT 45/28/5990, *Keyless Padlock*, Smith Fleming & Co., 17 & 18 Leadenhall Street, 14/01/1878

207 BT 47/3/440, *Pick Prevention Key*, Joseph Schloss, 18 Friday Street, Cheapside, 01/07/1852

208t BT 45/11/2129, *Signal House for Height of Tides*, John Meik, Civil Engineer, Sunderland & Henry Watson, Brass Founder, Newcastle-upon-Tyne, 27/12/1849

208b BT 45/6/1107, *Day & Night Signal*, James Cocks, 18 Allen Street, Lambeth, 25/06/1847

209 BT 45/16/3124, *Apparatus to Ascertain the Height of Clouds*, William Mageough, Grenville Priest House near Dublin, 14/02/1852

210–11, BT 45/13/2458, *Life Raft*, Walter Raymond, Master mariner, 4 (East) Albion Square, Queen's Road, Dalston, Middlesex, 01/10/1850

212 BT 47/3/325, *Anti-Pickpocket*, Alfred Augustus Hely, Civil Engineer, 13A Cannon Row, Westminster, 14/11/1851

213 BT 45/23/4530, *Anti-Garotting Cravat*, Walter Thornhill, 144 New Bond Street, London, 18/12/1862

214t BT 45/1/165, *Pneumatic Chimney Top*, John Wallis Allen, Weymouth 12/04/1844

214b BT 45/17/3307, *Ventilating Wind Guard*, Alfred Suter, 65 Fenchurch Street, City, 19/06/1852

215 BT 45/19/3733, *The Luffer Chimney Top*, John Martyn Fisher, Ironmonger, Fore Street, Taunton in the County of Somerset, 26/06/1855

216tl BT 45/10/1931, *Defiance Windguard*, William Henry Dupré, 14 Charing Cross, Jersey, Channel Islands, 23/06/1849

216tr BT 45/16/3143, *Smoke Preventative*, Charles Neale May, Broad Street, Reading, 26/02/1852

216b BT 45/2/354, *Life Buoy*, Thomas Daley Armitage of Louth, 17/01/1845

217tl BT 45/15/2984 *Candle Shield*, Henry Batchelor, 13 Terrace, Kennington Common, 16/10/1851

217tr BT 45/20/3870, *Candle Lamp*, Price's Patent Candle Company Ltd., Belmont, Vauxhall, 27/08/1856

217b BT 47/3/422 *Self-Adjusting Candle Shade*, M. Paul, Prevost, Brouillet 4 South Street, Finsbury, 29/05/1852

224 BT 47/5/1214, *Tombstone Socket*, Thomas Long, 2 London Road, Croydon, Surrey, 08/03/1861

INDEX (A–F)

PAGE NUMBERS IN *ITALICS* INDICATE ILLUSTRATIONS

accessories:
  Combined Umbrella Handle and Railway Carriage Door Key *127*
  Combined Walking Stick and Railway Carriage Door Key *127*
  Design of an Improved Combined Glove and Purse *102*
  Design for the Mimosa or Flower Cornet *114*
  Design for a Porte Monnaie *115*
  see also pipes, cigars and smoking; travel; umbrellas
advertising 59–60, 87, 171;
  The Epanalepsian Advertizing Vehicle 16, *78*
  The Rotatary Advertizing Vehicle *78*
Africa 122
agriculture 56;
  Improved Machine for Cutting Turnips *84*
  Mechanical Poultry Feeder 17, *69*
  New and Useful Design for a Portable Sheep House *73*
  see also horticulture
anaesthesia 146 see also pain relief
Anderson, Will 59
anti-theft devices:
  'Antipickpocket' or Pocket Protector 193, *213*
  Design for a Pick Prevention Key *206*
Arkwright, Richard 11
athletics 169

'Baby Jumper', Design for a Nurse's Assistant or *40*
banking and accountancy 60–61
baths 15, 16, 18, 20, 23, 53;
  Design for the 'Hydro-Vapour Bath' 15, *45*
  'Somapantic bath' 16, 18, 20
  Useful New Design for 'A Portable Bath' *42*
  see also showers
'Beard and Moustache Movement' 91
beds see furniture
'Bible and Prayer Case, Spring' *4*, 17
bicycles 121–22
  'penny farthing' 122
  'safety bicycle' 122
Blacksmith's Hearth, Portable *85*
boilers 195, 196;
  Design for a Vertical Tubular Firebox Boiler *84*
bonnets 89 see also hats
boots see footwear
Bottle, Design for Split 53
Bowden, William John 146
braces 91;
  Design for 'Cantab' Braces 16, 91
  Design for a Combined Brace and Purse *102*
  Design for the Unique Braces 89
  Life-Preserver Braces 194
British Empire 118, 122
broadsheets 193, 194 see also newspapers; press, popular
Brunel, Isambard Kingdom 11, 119
buses see omnibuses

Calico Printers' Act (1787) 13
candles 12, 24, *31*;
  Candle Shield, The 217
  Design for a Counterbalance Candle-holder *31*
  Design for the Shape or configuration of a Candle Lamp 217
  Self Adjusting Candle Shade 217

Spiral Grooved Candle 12
  see also lighting
car see motor cars
carriages 120 see also travel and transport
chairs see furniture
Chandeliers, Apparatus for Raising and Lowering *38*
cholera 22, 144, 146, 147–48, 149;
  Design for the Chemical Sanitary Belt and Cholera Repellent 165
  Design for a Cholera Belt 147
cigars see pipes, cigars and smoking
cisterns see water closets
class and social status 11, 20, 22, 24, 57–58, 60–61, 88, 89, 93, 118–19, 120, 168
cleanliness see hygiene and cleanliness
Clock, Illuminated Night *31*
Clod Crusher, Design for Improved *69*
clothing 16;
  Design for Drawers or Pantaloons 91, *99*
  Design for a Spring Muffler 88
  Trouser Alliance, The *99*
  Volunteer Reversible Trowsers *99*
  see also accessories; braces; corsets; fashion; footwear; garotting; hair and grooming; hats; ladieswear; menswear; shirt fronts
clouds, Design for an Apparatus to Ascertain the Vertical Height of *209*
communications technology 11, 119, 123;
  Carriage Telegraph, The *130*
  Submarine Communicator *187*
  Useful Design: An Early Calling Machine *74*
  Useful Design: Improved Telekouphonon *74*
Compasses, Design for Elliptical *79*
consumerism 11, 20, 21, 57, 59 see also mass production
cooking see kitchen equipment
copyright 10–11, 12, 13, 16
Cornice-Pole and Ring, Design for Noiseless 53
corsets 92, 93;
  Design for a Corset with Expansible Busts 93, *111*
  see also clothing; ladieswear
Crapper, Thomas 23
cricket 169
crime 192–94 see also anti-theft devices
crockery:
  Design for a Gravy Dish *34*
  Design for the Imigrant's Companion 141
croquet 170;
  croquet clog 171
  Design for a Croquet Clog *176*
  Design for the Umpire Croquet Register 171, *176*
cutlery 17, 20, 21, 22, 53 see also forks; knives

dentistry 144–45, 146;
  New Metallic Masticating Plates for Artificial Teeth *158*
  Toothless, The 144
  see also knives
department stores 58–59, 88, 90
Design Registers 8, 10–11, 12
design registration 12, 13, 14–15
Designs Act (1850) 16
Designs Registry, Somerset House, London 10, 12, 14
disease 22, 146–47, 149 see also cholera; syphilis
Diving Dresses, Improvement in *187*
drowning 194 see also life-saving; swimming

drugs 144;
  Design for a Mill for Grinding Drugs and Groceries 149
  see also medicine and medical treatments

elastic 91 see also hats
electricity 24, 172 see also lighting
Ellis, Mary Stickney 21
entertainment industry 171–73, 193–94
etiquette 21, 88 see also class and social status
exploration 15, 122–23 see also travel and transport
eyesight 145–46;
  Design of a Typograph for the Blind *161*
  see also spectacles

facial hair 91–92 see also hair and grooming
factories 11, 20, 24, 56, 57
fashion 88, 90–91, 196–97, see also accessories; clothing; hair and grooming; ladieswear; menswear
Fashion magazine 92, 93
Filing Papers, Bills &c, Design for a File for *82*
fire and firefighting 195–98;
  Apparatus for Extinguishing Accidental Fires in Dwelling Houses or Other Buildings, An *203*
  Design for a Ventilating Windguard *215*
  Non-Ornamental Design for a Smoke Preventitive 216
  Pneumatic Chimney-Top or Cowl *215*
  Portable Economic Fire-Proof Building 17, *72*
  Safer Chimney Top, The *215*
  see also fire escapes; safety
fire escapes 197;
  Design for a Fire-Escape (1843) 197, *198*
  Design for a Fire-Escape (1846) 6–7, 15
  Design for a Fire Escape (1845) *190*
  Portable Apparatus with Self-Acting Friction Band, Spring, or Grip, for Escape from Elevated Places in Cases of Fire &c; and for Lowering Goods or Persons Generally 197, *198*
  Useful Design for a Family Fire Escape (1855) 196
  see also fire and firefighting
fitness 169 see also health
flying machines 15;
  Design for a Flying or Aerial Machine for the Artic Regions 15, 123, *135*
football 169–70
foot-warmers see warmers
footwear:
  Amphitrepolax boot 17, 90, *104*
  Design for a 'Jack' for Putting On and Pulling Off Boots *27*
  Design for Spring Soles for Boots and Shoes *104*
  see also warming devices
Forge, Design for a Portable *64*
forks 17, 20, 21, 22, *28*, *32*, 53
  Desideratum Combined Knife and Fork 17, 20, *33*
  Design for an Improved Pickle Fork 17, 53
  Design for a Knife and Fork Cleaner 20, 22, *28*
  Improved Masticating Knife and Fork, An *158*
furniture:
  Design for an Expanding Dining-Table 52
  Design for an Extending Table 21
  Design for an Invalid's Exercising chair *161*
  Invalid's Reclining Bed Couch 164
  Supporter or Bed Rest *38*
  Unique Folding Stool, The *132*

INDEX (G–Z)

gadgets 20
gardening 24–45 *see also* horticulture
garotting 192, 193;
    Design for an 'Anti-Garotting Cravat' 15, *213*
    see also anti-theft devices; safety
gas *see* lighting
glasses *see* spectacles
Glue Pot and Stand, Design for a *85*
gold prospecting 118, 123;
    Design for a Gold-Digger's Dwelling 123, *130*
    J. Symonds and Co's Gold-Washing Cradle 123, *130*
golf 171
Great Exhibition, London (1851) 16, 21, 23, 120
Great Stink (1858) 23
guns and hunting:
    Design for an 'Artificial Bird' Shooting Machine *179*
    Design for a cartridge belt 189
    Rifle Ball 189
    Design for a walking stick gun 166
    see also horses and horseriding; spectacles
gymnasiums 170

hair and grooming 91–92;
    Design for a Moustache Protector 91
    Portable Rotary Hair Brushing Machine *112*
    Triple Hair Brush, A *112*
hats 17, 89, 91;
    Bona Fide Ventilating Hat, The *86*, 91
    Clark's Hat Suspender *94*
    Design for an Elastic Dress and Opera Hat 91, *94*
    Design for a Folding Trencher Cap *82*
    Design for a Hat Brush to be Carried Inside a Hat 91, *115*
    Design for an Instrument for Measuring Persons' Heads *96*
    Duplex Hat, The *94*
    Portable apparatus for shaping hats 91, *96*
    see also accessories
health 15, 21–22, 56, 60, 144, 148, 194 *see also* fitness
heaters/heating systems *see* boilers; warming devices
Hoare and Company 61
holidays 117, 171, 194, 197
horses and horseriding 118, 119–21, 167;
    Design for a Fan Riding Whip 188
    Design for a Plantoform or instrument for measuring the feet of Horses for facilitating Shoeing 118
horticulture 24–25
    Apparatus to be Used for Distroying Insects on Trees *47*
    Clover Rubber for Extracting the Seed From Clover Head's *66*
    Design for a Flower- and Fruit-Gatherer *51*
    Design for a Hot Water circulator Suitable for Horticultural, Domestic and other purposes 25
    Fruit Gatherer *51*
    Greenhouse Peach Protector *47*
    Irrigator, Improved *47*
    see also agriculture
housework 21–22
hydrotherapy 15, 144
hygiene and cleanliness 20, 21–22
    Design for Bar of Soap 22
    see also sanitation

'improved' designs 17 *see also under individual entries*
industry and industrialization 11, 12, 13, 16, 20, 56–57, 88, 92, 168 *see also* factories; manufacturing; machinery and mechanization
Inkstand, J. & E. Ratcliff's Universal Reservoir *82*
intellectual property 12 *see also* copyright
iron and steel industry 56–57, 92

Jones, Jane 193

kettles:
    Kettle or Saucepan, Design for the Bottom of a 52
    Swing Kettle-Stand, Design for a 52
Kiln, Design for a Portable or Stationary 58
kitchen equipment 52, 196;
    Oyster Opener, Design for an *34*
    Spatula, Design for the shape or configuration of a *28*
    see also crockery; forks; kettles; knives
knives 17, 20, 21, 22;
    Castrating Knife, The *85*
    'Cigar-holding Pencil Case Knife' 17, *107*
    Desideratum Combined Knife and Fork 17, 20, *33*
    Design for a Knife and Fork Cleaner 20, 22, *28*
    Improved Bread Knife *32*
    Improved Masticating Knife and Fork, An *158*

labour-saving devices 19, 20, 22, 57
ladieswear 88–89, 92–93
    Design for an Improved Economic Button for Ladies Wear 17, *114*
    Design for an Instrument for Holding Up Ladies' Dresses *114*
    see also clothing; corsets
lavatories 22 *see also* water closets
lawn tennis *see* tennis
Lead, A Design for the Shape or Configuration of a Block of *84*
leeches 144;
    Artificial Leeches 144, *150*
    Improvements in the Shape or Configuration of Mechanical or Artificial Leeches and the Lancet Used Therewith *150*
    see also medicine and medical treatments; pain relief
leisure 168, 173, 197 *see also* entertainment industry; holidays; sport and exercise; theatre and performance
life-saving 194–95;
    Apparatus for Saving Lives From Drowning *198*
    Design for a Life Raft *212*
    Yarborough Life Buoy, The *216*
    see also safety
lighting 24, *31*, 195, 196
    Combined Lamp and Oil Can, A *71*
    electric lighting 24, 172
    gas lighting 24, 195, 196
    oil lamps 24, 195, 196
    see also candles
locomotives *see* railways
Loftie, Mrs 21
London Swing, Design for 188
Lutas Leathley & Co. 87

machinery and mechanization 56, 57;
    Cordwainer's Standing or Sitting Machine *63*
    Design for the Hand Hard Labor Machine *54*

Design for a Machine for Folding Paper Bags *66*
'Improved Sausage Machine' 17
    see also industry and industrialization
magazines 11, 12, 13, 59, 61, 88, 92, 93, 122, 170, 171
Major Gunter's Field Sketching Holdall, Design for 140
Major Gunter's Field Sketching Protractor, Design for 140
'manliness' 168–69, 170, 194, 195–56
manufacturing 11, 13, 21, 56–57, 88, 92 *see also* consumerism; factories
Maps Charts &c, Design for a Distance Measurer for 60
mass production 11, 20, 88, 120
Mechanics Magazine 12, 13
medicine and medical treatments 144, 148–49;
    Continuous Stream Enema Fountain Syringe *156*
    Design for a Fastening For Bandages and Stays 165
    Design for a Graduated Medical Galvanic Machine 145
    Design for an Improved Pneumatic Inhaler 17, *153*
    Design for an Improved Surgical Syringe 144
    Design for the 'Pessary' For the Relief of 'Prolapsus Uteri' or 'Prolapsus Ani' *156*
    Design for a Truss (1844) *142*
    Design for a Truss (1845) *156*
    Dr. Torbock's Apparatus for the Treatment of Fractures of the Leg *161*
    Elastic Pessary (Surgical Instrument) 164
    Forceps and Scissars Joint 164
    Gum Elastic Breast Reliever, The 164
    Improved Scarificator 153
    Non-Ornamental Design for a Nipple Protector 165
    Parturition Forceps 164
    Pessary for Prolapsus Uteri *156*
    Springs and Belts for Fractured Clavicle and Other Injuries of the Shoulder 165
    see also baths; cholera; dentistry; drugs; eyesight; furniture; leeches; syphilis; warming devices
menswear 89–90, 91, 93 *see also* accessories; clothing; shirt fronts
mice and vermin:
    Perpetual Mouse-Trap *204*
    Design for an Improved Vermin Trap *204*
motor cars 119, 122
murder 192, 193
music and musical instruments 171, 173
    Design for Rolling Valve Brass Instruments 189
    Design for a Sax-Horn (A Musical Wind Instrument) *181*
    Design for a Self-Acting Music Turner 173
    Design for a Solocornu *182*
    Design for a Useful Provisional Accordion Stand 172
    Design for a Valve Perfecting Spring Slide for Cornets &c. *181*
    'innovations for brass instruments' 173
    Plan of the Newly Invented Geometrical Key Board for the Pianoforte *182*
music halls 173

National Archives, London 10–11
newspapers 59, 122, 171, 193, 194
Northwest Passage, the 122–23
Nurse's Assistant or 'Baby Jumper', Design for a *40*

office work 57, 58, 60–61
oil *see* lighting
omnibuses 120
ophthalmoscope 145
'ornamental designs' 12, 13
Ornamental Designs Act (1842) 13

pain relief 146;
    Design for a Portable Regulating Ether Inhaler 146
Panton, Jane Ellen 21
paraffin lamps 24 *see also* lighting
Patent Law Amendment Act (1852) 16
patents agents 14
patents/patent system 12–13, 14, 16
Patterson, Mr T. 89, 93
Pedo-manu-motive 15, 16–17
pens and pencils:
    Oblique Penholder, The *79*
    Design for the Optical Pencil 59
    Design for a Pen and Pencil Case-Calendar and Tape Measure *107*
    Shaw's Revolving Holder for Pen, Pencil, or Toothpick *107*
pipes, cigars and smoking:
    Design for a Cigar Case with Self Lighting Matches *115*
    Design for a Hat Cigar Holder 90
    Design for a Smoking Pipe *108*
    Provisional Useful Design: Cigar Tube *108*
    Provisionally Registered Cigar Cane *108*
    Provisionally Registered Pipe Cane *108*
    see also knives
placard holder 4–5
plumbing systems 23 *see also* baths; showers; water closets
police 192
'portable' designs 17 *see also under individual entries*
press, popular 11, 88, 192, 193, 194 *see also* newspapers; publishing
publishing 11–12, 21, 59, 88, 92

railways 11, 117, 118–19, 121, 168, 171, 194
    Design for Bennett's Locomotive Regulator 140
    Design for a Clack Box Feed Pipe for Locomotives 141
    Design for an Improved Pole and Bolster for Railway and Other Trucks 119
    Design for a Railway Rug or Carriage Wrapper *124*
    underground 121
    see also accessories; steam power; travel and transport; umbrellas
Raverat, Gwen 24
registration agents 14–15
'remedies' 144 *see also* medicine and medical treatments
Rocking Horse, Non-Ornamental Design for a *40*
Roller Blind, Design for a Curved *38*
roller skating 171
rowing 169
Royal Geographical Society 122

safety 15, 56, 192, 194–95;
    Design for an Anti-explosive Alarm Whistle 193, 194
    Design for Lee's Marine Life Preserver 194, 195
    Design for the Safety Pocket 192, 193

Improved Alarm Gun, An 194, *203*
    see also anti-theft devices; braces; fire escapes; life-saving
sanitation 22, 23, 148
Sausage Machine, Design for an Improved 17, 57
Sawing Instrument *47*
Scaffold, Design for a Portable *64*
School Room, Design for a *82*
security 192 *see also* anti-theft devices
'Sheep House, Portable' 17
shirt fronts 89–90
    New Uniform Front, The *111*
shoes *see* footwear
shooting *see* guns and hunting
shops and retail 58–59, 88
showers 24, 42;
    Shower-Bath, Design for 53
    Shower Bath, Design for a Portable *45*
signalling:
    Design for a Day and Night Signal *209*
    Design for a Signal House *209*
Smelting Apparatus, Design for a Portable 17, *64*
Smiles, Samuel 12, 16, 55
smoking *see* pipes, cigars and smoking
Snow, John 146, 148
Soap, Design for Bar of 22
social status *see* class and social status
spectacles 145, 146;
    Design for Dallman's Patient Invisible Spring Hunting Eye Glass & Spectacles 188
    Design for Double Spectacles *161*
    see also eyesight
sport and exercise 168–71;
    'An Apparatus' for Gymnastic Performances *181*
    Design for a Game Register *179*
    Design for an Invalid's Exercising chair *161*
    Design for a Portable Wager Boat 168
    'non-combustible person propeller' 168
    Saddle Spring Bar *181*
    tennis scoring system 168
    walking stick gun 168
    see also croquet; furniture; leisure; shooting; tennis
steam power 11, 16, 56, 118;
    Design for an Improved Link-Motion for Steam Engines 141
    see also railways
Stephenson, George 11
Stink Trap, Design for a *204*
swimming 194–95;
    Design for swimming apparatuses 194
    see also life-saving
syphilis 148, 149;
    Design for a Fumigating Apparatus to Cure Syphilis 148

tables *see* furniture
Tailor's Measure, Design for a 92
taste 20–21
technology 11, 12, 16, 88, 192 *see also* communications technology; steam power
telegraph, the 11, 119 *see also* communications technology
Tell-Tale Keyless Padlock, A *206*
tennis 170;
    Apparatus for Scoring the Game of Lawn Tennis &c. *176*

New and Useful Design for an Instrument to be attached to Lawn tennis Rackets for picking up balls from the ground, A 171
    Receptacle for Containing the Ball (and Arranged to the Belt) Employed in the Game of Lawn Tennis *176*
Tent or Sleeping Cabin, Design for a Universal Portable 123
textile industry 11, 13, 56, 88
textiles 21–22 *see also* clothing
theatre and performance 171–73, 193, 195 *see also* music and musical instruments
toilets *see* water closets
Tombstone Socket 224
top hats 17, 89, 91 *see also* hats
tourism 117, 197
trade/trade routes 11, 122
trains *see* railways
trams 120
travel and transport 11, 15, 118–22, 123, 168;
    Design for a Campaigning Waterproof Sheet and Valise 135
    Design for the Imigrant's Companion 141
    Design for an Improved Travelling Label *127*
    Design for the Pillow Cap for Travellers *124*
    Design for a Portable Cooking Apparatus *132*
    Hearse *138*
    New and Useful Design for a Luncheon Casket *140*
    Travelling Bottle and Glass *127*
    United Service Travelling Case, The *116*
    see also accessories; communications technology; exploration; flying machines; furniture; horses and horseriding; railways
Trevithick, Richard 11
Turner, Thomas 14
Tussaud, Mme 172–73, 193–94

umbrellas:
    Combined Umbrella Handle and Railway Carriage Door Key *127*
    Design for a Portable Carrier for Multiple Umbrellas *114*
    Lunette Parasol or Umbrella *138*
urbanization 56, 58, 118, 146
Utility Designs Act (1843) 13, 14

velocipedes 121–22
venereal disease 148 *see also* syphilis
ventilation:
    'Defiance Windguard and True Ventilator, A' 216
    ventilating window pane 1
    Ventilator for Buildings, A 56
    see also fire and firefighting; hats
vermin *see* mice and vermin

warming devices 119;
    Design for a Foot-Warmer and Influenza Vapour Bath 165
    Design for a Portable Bed Warmer 17, *38*
    Design for the Shape or Configuration of a Boot or Shoe Warmer , A 17, *27*
Washing Machine, Bradford's Patent 'Vowel' 19
water closets 22–23;
    Design for a Self-Acting Water Closet 23
    Improved Self-Acting Service Cistern for Water Closets 42
Wheel Supporter *71*
windows *see* ventilation
work/working life 56, 57

ACKNOWLEDGMENTS

TRISTAN DE LANCEY, JON CRABB & RACHEL HELEY
AT THAMES & HUDSON

TZORTZIS RALLIS AND JODIE GAUDET

STEPHEN TWIGGE, PAUL CARTER, ED FIELD,
HESTER VAIZEY, GARY THORPE AND DEAN HANLON
AT THE NATIONAL ARCHIVES

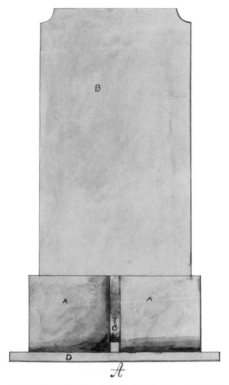

TOMB·STONE SOCKET or SHOE